The Oxford Book of

OXFORD

Erratum slip

The Oxford Book of Modern Australian Verse edited by
Peter Porter
ISBN 0 19 553376 3

p. vi: Gwen Harwood died in 1995, not 1996.
p. xv: Lionel Fogarty's entry should not include a
death date.
p. 86: line 32 of 'All Friends Together' by R. A. Simpson
should end with a comma, not a full stop; line 35 should
end with a dash. Line 11 of 'My Funeral' should read:
'of this symphony'.
p. 87: line 26 of 'My Funeral' by R. A. Simpson should read:
'is—I'm being burnt'.

The Oxford Book of
modern
Australian Verse

Edited by **Peter Porter**

BRN 21458

Melbourne

OXFORD UNIVERSITY PRESS

Oxford   Auckland   New York

OXFORD UNIVERSITY PRESS AUSTRALIA

Oxford   New York
Athens   Auckland   Bangkok   Bombay
Calcutta   Cape Town   Dar es Salaam   Delhi
Florence   Hong Kong   Istanbul   Karachi
Kuala Lumpur   Madras   Madrid   Melbourne
Mexico City   Nairobi   Paris   Port Moresby
Singapore   Taipei   Tokyo   Toronto

and associated companies in
Berlin   Ibadan

OXFORD is a trade mark of Oxford University Press

Introduction and selection © 1996 Peter Porter
First published 1996

National Library of Australia
Cataloguing-in-Publication data:

The Oxford book of modern Australian verse.

Includes index.
ISBN 0 19 553376 3.

1. Australian poetry—20th century. I. Porter, Peter,
1929– . II. Title: Book of modern Australian verse.

A821.308

This project has been assisted by
the Commonwealth Government
through the Australia Council, its
arts funding and advisory body.

Edited by Cathryn Game
Indexed by Carol Goudie
Text designed by Sarn Potter
Cover design by Guy Mirabella
Typeset by Desktop Concepts P/L, Melbourne
Printed by Australian Print Group
Published by Oxford University Press,
253 Normanby Road, South Melbourne, Australia

Contents

Introduction

It is hardly possible to read an article or essay on art or litera-
ture today without having to negotiate the contentious pre-
fixes—*late*, *post* and *after*. It seems that everything we do and
make is aware of its place in a sequential pattern or historic
declension. However heartily we might deplore concepts such
as 'post-modern', 'late twentieth century' and their numerous
clonings, we are scarcely capable of thinking other than in his-
torical terms. I confess to having roped off the catchment area
of this anthology in my mind while compiling it as 'Australian
poetry since the Second World War'. But my mind was formed
before 1945, when hostilities ceased, and the great majority of
my potential readers was born after that date, many of whom
would be hard pressed to know quite what is meant by the
term *Second World War*.

In terms of creativity and invention, Australian poetry before
1945 compares not unfavourably with what is gathered in this
anthology, but if we consider stylistic self-consciousness, then
the first half of the present century in Australia was a time of
innocence and straightforwardness almost inconceivable today.
And this despite such artistic analogues as the Eureka Stockade
(1854) and the Ern Malley affair (1944). Since 1945 Australia has
become an independent source of English-language literature.
Before that time, Australian writers tended to be considered
individually or as offshoots of the larger tree of English litera-
ture. This wasn't because of their subject matter or talent—it
was an expression of Australia's standing in the world in gen-
eral. The less that readers in the UK and US knew of Australian
writing, the more shrill certain Australian nationalists became
and the more dependent on overseas models most of the rest
seemed to be. Perhaps the least helpful of all slogans bandied
about in Australia in recent years has been 'cultural cringe', but
it does exemplify some writers' and critics' discomfiture when
faced by home productions. At this point I'm tempted to add—
how very different matters are now! Australian nationalism is in
the saddle: the chief danger critics of poetry and fiction face is an
almost hermetic concern with Australia and its topics and a
neglect of what is being written in Europe, America and else-
where. Can we be as good as we say we are? The answer must
be a qualified Yes—current Australian literature is as impressive

overall as that of any of the main countries writing in English. We still aren't as famous in the world as we feel we ought to be. And nothing will quiet those voices that, on looking at what is published by Australians today, see only decline of ability hiding behind the manipulations of fashion. To such I send a plea: please read properly what is being written by your compatriots—it might surprise you.

The change in awareness of what is happening throughout the world of poetry in English is particularly well demonstrated by comparing anthologies compiled in the first half of the century and those that hail from the second. One comparison that affected me personally might prove a fruitful example here. In 1936 Michael Roberts's *Faber Book of Modern Verse* was first published. At that time, it was possible for an English editor such as Roberts to assume that an anthology of contemporary verse would be based on what was being written in the British Isles, with a few representative American figures. Roberts would have been surprised if his anthology were to have been described as 'English' or 'British', or characterised as nationalist. That poetry in English was British or American would have been his unconscious assumption. The defining adjective in his title was *modern*, as it was even in W. B. Yeats's *Oxford Book* (1937), despite that volume's eccentric and markedly unmodern tone. Roberts's book proved both influential and successful in marketing terms, and was twice revised between its original issue and 1974, when I was asked to undertake the final revision. In my introduction to this recension I touched on the impossible task of keeping fairly strictly to Roberts's criteria while attempting even cursorily to reflect the enormous expansion of poetry in English since 1936.

Even more significant than the sheer weight of verse that had to be considered was the shift in emphasis away from the British Isles towards the United States. Taste-makers and style models were seldom British any more; by 1970 most poets writing in English, and even a significant number in Britain itself, looked to America. The unconscious Britishness of Roberts's taste could no longer aspire to any kind of objectivity. Many British poetry anthologies since the Second World War had to accept a more modest labelling and include *English* or *British* in their titles. The right to use unadorned descriptive labels like *new* or *modern* passed to American editors.

I have to confess that, while attempting to freshen up Roberts by including significant Americans, I still did not manage to find a place for a single Australian poet. I was aware of fine verse by Australian writers that deserved inclusion, but my British editors were not. They were at that time unready to acknowledge something that I believe every critic and publisher in the English-speaking world has now to come to terms with: namely, we are truly in a post-modern position where considerations of worth in contemporary poetry cut across borders and national identities.

This, however, bogs us down in sheer superfluity of choice. Faced by the need to distinguish the best poets over a particular span of time and chosen from among several thousand contenders and some dozens of countries, the anthologist might be tempted to fall back on fame, notoriety, fashion and other indicators not synonymous with merit. This, in turn, gives a considerable advantage to literature that comes from the more powerful societies, the ones that control both literary comment and commercial publishing.

Consequently, there has been an acute need for individual countries to produce anthologies of their own verse in English. This can suggest a misleading narrowness of theme, or promote an orthodoxy that fits national requirements rather than literary value. Almost any poet will tell you that the influences on his or her work have not been confined to things written by compatriots but range widely outside national borders. This has been sharply demonstrated by Australia's 'School of '68', under the guidance of John Tranter, whose manifesto deliberately pledged allegiance to American poetry and its several avatars. However, for all its reliance on external models, the Tranterites' work is no less Australian. What is striking is the insistence that by choosing exemplars from America they were marking out the only permissible Australianness. They would deny any such Australianness to the Melbourne poets who are their slightly older contemporaries—those who might be held to lean more to Irish writers, such as Seamus Heaney, or to British examples, such as the Movement and Philip Larkin, and further back to Auden and Thomas Hardy. Such disagreement can come to seem more like the traditional tussle between Bohemia and Academia. A poetry without influences from the outside would be impossibly hermetic, but the quarrels between the makers of taste blur real distinctions in skill and achievement.

Another way to see a national poetry coming together is to group it around some major figure. Australia has been given to this Führer-Prinzip. From Brennan to Slessor to Judith Wright and on to Les Murray, the baton-passing has gone on. Such key figures can also be rallying-points for ideologies, although not necessarily perceived as such. I think it appropriate that this anthology should be published in the lead-up to the new millennium, at a time when, in the opinion of many judges, myself included, Australia possesses in Les Murray a poet equal to any in the world. I should be happy to point to Murray and say, not that he epitomises any special Australian qualities or that he would be likely to endorse my selection of Australia's best recent work, but that a literature in which he is *primus inter pares* has indeed come of age and is worthy of international attention.

I have already emphasised that the Australian struggle with 'cultural cringe' has led to national self-consciousness of a highly assertive kind. In consequence, an extraordinary number of poetry anthologies has been issued in Australia since the 1970s. They range from the polemical to the resource book for teachers. Although their compilers might have seen themselves as ideologically entrenched and therefore opposed to each other, their intense survey-making has bred an unintended orthodoxy. It is easy for good poets to fall through the mesh of institutional taste-making, and I would not claim to have wholly avoided that danger myself. But I have been guided by different principles from those of many of my predecessors, the chief of which has been a refusal to make my selection on historical grounds.

At first, Australian anthologies of contemporary verse were national gatherings usually from a consolidating point of view. They were often useful. Their chief drawback was a tendency to date quickly and on occasion to suffer from editorial cronyism. It is hard today to appreciate how strongly various Australian literary establishments resisted what they perceived to be the pernicious influence of modernism. One unintended effect of this, well illustrated by the Ern Malley affair, was the uncritical attitude adopted by the early supporters of experiment towards their own talents. There are two special ironies in the furore created by Ern Malley. McAuley's and Stewart's parodies were so exact because they understood modernism as profoundly as they disliked it. Ern's poems are richer than most of what Australian modernists were producing in imitation of European and American models. This meant that admirers of the Malley forgeries were never really taken in; instead they were enjoying better examples of how to cultivate modernism than almost any offered seriously by their Australian contemporaries. A look through *Angry Penguins* and the early works of Max Harris will confirm this. The second irony has often been remarked on: the Malley poems are more energetic and show a richer response to imagination than much of McAuley and Stewart's seriously intended verse.

The Malley affair is sometimes credited with putting Australian literature back by a couple of decades. It would be more truthful to say that its 'early frost' effect meant that when poetry in Australia suddenly emerged into the full light of national awareness there was a lot of catching-up to do, and distinctions of style became the spur rather than distinctions of quality. This had a beneficial side-effect; the sudden burst of creativity meant that Australia became a pioneer of post-modernism among English-language countries. So much was vying for recognition; so many different rigs were tried out. From the beginning of the 1960s, Australian poetry became more than just visible; it adopted a leading role in the country's sense of nationhood. Also, from this time onwards, poetry was boosted by consistent support from government agencies. University English departments began to include contemporary verse in their teaching of Australian literature. The effect of such activity was to project suddenly a corpus of work into public consciousness—work not necessarily better than that of previous decades, but one undoubtedly more acutely aware of contemporary life. The anthologists had plenty to choose from.

I doubt that I have read every anthology available, but I have certainly consulted the bulk of them. Thus I have met many of the same names in different contexts (and rather too often the same poems). John Thompson's Penguin of the 1950s breathes a different air from Harry Heseltine's of the 1960s, and his in turn is unlike the latest Penguin edited by John Tranter and Philip Mead. Specialist anthologies (i.e. those with a program from a recognisable literary camp) date fastest but still harbour much interesting writing.

During the 1960s and 1970s, when enthusiasm for American experiment was at its height, Australian collections proliferated and, if they have now the slightly stale look of leftovers in a patisserie window, nevertheless gifted writers jostled along with time-travellers in their pages. For instance, the highly original poetry of j.s. harry first appeared then. Time's winnowing shows that such originality keeps its freshness, and harry seems a different and more impressive poet than she did when her work was first published. A marker to this age was the anthology devised by Tom Shapcott in which Australia's best poetry was printed alongside his choice from American contemporaries. Australia did not emerge from this juxtaposition particularly well, but then the notion was false. Shapcott's intention was to illustrate an Australian maturity through the embracing of international styles, but the Australian contingent was not as convincingly unlaced as the American.

Poetry anthologies tend to be seen by literary journalists as fixtures in which contending names vie for superiority in the manner of AFL football teams. Thus Geoffrey Lehmann and Robert Gray's Longman anthology is deliberately *parti pris*, excluding or under-representing not only American-directed modernists but also failing to find a place for such a noted native experimenter as Bruce Beaver. Tranter and Mead's *Penguin Book of Modern Australian Verse* is more wide-ranging but could be accused of bias in its emphasis on Tranter's team of Sydney/Melbourne modernisers. The exclusion of Beaver by Lehmann and Gray is strange since Beaver is a writer whom almost all sides in poetic controversy unite in admiring. He stands apart from any sort of Sydney-or-the-Bush or Boeotia/ Athens antinomy and represents originality *sui generis*. His poetry demonstrates that you become more yourself by reading and sympathising widely in all sorts of literatures. It was always going to be a fact that the circumstances of Australian life and the idiom of Australian speech (I do not mean slang or jargon) would be the chief factors in establishing a natural Australian style. Subject matter and the inflections of ordinary colloquy are more important in the long run than stylistic strait-jacketing. Subject matter alone, of course, can be misleading, as the Jindyworobaks have shown. But there, perhaps, it was not their subjects that turned out to be factitious but the manner of presentation, an adoption of supposed

Aboriginal modes not emotionally paid for. Again Les Murray provides an excellent example of the rewards of confidence in a writer. Murray is certainly expert in the ways of bush communities and is willing to stand guard over a rural morality under threat from international conformity. But the rations of Roman legionaries ('sour fish sauce') is a reference as readily to hand in his verse as any of the customs of people along the Coolongolook Road. In good writing the Stravinsky principle prevails: you take what you want from anyone, and always remain yourself.

Inevitably I have touched on the history of Australian poetry, but I have tried to keep it as background to the charting of recent activity. What then do I mean when I stress that this anthology is not compiled on historical principles? I can answer best by suggesting a metaphorical key: I have endeavoured to produce an on-the-spot survey of Australian poetry over the past fifty years almost as a Martian dropped suddenly in the midst of Australian society might do. He or she would go to a very good library and order all obtainable books by as many poets as possible, then read through the lot. From each poet a selection would be made of what seemed outstanding (in some cases nothing might be chosen). From this pile refinement would lead to an ultimate selection, which would be offered to the world outside and within Australia as a quintessence derived from one person's concentrated reading and assessment.

My metaphor begs several questions. First, isn't this what every anthologist does? My response must be No. Most begin with a point of view, a historical progression already in place, or even a crusading fervour in a particular direction. They follow this Ariadne's thread and proclaim a literary precedence among the maze of work on offer. While I was reading the work of more than 150 poets for this book I sought any poem that struck me as outstanding, whether it fitted in with my own tastes or not. What I was seeking was whatever I could recognise as excellent, and I was indifferent to whether such a poem was characteristic of its place, society or author. The 'characteristic' has for too long bedevilled the judging of poetry in Australia. Topics, attitudes and themes should not become favoured any one above another.

If I have come to any conclusion about the nature of poetry written by Australians, I have done so from reading works assembled independently of each other or of any thematic sympathy or empathy. I have not started out with the conviction that certain matters are *echt* Australian and searched for poems that would confirm my view. Looked at this way, the contending loyalties of city and country, tradition and modernity, nationalist and internationalist, lose much of their force. I hope that any pigeon-holer or gestalt-maker will find that this collection of poems suggests categories rather different from the usual ones poetry is lumped into. There is palpable Australianness in this anthology, but it never declares itself by observance of notionally Australian themes. Instead, the total body of work makes one major claim: these are all good poems, all written by Australians in the second half of the twentieth century.

Another question begged might be my assertion that I am not prejudiced. I have quite pronounced tastes, but I believe that my bias is to what is well done and well thought-through, not to any prescriptive notion—such as 'make it new' or 'the age demands ...' or 'we are in a new land and must therefore explore new themes'. Equally, I do not deplore the innovative, the experimental or the obsessive. I have no preference for the solemn over the light or any view of what forms are appropriate to the present. No topic is beyond the pale. The Bush is still here, and the ballads; the formal odes and the dramatic monologues are alongside poems of pure idea and poems about travel, foreign scenes and subjects. I am not averse to abstraction. The range is wide and liberatingly varied.

I must enter an explanation concerning my attitude to Aboriginal poetry. I do not care for verse that smells of anthropology. From the beginning, I insisted that to get into this book a poem must have been written in English. In poetry composed by Aborigines, this condition excludes the cycles and songs that exist in various Aboriginal tongues. Besides being basically shamanistic or liturgical (not perhaps a disqualification if one considers Christian poetry in English), it seems to me that there is no way of knowing when they were written—last week, last year, a thousand years ago? Are they group or individual productions? Have they been correctly transcribed, and does our language permit the recording of their idiosyncratic excellence? Any of the many song cycles that have been included in recent anthologies will inevitably be in English translation, not even transcription. As such they are almost 'found poetry', and I prefer to give severely restricted space to work conceived and written in the one language—English. Naturally, however, there are poems by Aboriginal authors composed in English.

Apropos my sticking to poems in English, I appreciate that some verse has been written in various languages—European, Asian or Polynesian—in contemporary Australia. Today's emphasis on multiculturalism might condemn my restriction of choice to English. In this, though, I have been guided partly by American practice. The USA also went through exemplary changes after mass immigration from non-English-speaking countries. But anthologists of verse from the United States seldom include poems in French, German, Italian or Spanish. A poet writing in Greek who supervises his own renditions into English, such as Dimitris Tsaloumas, is a different case, although only his English versions qualify for inclusion. As anyone who has observed Australians travelling abroad will testify, we are indeed multicultural, but we are still mainly monoglot. English (*Australian* English, not *English* English) is our language and the one we write our poetry in.

One final round-up of my editorial principles—I do not assign equal representation to all poets. That would be to deny merit and become an absurdity. The text is arranged in chronological order of the poets' births; it would not be possible to determine an order based on date of composition of the poems themselves. I have tried to ensure that no poem written before my starting date of the end of the Second World War (August 1945) is included. Certainly, I have not taken a poem from a book published before that time, although some poems whose original appearance falls within my catchment area might have been written previously. I have had to exclude so famous a poet as Kenneth Slessor in consequence of my time range. He was virtually silent after the war. At first I thought this a calamity, since Slessor is a founding father of modern Australian poetry. But then his absence came to seem a useful demarcation. I could conceive of my book as 'heirs of Slessor'. And Slessor's poetry is readily accessible elsewhere. The Ern Malley poems are missing, too. I didn't want to include them, although not on quality grounds, but because they offer too easy a signpost to duelling aestheticians. As it happens, they are excluded anyway by virtue of their original publication date.

The book had to stop somewhere, although I was revising my selection right up to copy date. The most recent poems considered were written in 1995, so the anthology has good millennial credentials. Some names and even more poems loved by readers are not here. I can hope only that annoyance caused by the absence of favourite pieces will be somewhat mollified by pleasure at encountering works and talents either not previously known or insufficiently regarded.

Poetry in English worldwide is changing continuously. One lexicon of living poets of the English language is approaching an entry of 2000 names. None of these is a Sunday writer—all are serious and professional, and have published several books. But the incidence of poets remains proportional to world population. If, in Yeats's words, 'We are too many', the observation applies to mankind in general and not just to poets. It is unlikely that if an undoubted genius is working among us, he or she will not be prominent in some anthology. (Emily Dickinsons are rare indeed.)

Much that is written today arouses the polemicist in literary critics. My contention is that all such diatribe or advocacy is less important than a wider diffusion of poetry itself among the reading public. I hope this anthology will serve poetry and not polemics, histories of literature or artists' biographies. Modern Australian poetry is worth reading. Our celebrated fiction writers should not be allowed to eclipse the fame of our poets.

Editor's acknowledgments

A large number of people and institutions came to my aid during the several years that this anthology was in preparation. First acknowledgment must go to Peter Rose, my editor and commissioner of the book at OUP. He has helped in a great number of ways and overseen the anthology at every turn. Next is Professor Bruce Bennett, head of the English Department at the Australian Defence Force Academy, Canberra, who arranged for me to spend time in his department as a Visiting Fellow with the specific intention of reading towards completing the compilation. My indebtedness extends further—to Professor Harry Heseltine, until recently the Rector of ADFA, whose support reinforced Professor Bennett's help with time, money and facilities. Chief among these was access to the unrivalled collection of contemporary Australian poetry held at the ADFA library, whose only begetter is the Chief Librarian, Lynn Hard, to whom I am indebted also. And to the secretarial and administrative staff at the English Department and the library. My roll call of gratitude beyond them is to individual poets, critics and enthusiasts, including the following: Chris Wallace-Crabbe, Peter Steele, SJ, the late Philip Hodgins, Evan Jones, John Forbes, Robert Gray, Adrian Caesar, Jeff Doyle, Jennifer Strauss, Susan Lever, Professor Brian Matthews and Professor Roger Covell.

Robert D. Fitzgerald

*E*LEVEN COMPOSITIONS: ROADSIDE

III

Having said that all the gums have not been cut
and dry sticks break beneath them; and having said
the grass is good this year, but shows a rut
developing here and there and looking red

along worn sides of hills; that as I walked
kicking up dust and powdered dung of sheep,
a hare came loping towards me, saw me, baulked,
crouched—then lost his nerve and fled with a leap;

that magpies gossiped above me on big boughs;
that tanks are three parts full though hard earth bakes;
that there are sheep, of course, a few dry cows,
not many rabbits, and I stirred no snakes;

having said this much I know and regret my loss,
whose eye falls short of my love for just this land,
too turned within for the small flower in the moss
and birds my father all but brought to his hand.

*T*HE WIND AT YOUR DOOR

To Mary Gilmore

My ancestor was called on to go out—
a medical man, and one such must by law
wait in attendance on the pampered knout
and lend his countenance to what he saw,
lest the pet, patting with too bared a claw,
be judged a clumsy pussy. Bitter and hard,
see, as I see him, in that jailhouse yard.

Or see my thought of him: though time may keep
elsewhere tradition or a portrait still,
I would not feel under his cloak of sleep
if beard there or smooth chin, just to fulfil
some canon of precision. Good or ill
his blood's my own; and scratching in his grave
could find me more than I might wish to have.

Let him then be much of the middle style
of height and colouring; let his hair be dark
and his eyes green; and for that slit, the smile
that seemed inhuman, have it cruel and stark,
but grant it could be too the ironic mark
of all caught in the system—who the most,
the doctor or the flesh twined round that post?

There was a high wind blowing on that day;
for one who would not watch, but looked aside,
said that when twice he turned it blew his way
splashes of blood and strips of human hide
shaken out from the lashes that were plied
by one right-handed, one left-handed tough,
sweating at this paid task, and skilled enough.

That wind blows to your door down all these years.
Have you not known it when some breath you drew
tasted of blood? Your comfort is in arrears
of just thanks to a savagery tamed in you
only as subtler fears may serve in lieu
of thong and noose—old savagery which has built
your world and laws out of the lives it split.

For what was jailyard widens and takes in
my country. Fifty paces of stamped earth
stretch; and grey walls retreat and grow so thin
that towns show through and clearings—new raw birth
which burst from handcuffs—and free hands go forth
to win tomorrow's harvest from a vast
ploughland—the fifty paces of that past.

But see it through a window barred across,
from cells this side, facing the outer gate
which shuts on freedom, opens on its loss
in a flat wall. Look left now through the grate
at buildings like more walls, roofed with grey slate
or hollowed in the thickness of laid stone
each side the court where the crowd stands this noon.

One there with the officials, thick of build,
not stout, say burly (so this obstinate man
ghosts in the eyes) is he whom enemies killed
(as I was taught) because the monopolist clan
found him a grit in their smooth-turning plan,
too loyally active on behalf of Bligh.
So he got lost; and history passed him by.

But now he buttons his long coat against
the biting gusts, or as a gesture of mind,
habitual; as if to keep him fenced
from stabs of slander sticking him from behind,
sped by the schemers never far to find
in faction, where approval from one source
damns in another clubroom as of course.

This man had Hunter's confidence, Kings's praise;
and settlers on the starving Hawkesbury banks
recalled through twilight drifting across their days
the doctor's fee of little more than thanks

so often; and how sent by their squeezed ranks
he put their case in London. I find I lack
the hateful paint to daub him wholly black.

Perhaps my life replies to his too much
through veiling generations dropped between,
My weakness here, resentments there, may touch
old motives and explain them, till I lean
to the forgiveness I must hope may clean
my own shortcomings; since no man can live
in his own sight if it will not forgive.

Certainly I must own him whether or not
it be my will. I was made understand
this much when once, marking a freehold lot,
my papers suddenly told me it was land
granted to Martin Mason. I felt his hand
heavily on my shoulder, and knew what coil
binds life to life through bodies, and soul to soil.

There, over to one corner, a bony group
of prisoners waits; and each shall be in turn
tied by his own arms in a human loop
about the post, with his back bared to learn
the price of seeking freedom. So they earn
three hundred rippling stripes apiece, as set
by the law's mathematics against the debt.

These are the Irish batch of Castle Hill,
rebels and mutineers, my countrymen
twice over: first, because of those to till
my birthplace first, hack roads, raise roofs; and then
because their older land time and again
enrols me through my forbears; and I claim
as origin that threshold whence we came.

One sufferer had my surname, and thereto
'Maurice', which added up to history once;
an ignorant dolt, no doubt, for all that crew
was tenantry. The breed of clod and dunce
makes patriots and true men: could I announce
that Maurice as my kin I say aloud
I'd take his irons as heraldry, and be proud.

Maurice is at the post. Its music lulls,
one hundred lashes done. If backbone shows
then play the tune on buttocks! But feel his pulse;
that's what a doctor's for; and if it goes
lamely, then dose it with these purging blows—
which have not made him moan; though, writhing there,
'Let my neck be,' he says, 'and flog me fair.'

One hundred lashes more, then rest the flail.
What says the doctor now? 'This dog won't yelp;
he'll tire you out before you'll see him fail;
here's strength to spare; go on!' Ay, pound to pulp;
yet when you've done he'll walk without your help,
and knock down guards who'd carry him being bid,
and sing no song of where the pikes are hid.

It would be well if I could find, removed
through generations back—who knows how far?—
more than a surname's thickness as a proved
bridge with that man's foundations. I need some star
of courage from his firmament, a bar
against surrenders: faith. All trials are less
than rain-blacked wind tells of that old distress.

Yet I can live with Mason. What is told
and what my heart knows of his heart, can sort
much truth from falsehood, much there that I hold
good clearly or good clouded by report;
and for things bad, ill grows where ills resort:
there were bad times. None know what in his place
they might have done. I've my own faults to face.

A. D. Hope

THE LINGAM AND THE YONI

The Lingam and the Yoni
Are walking hand in glove,
O are you listening, honey?
I hear my honey-love.

The He and She our movers
What is it they discuss?
Is it the talk of Lovers?
And do they speak of us?

I hear their high palaver—
O tell me what they say!
The talk goes on for ever
So deep in love are they;

So deep in thought, debating
The suburb and the street;
Time-payment calculating
Upon the bedroom suite.

But ours is long division
By love's arithmetic,
Until they make provision
To buy a box of brick,

A box that makes her prisoner,
That he must slave to win
To do the Lingam honour,
To keep the Yoni in.

The mortgage on tomorrow?
The haemorrhage of rent?
Against the heart they borrow
At five or six per cent.

The heart has bought fulfilment
Which yet their mouths defer
Until the last instalment
Upon the furniture.

No Lingam for her money
Can make up youth's arrears:
His layby on the Yoni
Will not be paid in years.

And they, who keep this tally,
They count what they destroy;
While, in its secret valley
Withers the herb of joy.

$\mathcal{M}$OSCHUS MOSCHIFERUS

A SONG FOR ST CECILIA'S DAY

In the high jungle where Assam meets Tibet
The small Kastura, most archaic of deer,
Were driven in herds to cram the hunter's net
And slaughtered for the musk-pods which they bear;

But in those thickets of rhododendron and birch
The tiny creatures now grow hard to find.
Fewer and fewer survive each year. The search
Employs new means, more exquisite and refined:

The hunters now set out by two or three;
Each carries a bow and one a slender flute.
Deep in the forest the archers choose a tree
And climb; the piper squats against the root.

And there they wait until all trace of man
And rumour of his passage dies away.
They melt into the leaves and, while they scan
The glade below, their comrade starts to play.

Through those vast, listening woods a tremulous skein
Of melody wavers, delicate and shrill:
Now dancing and now pensive, now a rain
Of pure, bright drops of sound and now the still

Sad wailing of lament; from tune to tune
It winds and modulates without a pause;
The hunters hold their breath; the trance of noon
Grows tense; with its full power the music draws

A shadow from a juniper's darker shade;
Bright-eyed, with quivering muzzle and pricked ear,
The little musk-deer slips into the glade
Led by an ecstasy that conquers fear.

A wild enchantment lures him, step by step
Into its net of crystalline sound, until
The leaves stir overhead, the bowstrings snap
And poisoned shafts bite sharp into the kill.

Then as the victim shudders, leaps and falls,
The music soars to a delicious peak,
And on and on its silvery piping calls
Fresh spoil for the rewards the hunters seek.

But when the woods are emptied and the dusk
Draws in, the men climb down and count their prey,
Cut out the little glands that hold the musk
And leave the carcasses to rot away.

A hundred thousand or so are killed each year;
Cause and effect are very simply linked:
Rich scents demand the musk, and so the deer,
Its source, must soon, they say, become extinct.

Divine Cecilia, there is no more to say!
Of all who praised the power of music, few
Knew of these things. In honour of your day
Accept this song I too have made for you.

*H*AY FEVER

Time with his scythe honed fine,
Takes a pace forward, swings from the hips; the flesh
Crumples and falls in windrows curving away.
Waiting my turn as he swings—(Not yet, not mine!)
I recall the sound of the scythe on an earlier day:
Late spring in my boyhood; learning to mow with the men;
Eight of us mowing together in echelon line,
Out of the lucerne patch and into the hay,
And I at the end on the left because I was fresh,

Because I was new to the game and young at the skill—
As though I were Time himself I remember it still.

The mild Tasmanian summer; the men are here
To mow for my minister father and make his hay.
They have brought a scythe for me. I hold it with pride.
The lucerne is up to my knee, the grass to my waist.
I set the blade into the grass as they taught me the way;
The still dewy stalks nod, tremble and tilt aside,
Cornflowers, lucerne and poppies, sugar-grass, summer-grass, laced
With red-stemmed dock; I feel the thin steel crunch
Through hollow-stalk milk thistle, self-sown oats and rye;
I snag on a fat-hen clump; chick-weed falls in a bunch,
But sorrel scatters; dandelion casts up a golden eye,
To a smell of cows chewing their cuds, the sweet hay-breath:
The boy with the scythe never thinks it the smell of death.

The boy with the scythe takes a stride forward, swings
From the hips, keeping place and pace, keeping time
By the sound of the scythes, by the swish and ripple, the sigh
Of the dying grass like an animal breathing, a rhyme
Falling pat on the ear that matches the steel as it sings
True through the tottering stems. Sweat runs into my eye.
How long to a break? How long can I hold out yet?
I nerve my arms to go on; I am running with, flooding with, sweat.

How long ago was it?—Why, the scythe is as obsolete now
As arrows and bow. I have lived from one age to another;
And I have made hay while I could and the sun still shone.
Time drives a harvester now: he does not depend on the weather
Well, I have rolled in his hay, in my day, and now it is gone;
But I still have a barn stacked high with that good, dry mow,
Shrivelled and fragrant stems, the grass and the flowers together
And a thistle or two in the pile for the prick of remorse.
It is good for a man when he comes to the end of his course
In the barn of his brain to be able to romp like a boy in the heap …
To lie still in well-cured hay … to drift into sleep.

SPÄTLESE

A late picking—the old man sips his wine
And eyes his vineyard flourishing row on row.
Ripe clusters, hanging heavy on the vine,
        Catch the sun's afterglow.

He thinks: next vintage will not be too bad.
The *spätlese* at last, as I recall,
Has caught the grace I aimed at as a lad;
        Yet ripeness is not all.

Young men still seek perfection of the type;
A grace that lies beyond, one learns in time.
The improbable ferment of the overripe
    May touch on the sublime.

Old men should be adventurous. On the whole
I think that's what old age is really for:
Tolstoy at Astapovo finds his soul;
    Ulysses hefts his oar.

THE MAYAN BOOKS

Diego de Landa, archbishop of Yucatan
—The curse of God upon his pious soul—
Placed all their Devil's picture-books under ban
And, piling them in one sin-heap, burned the whole;

But took the trouble to keep the calendar
By which the Devil taught them to count time.
The impious creatures had tallied back as far
As ninety million years before Eve's crime.

That was enough: they burned the Mayan books,
Saved souls and kept their own in proper trim.
Diego de Landa in heaven always looks
Towards God: God never looks at him.

INSCRIPTION FOR A WAR

Stranger, go tell the Spartans
we died here obedient to their commands.
    Inscription at Thermopylae

Linger not, stranger; shed no tear;
Go back to those who sent us here.

We are the young they drafted out
To wars their folly brought about.

Go tell those old men, safe in bed,
We took their orders and are dead.

Elizabeth Riddell

Tom

Tom Tom whoever's son
chose the way south and away he run.

Past the mango tree by day,
past the pearly beach by night
ran, he thought, towards the light,
lifting, floating, different kind
of life. Left the warped window frame,
the narrow door, the fretted path
and a shell, the cast turban of Cypraea Tigris,
far, far behind.

Whose were the sharp cries
and whose the cutting stones along his way?

Tom ran, the russet boy, on leaves,
on sand and on the flaking bones
of birds and fish. Quartz blinded him
but rain gave back his eyes their glittering blue.

We walked trudged limped behind him where he ran
on tussock, dune and over creek,
ran, he thought, towards a spire
cracked by thunder, ringed by fire,
comets roaring at its shivering peak.

Came other turnings, other signs
showing us a lemon grove, a shearing shed,
cockpit, kitchen, monastery,
a cave, a waterfall,
pastures and promises. We dropped away.
Tom ran south, as if the south were all.

The end of the affair

I do not forgive your old age.
I have liked lavishness, a splurge,
so I do not forgive caution, nor
the desire blurred, scribbled over, half-erased,
nor the corner of the mouth turned down
as if dragged by an aching critical tooth.

I do not forgive the tufts, the patches, the stained skin.
Not your fault, of course, but still unforgivable
to go russet from red and white to dark in
so few years, to lose the spring,
the stretch, the hair, the glistening eye.

Most of all I do not forgive your tolerance
when I reject you. It is no substitute for rage.
(And most of all I do not forgive myself,
mirror image of your decay, the soon-shredded flesh.)

Give me this, do not sleep through the cavatina
and I will stay awake for you, for the last time.

WAKEFUL IN THE TOWNSHIP

Cries the lonely dog all night,
Swims in the stream the shadowy fish.
Who would live in a country town
If they had their wish?

When the sum comes hurrying up
I will take the circus train
That cries once, once in the night
And then not again.

In the stream the shadowy fish
Sleeps below the sleeping fly.
Many around me straitly sleep
But not I.

Near my window a drowsy bird
Flickers its feathers against the thorn.
Around the township's single light
My cousins die and are born.

I will join the circus train
For mangy leopard and tinsel girl
And the galloping horses' great white haunches,
Whiter than a pearl.

When to the dark blue mountains
My captive pigeons flew
I'd no heart to lure them back
With wheat upon the dew.

When the dog at morning
Barks upon the frost
I shall be in another place
Lost, lost, lost.

SUBURBAN SONG

Now all the dogs with folded paws
Stare at the lowering sky.
This is the hour when women hear
Their lives go ticking by.

The baker's horse with rattling hooves
Upon the windy hill
Mocks the thunder in the heart
Of women sitting still.

The poppies in the garden turn
Their faces to the sand
And tears upon the sewing fall
And on the stranger's hand.

Flap flap the washing flies
To meet the starting hail.
Close the door on love and hang
The key upon the nail.

Roland Robinson

DRIFTING DUG-OUT

Now that the fig lets fall her single stars
of flowers on these green waters I would be
withdrawn as Gul-ar-dar-ark the peaceful dove
sending his callings over the many springs,
over the fountains and the jets of song
of Nin the finch and Geek-keek the honeyeater.
I would be withdrawn as Gul-ar-dar-ark calling
out of the distant sky and tresses of the leaves,
now that the fig lets fall her single flowers
like stars to pass beyond my trailing hand.

CURRACARANG

A whip's crack wakes him. He feels the bed
of tea-tree branches he broke and spread
down when he came there. Now it is light
and the oval cave's mouth frames the white
sea, and the gully of Curracarang
where the wind, that all night howled and sang,
travels the tea-tree scrub and comes
silvering the banksias and the sapling gums.

All night he has slept there and the cave
has sheltered and kept him warm from the rave
of rain and wind that howled as it tore
at the break of branches. You shall be poor;
you shall lose faith, be desolate,
follow a star, that star curse your fate.
You shall lie down and with last breath
pray not to waken from that death.
From this despair, the wind cried in scorn,
shall your fierce exultation be born.
This he remembers the wind howled and sang
all night through the gully of Curracarang,
now that the whip-bird's tongue has uncurled
the shattering crack of its thong at the world.

CAPTAIN COOK

RELATED BY PERCY MUMBULLA

Tungeei, that was her native name.
She was a terrible tall woman
who lived at Ulladulla.
She had six husbands,
an' buried the lot.

She was over a hundred, easy,
when she died.
She was tellin' my father,
they were sittin' on the point
that was all wild scrub.

The big ship came and anchored
out at Snapper Island.
He put down a boat
an' rowed up the river
into Bateman's Bay.

He landed on the shore of the river,
the other side from where the
church is now.
When he landed he gave the Kurris clothes,
an' those big sea-biscuits.
Terrible hard biscuits they was.

When they were pullin' away to go back
to the ship, these wild Kurris
were runnin' out of the scrub.
They'd stripped right off again.
They were throwin' the clothes an' biscuits
back at Captain Cook
as his men were pullin' away in the boat.

John Blight

CORMORANTS

The sea has it this way: if you see
cormorants, they are the pattern for the eye.
In the sky, on the rocks, in the water—shags!
To think of them every way: I see them, oily rags
flung starboard from some tramp and washed
onto rocks, flung up by the waves, squashed
into sock-shapes with the foot up; sooty birds
wearing white, but not foam-white; swearing, not words,
but blaspheming with swastika-gesture, wing-hinge to nose:
ugly grotesqueries, all in a shag's pose.
And beautifully ugly for their being shags,
not partly swans. When the eye searches for rags,
it does not seek muslin, white satin; nor,
for its purpose, does the sea adorn shags more.

GARFISH

Creatures that live in a wave, glass-housed,
luxury-living garfish, yellow-lipped
and pretty as flat-women. Slim-hipped,
bubble-sipping surface-livers, espoused
by the sun. Garfish that are not fish
but meteors, in the eyes of the star-gazer
—star-dripping meteors that the dozer
on the mud bottom would trap in a wish.
Sinker-sodden star-gazer, sick and sorry fish:
while the flappers are storeys up—gars
in the planetarium drinking bubbling spas;
off-this-planet plankton, trifling, for a dish;
and catching a breaker now and then—
it, a late tram crammed with white-shirted men.

BLACK

Soon, I said to my atoms, you must go back
to the no-land of unknowable black;
peer through its sea of loss at that blanketing lack
of light, at that solid void. There can you swim
in dreams, or fly, my atoms? There can your dim
beginnings remember the ungainly fish
that swam into fowl of the air, with flash
of insight into inconsolable man?

Think, as you ever think in the monotone
of oneness that is nothing, the numbness of black;
and as nothing think, and from such thinking make,
again, your mistake of man—embody shape;
because you must have shape and, with it, hope
and life; throw off death's awesome cape.

The Limousine

The willows that fled past us
in our limousine are shadows
and the old bus is our hens' coop
now, blue night with pride enamels its
svelte silhouette in our backyard.

Chariots of time, old cars, sweep past
(when I believed I had to own a car, to
own you too) now dispossessed by
daybreak's poultry cackling while

I wait on two eggs for my breakfast;
going down the yard with a full
tin of scraps to find only the dupe
china egg we planted as
encouragement. Give the

old bus to them, the chooks choose
their own time for laying breakfasts out.
I'll have to park the old car now at
their convenience—as patiently
as when, lovesick, I couldn't eat.

Kenneth Mackenzie

Sick men waking

Half light, half light … the dissolution of dreams
in the huge panes of dawn that soaks up sleep and the sleeper
into a fountain of day
Half light and a crash of running water
signal sleep's over. Turn over, my easy heart,
and listen content to the steps quick with purpose, to the voices
murmuring, an aweless invocation of life
among sick men at sunrise.
All this estate of patterned whiteness and light is mine
to shape for a moment backward into a dream of night
then thrust towards morning:

the steps and the little wheels that run and click
like strips of time laid flat on the shine of the floor
are mine,
clawed under the blanket with me, a rat's nest of fragments,
bits and scraps and chewed corners of thought
woven together by noises—the sigh of grief or pleasure
as men wake; the increasing voices,
always the voices, taking courage from daylight
like children, as wakefulness draws on
self and personality—like a glove—
neat, perhaps worn by the rub of the wheel of years,
or raw and bright and happily insolent with youth.
No rough-and-tumble until on a lingering course
the beloved tea-wagon passes and doles out
hot comfort and a warning of time still passing, time
building a day already out of bricks of minutes
and the thin cement of talk that sets in thought
hardening course by course, a hollowed monument
of waiting and wishing, of day and day
and night infinitely repeated.
Many tomorrows lie in wait like thieves
to rob us of some hours of half living
here in the rooms of day, after the half-light
melts sleep with its cool dispassionate flame
and dreams dissolve in the blue panes of dawn,
the yawning stretch of unattainable heaven,
the stretch and yawn and self-conscious exhalations
of sick men waking.

An old inmate

Joe Green Joe Green O how are you doing today?
I'm well, he said, and the bones of his head looked noble.
That night they wheeled Joe Green on a whisper away
but his voice rang on in the ward: I'm a terrible trouble
to all you girls. I make you work for your pay.
If I 'ad my way I'd see that they paid you double.

Joe Green Joe Green for eighty-two years and more
you walked the earth of your grandad's farm down-river
where oranges bigger than suns grow back from the shore
in the dark straight groves. Your love for life was a fever
that polished your eye and glowed in your cheek the more
the more you aged and pulsed in your voice for ever.

Joe Green looked down on his worked-out hands with scorn
and tears of age and sickness and pride and wonder
lay on his yellow cheek where the grooves were worn
shallow and straight: but the scorn of his look was tender

like a lover's who hears reproaches meet to be borne
and his voice no more than echoed its outdoor thunder:

Gi' me the good old days and the old-time folk.
You don't find that sort now you clever young fellers.
Wireless motorbikes all this American talk
and the pitchers and atom-bombs. O' course it follers
soon you'll forget 'ow to read or think or walk—
and there won't be one o' you sleeps at night on your pillers!

Joe Green Joe Green let us hear what your grandad said
when you were a lad and the oranges not yet planted
on the deep soil where the dark wild children played
the land that Governor King himself had granted
fifteen decades ago that the Green men made
a mile-square Eden where nothing that lived there wanted.

Joe Green lay back and smiled at the western sun:
'Fear God and the women, boy,' was his only lesson,
'and love 'em—but on the 'ole just leave 'em alone,
the women specially.' Maybe I didn't listen
all of the time. A man ain't made of stone …
But I done my share of praying and fearing and kissing.

No. I 'ad no dad nor mum of me own—
not to remember—but still I'd a good upbringing.
The gran'ma raised thirty-two of us all alone
child and grandchild … Somewhere a bell goes ringing.
Steps and the shielded lanterns come and are gone.
The old voice rocks with laughter and tears and singing.

Gi' me the good old days … Joe Green Joe Green
how are you doing tonight? Is it cold work dying?
Not 'alf so cold as some of the frosts I've seen
out Sackville way … The voice holds fast defying
sleep and silence, the whisper and the trifold screen
and the futile difficult sounds of his old girl's crying.

THE AWAKENING

No glistening cowpat, after all, but the first, worst
snake of the season, dissatisfied with the sun
of October, though the branches began to burst
a month ago, and the fruit has set too soon
this dry and wind-wrung spring.

Apart from the thread of cattle-track, in a whorl curled
outward from its hard and angry little head
it lay shining deceptively at the world
that stepped aside with quick and careful heed
for the shy, savage thing.

Winter melted slowly from the delicate frail scales
that sheathed its devil where it lay so sleek and still
forming a deathly purpose that seldom fails:
for it has all the rapier-speed and steel
of death for a heritage,

and today (I thought) or tomorrow, in the bright light
with shining topaz eye and wide mouth extended
it will move; or in the quiet hours of night,
perhaps, it will move and kill and with the deed
quench its herpetic rage

and winter's fast in one; each will smother the other
in very repletion, and no more manifest
this cold malice: it will have become blood-brother
to warm life by virtue of that feast
swallowed alive and whole ...

But now it waited until I had looked, gone on
and returned: it was there still on the starved grass,
deadly, lovely, painfully absorbing the sun
into its smooth self-seeking coils of grace,
into its dark soul.

David Campbell

At THE SHEEP-DOG TRIALS

What ancestors unite
Here in this red and white
Kelpie to define
His symmetry of line,

As crouched in burning dust
He halts both Time and beast?
The wethers stamp the ground,
At his will turn around.

He is of collie stock:
Austerity of rock
Lent his mind and bone
The toughness of its stone;

And though for Border flocks
The collie and the fox
Fought tooth to tooth, they joined
And have the kelpie coined

Whose ears acutely set
Across the centuries yet
Hear the concordant sound
Of coupled horn and hound;

And as the moon the tides
The hidden vixen guides
With craft the blood that strains
And surges in his veins.

Those who stand and stare
At cripples in the fair
Have not the eyes to see
His blood's dignity

Where old adversaries meet,
As now on velvet feet
He moves to his master's call,
In action classical.

THE HOUSE RISES

They have taken their briefs,
Their griefs and their faces.
It's the end of a day.
In the garden a snail
Deliberately munches a leaf.

They have gone in the rain
With their talk in high places,
Their cares and despairs
And their confident phrases,
Their wish to explain;
And the delicate thief
In his back-street of slime
Waves an antenna wand,
Gropes with a horn.
Is it good to eat? Eat.
Is it good to eat you?

They have gone like the wind
With their grief and distinctions,
Gone like a leaf
Or the voice of the news,
Like death on the air
With a rustle of paper;
And in the garden
The blind beast chews.

Mothers and Daughters

The cruel girls we loved
Are over forty,
Their subtle daughters
Have stolen their beauty;

And with a blue stare
Of cool surprise,
They mock their anxious mothers
With their mothers' eyes.

Strzelecki

FOR MANNING CLARK

And so Strzelecki set out from Hannibal
Macarthur's station, leaving the girls behind
In Sydney.—All night the Nacki washed my mind
Like willow roots in water.—From the Geehi wall
The party climbed Mt Townsend through a whole
Avalanche of wild flowers only to find
The south peak topped it—much like one in Poland
Called Kosciusko, Strzelecki claimed. The Pole
Scaled it alone, and when a cloud came down
Shutting the alpine vastness in a room
With his brief triumph, Strzelecki picked the bloom
Of one of those rare snowflowers sprung from stone
Remembering Adyna Turno and her love,
And joined the others happily enough.

from Red Bridge: The Wolf of Gubbio

SASSETTA

In perfect line astern the heron
Describe like bombers after 'Bombs away'
An arc above the city

And the road swings through the wood
Between dead men's bones
        In the foreground
A head and naked leg are shrewd reminders

Send these courtiers to a tailor and you have
Any Peace Delegation
The wolf is a reasonable fellow

St Francis ('Hold it') holds his paw
Yesterday's Kissinger
        The airy delegates
Discuss the international weather

And the people look down from the walls
At the wood and the foreshortened group
About to smile
      The wolf will keep his word.

DEATHS AND PRETTY COUSINS

I   MR HUGHES

When my grandmother left the races with Mr Hughes,
She left at the same time eight children and a husband
The committee deeply loved. She waved a hand
And Mr Hughes was dressed in purples and blues.
He kissed the hand and listened to her views
Which did not surprise him. He bought newspapers and
Confectionery and said in yellow grand-
Mother looked delightful. He was a goose;
And she never regretted leaving the maids, the flies,
The paddocks and the children—not to mention
That house and its verandahs. Throwing up her eyes,
There was the ferry greening into Mosman—
So convenient. Her rooms were bright if snug.
Mr Hughes smiled like a tiger from the rug.

II   PORTRAIT OF A DAUGHTER

From PLC and dreaming and *The Girl's Own
Annual*, Madge worried home. But as the train
Blew in to the toy siding on the quicksilver plain,
She knew her true calling. There was father, and her brown
Eyes filled with selfless tears, though he swung her down
And around in a waltz, quite unlike the heroine
Of her high journey. 'And how is my little kitten?'—
She'd do anything for him.—'Wearing our first frown?'
For father would not be serious though the David Jones
Account swallowed the wool-cheque. 'There is Yarragreen.'
There were also nurse and the children, the maids and the men,
And cook whom she feared, though from her even tones,
Who would ever know? For there was her dream to sustain
Her; and her love for father. He became her romance.

III   JOSEPHINE

Jo was the first to go. She was four feet ten
And men and mirrors loved her. She said to cook:
'If I hear one word of you, I'll come straight back
And fire you from a cannon.' 'That Josephine!
She would, you know.' It took a cup and scone
To settle cook's ruffled feathers. Jo had no truck
With Gran whom she loathed, and her gigolo. 'Good luck

To the pair of them!' In six months she held the town
In her small gloved pointing hand. For Josephine
Could put a ring around the moment. It sang
With first-light innocence suddenly come of age.
So she endured seven engagements, maybe nine,
And an unhappy marriage. When men were tongue-
Tied, she listened. For months, they were the rage.

IV *NEWS OF THE FAMILY*

Shem loved her mother and horses. She rode at shows.
Bruce wrote from Yarragreen. Spring racing, Madge met
A green-eyed doctor who joked with father. At
Petty's her room filled up with flowers. A rose
Lay on her plate. She found one in her shoes
In the corridor. The doctor would sit and chat
For hours with father and then like father let
His eyes stray to her. Before he could propose
She left, but he caught her at the station. Reg
Played the piano and sailed for Gallipoli.
When the boys came home, he told young khakied Dan,
'It was bloody shocking,' and never spoke again.
The children were growing up. Behind the hedge
Norman rolled his pretty governess, and came to stay.

V *MEN!*

My mother and aunts were shocked but not surprised
by talk of Mr Hughes and an affair
With the wife of a French woolbuyer. But how dare
He! Surely being poor, the fellow realised
His duty of self-interest? He should be pleased,
Whisking Gran off and sponging on her. Where
Would she go now? My aunts were in despair;
And mother caught the ferry. Admiring, she paused
By a blue garden where a pink old man
Was fashioning a nosegay: 'For a friend,'
He said, 'who walks about this hour.' And grand-
Mother came round the corner. 'There you are!'
Her nose in flowers, she said, 'No harm, my dear;
Though men get jealous. Men! Have you a pin?'

VI *ULINDA*

There was a duck egg as green as the evening sky.
Trout hovered in the horse-trough. The road was white
And vanished like a headache in sheets of light
And pale blue mountains. The homestead creek was dry
And warm with pebbles. Grandfather said that *Why?*
Was a crooked letter. His beard got in his plate.
'Milk grandfather. Sugar grandfather.' 'Now that

Is just what I can't have.' And he winked the bluest eye.
It was like the duck egg. We were only playing a game,
But mother left the table; so we ran along.
One sundown they butchered a pig and I saw it scream.
I held my ears and it went on screaming. 'What's wrong?'
They said. 'It's only a dream.' But I sang in my dream:
'Grandfather's dying. He's going to die,' I sang.

VII   DEATHS AND PRETTY COUSINS

When Mr Hughes died at seventy-three, Gran
Was ninety. I looked after her for one day
In her Wahroonga flat. She had a way
Of sitting under her portrait, *Young Girl with Fan*:
Neither was good. She had a list that ran
To a dozen items. I could do it all by railway:
It meant four stops for I was not to pay;
She ran accounts. I felt sorry for that man
Hughes; and so were they. Dear Mr Wyatt:
They'd miss him. Always a smile. Each day he came
At the same time—you could set your watch—not that
He wasn't running down—for the Gold Top cream.
Of her death, I recall Gran's nose and some pretty cousins
I had not met before. They were Uncle Norman's.

John Manifold

THE TOMB OF LT JOHN LEARMONTH, AIF

*'At the end on Crete he took to the hills, and said he'd fight it
out with only a revolver. He was a great soldier ... '*
                                    One of his men in a letter.

This is not sorrow, this is work: I build
A cairn of words over a silent man,
My friend John Learmonth whom the Germans killed.

There was no word of hero in his plan;
Verse should have been his love and peace his trade,
But history turned him to a partisan.

Far from the battle as his bones are laid
Crete will remember him. Remember well,
Mountains of Crete, the Second Field Brigade!

Say Crete, and there is little more to tell
Of muddle tall as treachery, despair
And black defeat resounding like a bell;

But bring the magnifying focus near
And in contempt of muddle and defeat
The old heroic virtues still appear.

Australian blood where hot and icy meet
(James Hogg and Lermontov were of his kin)
Lie still and fertilise the fields of Crete.

      *   *   *

Schoolboy, I watched his ballading begin:
Billy and bullocky and billabong,
Our properties of childhood, all were in.

I heard the air though not the undersong,
the fierceness and resolve; but all the same
They're the tradition, and tradition's strong.

Swagman and bushranger die hard, die game,
Die fighting, like that wild colonial boy—
Jack Dowling, says the ballad, was his name.

He also spun his pistol like a toy,
Turned to the hills like wolf or kangaroo,
And faced destruction with a bitter joy.

His freedom gave him nothing else to do
But set his back against his family tree
And fight the better for the fact he knew

He was as good as dead. Because the sea
Was closed and the air dark and the land lost,
'They'll never capture me alive,' said he.

      *   *   *

That's courage chemically pure, uncrossed
With sacrifice or duty or career,
Which counts and pays in ready coin the cost

Of holding course. Armies are not its sphere
Where all's contrived to achieve its counterfeit;
It swears with discipline, it's volunteer.

I could as hardly make a moral fit
Around it as around a lightning flash.
There is no moral, that's the point of it,

No moral. But I'm glad of this panache
That sparkles, as from flint, from us and steel,
True to no crown nor presidential sash

Nor flag nor fame. Let others mourn and feel
He died for nothing: nothings have their place.
While thus the kind and civilised conceal

This spring of unsuspected inward grace
And look on death as equals, I am filled
With queer affection for the human race.

FIFE TUNE

FOR SIXTH PLATOON, 308TH ITCO

One morning in spring
We marched from Devizes
All shapes and sizes
Like beads on a string,
But yet with a swing
We trod the bluemetal
And full of high fettle
We started to sing.

She ran down the stair
A twelve-year-old darling
And laughing and calling
She tossed her bright hair;
Then silent to stare
At the men flowing past her—
There were all she could master
Adoring her there.

It's seldom I'll see
A sweeter or prettier;
I doubt we'll forget her
In two years or three,
And lucky he'll be
She takes for a lover
While we are far over
The treacherous sea.

Judith Wright

THE TRAINS

Tunnelling through the night, the trains pass
in a splendour of power, with a sound like thunder
shaking the orchards, waking
the young from a dream, scattering like glass
the old men's sleep; laying
a black trail over the still bloom of the orchards.
The trains go north with guns.

Strange primitive piece of flesh, the heart laid quiet
hearing their cry pierce through its thin-walled cave
recalls the forgotten tiger
and leaps awake in its old panic riot;

and how shall mind be sober,
since blood's red thread still binds us fast in history?
Tiger, you walk through all our past and future,
troubling the children's sleep; laying
a reeking trail across our dream of orchards.

Racing on iron errands, the trains go by,
and over the white acres of our orchards
hurl their wild summoning cry, their animal cry …
the trains go north with guns.

Camphor laurel

Here in the slack of night
the tree breathes honey and moonlight.
Here in the blackened yard
smoke and time and use have marred,
leaning from that fantan gloom
the bent tree is heavy in bloom.

The dark house creaks and sways;
'Not like the old days.'
Tim and Sam and ratbag Nell,
Wong who keeps the Chinese hell,
the half-caste lovers, the humpbacked boy,
sleep for sorrow, or wake for joy.

Under the house the roots go deep,
down, down, while the sleepers sleep;
splitting the rock where the house is set,
cracking the paved and broken street.
Old Tim turns and old Sam groans,
'God be good to my breaking bones';
and in the slack of tideless night
the tree breathes honey and moonlight.

Request to a year

If the year is meditating a suitable gift,
I should like it to be the attitude
of my great-great-grandmother,
legendary devotee of the arts,

who, having had eight children
and little opportunity for painting pictures,
sat one day on a high rock
beside a river in Switzerland

and from a difficult distance viewed
her second son, balanced on a small ice-floe,
drift down the current towards a waterfall
that struck rock-bottom eighty feet below,

while her second daughter, impeded,
no doubt, by the petticoats of the day,
stretched out a last-hope alpenstock
(which luckily later caught him on his way).

Nothing, it was evident, could be done;
and with the artist's isolating eye
my great-great-grandmother hastily sketched the scene.
The sketch survives to prove the story by.

Year, if you have no Mother's day present planned;
reach back and bring me the firmness of her hand.

BRUSH TURKEY

Right to the edge of his forest
the tourists come.
He learns the scavenger's habits
with scrap and crumb—
his forests shrunk, he lives
on what the moment gives:
pretends, in mockery,
to beg our charity.

Cunning and shy one must be
to snatch one's bread
from oafs whose hands are quicker
with stones instead.
He apes the backyard bird,
half-proud and half-absurd,
sheltered by his quick wit,
he sees and takes his bit.

Ash-black, wattles of scarlet,
and careful eye,
he hoaxes the ape, the ogre,
with mimicry.
Scornfully, he will eat
thrown crust and broken meat
till suddenly—'See, oh see!
The turkey's in the tree.'

The backyard bird is stupid;
he trusts and takes.
But this one's wiles are wary
to guard against the axe:

escaping, neat and pat,
into his habitat.
Charred log and shade and stone
accept him. He is gone.

And here's a bird the poet
may ponder over,
whose ancient forest-meanings
no longer grant him cover;
who, circumspect yet proud,
like yet unlike the crowd,
must cheat its chucklehead
to throw—not stones, but bread.

To ANOTHER HOUSEWIFE

Do you remember how we went,
on duty bound, to feed the crowd
of hungry dogs your father kept
as rabbit-hunters? Lean and loud,
half-starved and furious, how they leapt
against their chains, as though they meant
in mindless rage for being fed,
to tear our childish hands instead!

With tomahawk and knife we hacked
the flyblown tatters of old meat,
gagged at their carcass-smell, and threw
the scraps and watched the hungry eat.
Then turning faint, we made a pact,
(two greensick girls), crossed hearts and swore
to touch no meat forever more.

How many cuts of choice and prime
our housewife hands have dressed since then—
these hands with love and blood imbrued—
for daughters, sons, and hungry men!
How many creatures bred for food
we've raised and fattened for the time
they met at last the steaming knife
that serves the feast of death-in-life!

And as the evening meal is served
we hear the turned-down radio
begin to tell the evening news
just as the family joint is carved.
O murder, famine, pious wars …
Our children shrink to see us so,
in sudden meditation, stand
with knife and fork in either hand.

Finale

The cruellest thing they did
was to send home his teeth from the hospital.
What could she do with those,
arriving as they did days after the funeral?

Wrapped them in one of his clean handkerchiefs
she'd laundered and taken down.
All she could do was cradle them in her hands;
they looked so strange, alone—

utterly jawless in a constant smile
not in the least like his. She could cry no more.
At midnight she took heart and aim and threw
them out of the kitchen-door.

It rocketed out, that finally parted smile,
into the gully? the scrub? the neighbour's land?
And she went back and fell into stupid sleep,
knowing him dead at last, and by her hand.

Counting in sevens

Seven ones are seven.
I can't remember that year
or what presents I was given.

Seven twos are fourteen.
That year I found my mind,
swore not to be what I had been.

Seven threes are twenty-one.
I was sailing my own sea,
first in love, the knots undone.

Seven fours are twenty-eight;
three false starts had come and gone;
my true love came, and not too late.

Seven fives are thirty-five.
In her cot my daughter lay,
real, miraculous, alive.

Seven sixes are forty-two.
I packed her sandwiches for school,
I loved my love and time came true.

Seven sevens are forty-nine.
Fruit loaded down my apple-tree,
near fifty years of life were mine.

Seven eights are fifty-six.
My lips still cold from a last kiss,
my fire was ash and charcoal-sticks.

Seven nines are sixty-three, seven tens are seventy.
Who would that old woman be?
She will remember being me,
but what she is I cannot see.

Yet with every added seven,
some strange present I was given.

James McAuley

Vespers

The sunlight falling on the nursery floor
No longer brings the picture-books to life.
The blood dries unavenged upon the knife;
The jewelled nightingale will sing no more
To the dead emperor; magic hopes depart.
What tears shall melt the cold glass in my heart?

And was it after all no map of truth,
That land of Snakes and Ladders where we first
Practised the soul's ascent or fell accursed?
Were they deceitful meanings that in youth
Stories and games seemed anxious to impart,
Now fixed unfading in the frozen heart?

No, Wisdom's self has shed the warm salt tears
Which melt the glassy ice; and he has willed
Nothing whatever should be unfulfilled
That childhood promised to my later years;
Only this added, which I could not know,
That first the bitter tears, like his, must flow.

The inception of the poem

Midnight once more; the untended fire sinks low;
The lamp stares down upon the book unread;
The papers on my desk have nothing to show:
I have not learned the things I wished to know,
The things I wished to say remain unsaid.

Again the dead pause, the need for a new start;
The vanishing of every name and form
That seemed the very contours of the heart;

And all the working mystery of art
A queenless hive deserted by the swarm.

Then suddenly, unbidden, the theme returns
That visited my youth; over the vast
Pacific with the white wake at their sterns,
The ships of Quiros on their great concerns
Ride in upon the present from the past.

BECAUSE

My father and my mother never quarrelled.
They were united in a kind of love
As daily as the *Sydney Morning Herald*,
Rather than like the eagle or the dove.

I never saw them casually touch,
Or show a moment's joy in one another.
Why should this matter to me now so much?
I think it bore more hardly on my mother,

Who had more generous feelings to express.
My father had dammed up his Irish blood
Against all drinking praying fecklessness,
And stiffened into stone and creaking wood.

His lips would make a switching sound, as though
Spontaneous impulse must be kept at bay.
That it was mainly weakness I see now,
But then my feelings curled back in dismay.

Small things can pit the memory like a cyst:
Having seen other fathers greet their sons,
I put my childish face up to be kissed
After an absence. The rebuff still stuns

My blood. The poor man's curt embarrassment
At such a delicate proffer of affection
Cut like a saw. But home the lesson went:
My tenderness thenceforth escaped detection.

My mother sang *Because*, and *Annie Laurie*,
White Wings, and other songs; her voice was sweet.
I never gave enough, and I am sorry;
But we were all closed in the same defeat.

People do what they can; they were good people,
They cared for us and loved us. Once they stood
Tall in my childhood as the school, the steeple.
How can I judge without ingratitude?

Judgment is simply trying to reject
A part of what we are because it hurts.

The living cannot call the dead collect:
They won't accept the charge, and it reverts.

It's my own judgment day that I draw near,
Descending in the past, without a clue,
Down to that central deadness: the despair
Older than any hope I ever knew.

In the Huon Valley

Propped boughs are heavy with apples,
Springtime quite forgotten.
Pears ripen yellow. The wasp
Knows where windfalls lie rotten.

Juices grow rich with sun.
These autumn days are still:
The glassy river reflects
Elm-gold up the hill,

And big white plumes of rushes.
Life is full of returns;
It isn't true that one never
Profits, never learns:

Something is gathered in,
Worth the lifting and stacking;
Apples roll through the graders,
The sheds are noisy with packing.

Holiday

Sunlight runs like fluid gold in the veins,
A soft hilarity upon hair and skin.
    A bird's momentary shadow stains
        The stone paths we walk in.

It is good not to do what we should do,
But something good we needn't do—like spin
    Straw into gold, or living into
        Surprises, as this thin

Voltage of pale sunshine may incite.
For loving is a game where both can win,
    And freedom to do nothing right
        Is the flower of discipline.

Moulting Lagoon

Grant, if so it may be, still other seasons,
To watch the black swans at their early mating.
The hunters have left their hides, having thinned the numbers,
        And now the pairs are proudly nesting.

There's nothing I can do with brush or crayon;
My marks on papers are a kind of postscript.
I'm not afraid, but yet, if so it may be,
        Let me take note a little longer.

Late, it always seems too late, but it isn't:
The beauty almost destroyed, or the light fading;
The true proverb is still the Flemish master's,
        Als isch kan. It sounds so simple.

Explicit

So the word has come at last:
The argument of arms is past.
Fully tested I've been found
Fit to join the underground.

No worse age has ever been—
Murderous, lying, and obscene;
Devils worked while gods connived:
Somehow the human has survived.

Why these horrors must be so
I never could pretend to know:
It isn't I, dear Lord, who can
Justify your ways to man.

Soon I'll understand it all,
Or cease to wonder: so my small
Spark will blaze intensely bright,
Or go out in an endless night.

Welcome now to bread and wine:
Creature comfort, heavenly sign.
Winter will grow dark and cold
Before the wattle turns to gold.

Amy Witting

To THE UNBORN

Amphibian to mammal, you recalled
    the story of the race
as far as its last modish somersault,
    weightless in inner space.

We had a dialogue that man and wife
    can never hope to have:
when your dumb energy said 'I am life'
    I answered 'I am love'

with confidence, for once. In our shared night
    without a doubt I knew
the warmth and sustenance I gave were quite
    acceptable to you.

It was a love that knew its term, besides,
    approving transience.
I wish the other loves that time derides
    possessed of so much sense.

Beast OF BURDEN

Harnessed with muscle, nerve and will
she suffers out her mortal span,
hauling a cart piled high with logs
along a road in Sichuan.

The burden tyrannous as pain
sets to a grim, peculiar dance
her body twisted like a tree
around the stake of circumstance.

Seeing the rib-cage strain and sag
with the achievement of her breath,
I wish her the beast's privilege:
I wish her ignorance of death.

Lillipilli

The lillipilli tree by the gate is flowering:
tiny green fists are unclenching one after another
to show a magician's handful of knotted, springing
yellow-white silks from up Time's sleeve. How clever
the old wonderworker is, and, when the trick's over,
how extravagant, letting that silken mist
drift to the ground to settle into bright dust.

Rosemary Dobson

ONE SECTION

At the first doorway a child with a jug held carefully,
The cat with its back arched to a query, and the knocker
A little too high for her hand.

At the next a girl who leant on the iron railing
In a parroty dress with eyes on the tipsy soldiers—
Hands full of bottles and roses, buying a paper.

At the third, with the curtain bellying out from behind her
A woman waiting for something, or nothing—in slippers,
One hand to her eyes to shade the dazzle from distance.

Will you believe what I saw in the late afternoon from the tramway,
Going up William Street from the Past to the Future?
Who can deny it was Death in the final doorway?

Shut, shut, with the wind blowing outside from inside,
The bulb removed from the socket under the lampshade,
And the Vacancy notice swinging loose in the window.

COUNTRY PRESS

Under the dusty print of hobnailed boot,
Strewn on the floor the papers still assert
In ornamental gothic, swash italics
And bands of printer's flowers (traditional)
Mixed in a riot of typographic fancy,
this is the *Western Star*, the Farmer's Guide,
The Voice of Progress for the Nyngle District.
Page-proofs of double-spread with running headlines
Paper the walls, and sets of cigarette-cards
Where pouter-bosomed showgirls still display
The charms that dazzled in the nineteen hundreds.
Through gaping slats
Latticed with sun the ivy tendrils fall
Twining the disused platen thrust away
Under a pall of dust in nineteen-twenty.
Draw up a chair, sit down. Just shift the galleys.
You say you have a notice? There's no one dies
But what we know about it. Births, deaths and marriages,
Council reports, wool prices, river-heights,
The itinerant poem and the classified ads—
They all come homewards to the *Western Star*.
Joe's our type-setter. Meet Joe Burrell. Joe's
A promising lad—and Joe, near forty-seven,

Peers from a tennis-shade and, smiling vaguely,
Completes the headline for the Baptist Social.
The dance, the smoke-oh, and the children's picnic
Down by the river-flats beneath the willows—
They all come homewards and Joe sets them all,
Between the morning and the mid-day schooner.
Oh, *Western Star* that bringest all to fold,
The yarding sales, the champion shorthorn bull,
And Williams' pain-relieving liniment,
When I shall die
Set me up close against my fellow-men,
Cheer that cold column headed 'Deaths' with flowers,
Or mix me up with Births and Marriages;
Surround the tragic statement of my death
With euchre-drives and good-times-had-by-all
That, with these warm concomitants of life
Jostled and cheered, in lower-case italics
I shall go homewards in the *Western Star*.

DROWNED PERSON

After death fire must consume
hair, toenails, large bones and small
and then nothing can be told at all.

These bones, with pollen analysis
of their strata, provide a limited history;
for carbon-dating, deduction and analogy

do not reveal the dark side of the mind
nor betray the heart's deviousness,
the body's wilfulness,

the throbbing pulse, the fever,
divided longing, madness.
Down, down through the abyss

stratifications can be plotted
and set out on graph paper.
The following is deduced from existing data

and froth flotation of the surrounding
clay-bed: She was a young woman, gracile,
delicate. Died by water. Was vulnerable

and wounded—by love (but that's hypothesis)—
and carried with her to death such *weedy trophies*
as willow, nettles, crow-flowers and daisies.

Gwen Harwood

A SIMPLE STORY

A visiting conductor
    when I was seventeen,
took me back to his hotel room
    to cover the music scene.

I'd written a composition.
    Would wonders never cease—
here was a real musician
    prepared to hold my piece.

He spread my score on the counterpane
    with classic casualness,
and put one hand on the manuscript
    and the other down my dress.

It was hot as hell in the Windsor.
    I said I'd like a drink.
We talked across gin and grapefruit,
    and I heard the ice go clink

as I gazed at the lofty forehead
    of one who led the band,
and guessed at the hoarded sorrows
    no wife could understand.

I dreamed of a soaring passion
    as an egg might dream of flight,
while he read my crude sonata.
    If he'd said, 'That bar's not right,'

or, 'Have you thought of a coda?'
    or, 'Watch that first repeat,'
or, 'Modulate to the dominant,'
    he'd have had me at his feet.

But he shuffled it all together,
    and said, 'That's *lovely*, dear,'
as he put it down on the washstand
    in a way that made it clear

that I was no composer.
    And I being young and vain,
removed my lovely body
    from one who'd scorned my brain.

I swept off like Miss Virtue
    down dusty Roma Street,
and heard the goods trains whistle
    WHO? WHOOOOOO? in aching heat.

THE LION'S BRIDE

I loved her softness, her warm human smell,
her dark mane flowing loose. Sometimes stirred by
rank longing laid my muzzle on her thigh.
Her father, faithful keeper, fed me well,
but she came daily with our special bowl
barefoot into my cage, and set it down:
our love feast. We became the talk of town,
brute king and tender woman, soul to soul.

Until today: an icy spectre sheathed
in silk minced to my side on pointed feet.
I ripped the scented veil from its unreal
head and engorged the painted lips that breathed
our secret names. A ghost has bones, and meat!
Come soon my love, my bride, and share this meal.

DAYBREAK

The snails brush silver. Critic crow
    points his unpleasant beak, and lances.
Resumes his treetop, darts below
    his acid-bright, corrosive glances.

In the hushed corridors of sleep
    Professor Eisenbart plots treason.
Caretaker mind prepares to sweep
    the dusty offices of reason.

Eisenbart mutters, wakes in rage
    because crow's jarring *c-a-a-r-k-s* distress him.
His mistress grins, refers to age
    and other matters which oppress him.

He scowls purse-lipped. She yawns, and throws
    her arms in scarecrow crucifixion.
Clear of the hills, light's wafer shows
    in world-without-end benediction.

She makes him tea. He sips and calms
    his Royal Academic temper,
while Life and Day outside shout psalms
    in antiphon ... *Et nunc et semper.*

At the Arts Club

Kröte is drunk, but still can play.
Knick-knacks in shadow-boxes wink
at gewgaws while he grinds away
at Brahms, not much the worse for drink.

The hostess pats her tinted curls.
Sees, yawning surreptitiously,
a bitch in black with ginger pearls
squeezing the local tenor's knee.

Kröte lets the loud pedal blur
a dubious trill. The variations
on Handel's foursquare theme occur
to most as odd manipulations

of something better left alone.
They suffer. Kröte knows they do.
With malice adds some more, his own,
and plays all the repeats right through.

He was expected to perform
a waltz, or something short and sweet.
The coffee's made, the supper's warm,
the ravenous guests would love to eat.

Sober, Kröte's inclined to gloom.
Drunk, he becomes a sacred clown.
He puffs and pounds and shakes the room.
An ill-placed ornament falls down.

A pause. Chairs squeak. The hostess claps,
wrongly—there's still the fugue to play.
Tenor and Ginger Pearls, perhaps
for ever, boldly sneak away.

A Scattering of Ashes

Music alone can make me hold
my breath, thinks Kröte as he catches
his bus. A chill wind sighs. Bone cold
he rubs his hands as something scratches
a blank part of his memory.
Today's not right. Where should he be?

Beethoven's funeral. Torchbearer
Schubert held lilies bound in black;
afterwards with Randhartinger
and Lachner, heavy of heart, went back
to the Mehlgrüber Inn, to toast
the one whom death would summon first.

Schubert himself.
                Kröte recalls
why death is showing him its sting,
and why he thinks of funerals:
he must attend a Scattering
of Ashes, is engaged to play
at the crematorium today.

There he arrives immersed in gloom.
An earlier customer's not through.
The mourners, in a waiting room,
wait, since there's nothing else to do.
An old lady leans close to say,
'My beloved friend knew Massenet.'

Kröte's impressed. 'And Saint-Saëns too.
She was in Fauré's singing class.
Now I don't know what I shall do.
I thought I'd be the first to pass
away. We were friends for fifty years.'
She weeps, and Kröte's close to tears.

They are summoned. Kröte lifts the lid
of a fancy electronic job.
Is this an organ? God forbid.
He fiddles off a plastic knob,
fumbles the pedals with cold feet,
plays what's required, and takes a seat

beside Old Friend while prayers are said.
The chapel's neutral, shiny-clean.
No reason here to bow the head.
What God would visit this cool scene?
—O for a gorgeous requiem.
Old mittened claws: he watches them

extract from her capacious purse
a small carved wooden box, maybe
a reliquary made to nurse
an ash or two? She taps his knee
and puts the casket, like a grand
actress, in his unwilling hand.

—Pins? Needles? 'Whiskers! Our dead cats.
We've made provision in our wills
for those outliving us.' She pats
his hand confidingly. He spills
the box and contents on the floor.
Mourners are filing through a door,

but Kröte's kneeling to retrieve
whiskers. The cat is on the mat.
Lord, help me find them. I'll believe

in the resurrection of the cat.
She whispers on without concern,
'We couldn't keep whole cats to burn.

'Yes, fifty years we lived together.
Cats were our children.' Kröte leads
her gently into funeral weather
just as an unseen agent feeds
the ashes from a cross-shaped vent.
She shakes her casket. Whiskers sent

flying off on a sudden gust
fall on the unsuspecting crowd.
—Whiskers to whiskers, dust to dust.
'The cat's fugue!' she exclaims aloud.
Kröte begins to hum the theme
and feels her crazy joke redeem

the dismal day. He takes her arm.
She smiles at him, and he can guess
how bright she was, how full of charm.
—Such intervals! Let music bless
all hopes, all loves, however odd.
Music, my joy, my full-scale God.

Oyster Cove

Dreams drip to stone. Barracks and salt marsh blaze
opal beneath a crackling glaze of frost.
Boot-black, in graceless Christian rags, a lost
race breathes out cold. Parting the milky haze
on mudflats, seabirds, clean and separate, wade.
Mother, Husband and Child: stars which forecast
fine weather, all are set. The long night's past
and the long day begins. God's creatures, made
woodcutters' whores, sick drunks, watch the sun prise
their life apart: flesh, memory, language all
split open, featureless, to feed the wild
hunger of history. A woman lies
coughing her life out. There's still blood to fall,
but all blood's spilt that could have made a child.

Schrödinger's Cat Preaches to the Mice

To A. D. Hope

Silk-whispering of knife on stone,
due sacrifice, and my meat came.
Caressing whispers, then my own
choice among laps by leaping flame.

What shape is space? Space will put on
the shape of any cat. Know this:
my servant Schrödinger is gone
before me to prepare a place.

So worship me, the Chosen One
in the great thought-experiment.
As in a grave I will lie down
and wait for the Divine Event.

The lid will close. I will retire
from sight, curl up and say Amen
to geiger counter, amplifier,
and a cylinder of HCN.

When will the geiger counter feel
decay, its pulse be amplified
to a current that removes the seal
from the cylinder of cyanide?

Dead or alive? The case defies
all questions. Let the lid be locked.
Truth, from your little beady eyes,
is hidden. I will not be mocked.

Quantum mechanics has no place
for what's there without observation.
Classical physics cannot trace
spontaneous disintegration.

If the box holds a living cat
no scientist on earth can tell.
But I'll be waiting, sleek and fat.
Verily, all will not be well

if, to the peril of your souls,
you think me gone. Know that this house
is mine, that kittens by mouse-holes
wait, who have never seen a mouse.

Oodgeroo of the tribe Noonuccal

*N*ONA

At the happy chattering evening meal
Nona the lithe and lovely,
Liked by all,
Came out of her mother's gunya,
Naked like the rest, and like the rest
Unconscious of her body

As the dingo pup rolling about in play.
All eyes turned, men and women, all
Had smiles for Nona.
And what did the women see? They saw
The white hand-band above her forehead,
The gay little feather-tuft in her hair
Fixed with gum, and how she wore it.
They saw the necklet of red berries
And the plaited and painted reed arm-band
Jarri had made her.
And what did the men see? Ah, the men.
they did not see armlet or band
Or the bright little feather-tuft in her hair.
They had no eye for the red berries,
They did not look at these things at all.

BALLAD OF THE TOTEMS

My father was Noonuccal man and
          kept old tribal way,
His totem was the Carpet Snake,
          whom none must ever slay;
But mother was of Peewee clan,
          and loudly she expressed
The daring view that carpet snakes
          were nothing but a pest.

Now one lived right inside with us
          in full immunity,
For no one dared to interfere
          with father's stern decree:
A mighty fellow ten feet long,
          and as we lay in bed
We kids could watch him round a beam
          not far above our head.

Only the dog was scared of him,
          we'd hear its whines and growls,
But mother fiercely hated him
          because he took her fowls.
You should have heard her diatribes
          that flowed in angry torrents
With words you never see in print,
          except in D.H. Lawrence.

'I kill that robber,' she would scream,
          fierce as a spotted cat;
'You see that bulge inside of him?
          My speckly hen make that!'

But father's loud and strict command
         made even mother quake;
I think he'd sooner kill a man
         than kill a carpet snake.

That reptile was a greedy-guts,
         and as each bulge digested
He'd come down on the hunt at night
         as appetite suggested.
We heard his stealthy slithering sound
         across the earthen floor,
While the dog gave a startled yelp
         and bolted out the door.

Then over in the chicken-yard
         hysterical fowls gave tongue,
Loud frantic squawks accompanied by
         the barking of the mung,
Until at last the racket passed,
         and then to solve the riddle,
Next morning he was back up there
         with a new bulge in his middle.

When father died we wailed and cried,
         our grief was deep and sore;
And strange to say from that sad day
         the snake was seen no more.
The wise old men explained to us:
         'It was his tribal brother,
And that is why it done a guy'—
         but some looked hard at mother.

She seemed to have a secret smile,
         her eyes were smug and wary,
She looked as innocent as the cat
         that ate the pet canary.
We never knew, but anyhow
         (to end this tragic rhyme)
I think we all had snake for tea
         one day about that time.

*W*E ARE GOING

FOR GRANNIE COOLWELL

They came into the little town
A semi-naked band subdued and silent,
All that remained of their tribe.
They came here to the place
        of their old bora ground
Where now the many white men

hurry about like ants.
Notice of estate agent reads:
    'Rubbish May Be Tipped Here'.
Now it half covers the traces of the old bora ring.
They sit and are confused,
    they cannot say their thoughts:
'We are as strangers here now,
    but the white tribe are the strangers.
We belong here, we are of the old ways.
We are the corroboree and the bora ground,
We are the old sacred ceremonies,
    the laws of the elders.
We are the wonder tales of Dream Time,
    the tribal legends told.
We are the past, the hunts and the laughing games,
    the wandering camp fires.
We are the lightning-bolt over Gaphembah Hill
Quick and terrible,
And the Thunder after him, that loud fellow.
We are the quiet daybreak paling the dark lagoon.
We are the shadow-ghosts creeping back as the
camp fires burn low.
We are nature and the past, all the old ways
Gone now and scattered.
The scrubs are gone, the hunting and the laughter.
The eagle is gone, the emu and the kangaroo are
gone from this place.
The bora ring is gone.
The corroboree is gone.
And we are going.'

Lex Banning

Nursery Rhyme

There was a crooked man
who walked a crooked mile,
while the crooked hands ran backwards
around the crooked dial.

He found his crooked journey
led him through a crooked town,
where all his crooked neighbours
were running up and down,

and conducting crooked businesses
in crooked shops and stalls,

while their shadows capered crookedly
upon the crooked walls.

So he followed their example
and, as he passed along,
sold his birthright for a fortune:
he had got it for a song.

He thought he had a bargain,
and was overheard to say,
'That sometime every crooked dog
must have his crooked day.'

But even as he said it,
and drew a crooked breath,
he reached his crooked mile's end
and was straightened out by death.

$\mathcal{I}$XION

Turning and re-turning,
    the wheel returns once more,
once more the circus-master
    beckons through the door.
Will nothing stop the shadows'
    convolutions on the floor?

Will nothing stop the shadows?
    Must I once again perform
the usual limited number
    of variations from the norm?
Though the sky seems set for thunder
    there is never any storm.

Though the sky seems set for thunder,
    rest assured it will not rain;
at least till the appropriate season
    has everything in train.
There is never any reversal
    for the slayer and the slain.

There is never any reversal,
    the axe achieves the block,
denial produces only
    the crowing of the cock.
Turning and re-turning;
    no one stops the clock.

CAPTAIN ARTHUR PHILLIP AND THE BIRDS

Copper-green Phillip,
with a beak like a hawk,
perches on his pedestal
and will not talk
to the stuttering starlings
fluttering around,
or the crumb-seeking pigeons
patterning the ground;
and though, daylong,
bird calls to bird,
copper-green Phillip
says never a word.

Copper-green Phillip
just stares and stands
with a scroll and a flag
in his strong bronze hands,
and the birds may wonder
what's on the scroll:
is it the *Sirius*'s
pilgrims' roll;
or, perhaps, a commission;
or a declaration,
washing his hands
of the subsequent nation;
or, even, an inventory
of flocks and herds?
But Royal Navy captains
never talk to birds.

Copper-green Phillip
just stands and stares
away down the harbour
at the rolling years,
and the birds all gossip
of the nation's vices,
and of some of her virtues,
and of whom she entices;
but whether she's Magdalene,
or whether she's Martha,
it's all the same
to Captain Arthur.

Dimitris Tsaloumas

Note with interlude from the banks of the Brisbane in September

FOR MANFRED JURGENSEN

I sit with Spring by the Brisbane River
that gifts a city with loveliness. Fawn-thick
it flows across the level sun
in pools of purer light, and there it gleams
against the city's bastions, a distant blue.

A barge moves up below the gabled roofs
of garden houses. Serenely vibrant,
she folds the water equally at the bows.
Two men are talking on the deck.

It is so peaceful now that strange birds
land speechless at my feet
and look at me like children. And I write this
in shade unknown to you, antique,
the lily-blossomed tree, the canopy
of pale-scented years,

     ah true Bauhinia
my love, these must be days of happiness,
I know, for words come forth again
unfathomable, out of yellow-paged time
to walk with Thais in your train, she
of the slender throat, Beauty of conflagrations,
Aspasia the marble-obsessed, husky Lais
of sinful Corinth, and philosophic Lastheinia;
lush titian Phryne, lascivious Theodora
of the lustrous skin, mistress of palaces,
who dreamed of power in her youth
in Golden Horn and argued high Theology
through torrid vigils

      I write because
this ache gets sharper with the years
and my truth is but a husk of substance
wasted, my strength no longer adequate
to breast the song of the rock-bound sisters.
My message is this: in the old cupboard
in the wall, beside the mirror
opposite the bed, you'll find some papers
held in a roll with string:
please burn them. Youthful,
possibly happy stuff, I can't recall—

things one could redeem perhaps
in leaner times, but burn them nonetheless.
This has been preying on my mind of late,
but if I am to end this journey at all
it'll have to be as I began, expecting nothing.

AUTUMN SUPPER

Only this table by the draughty window
bare since the beginning of time:

a knife, black olives, a hunk of bread.
The bottle glows dark in the late

autumn light, and in the glass,
against the wind and the raging seas,

the one rose of the difficult year.
All my life long I've hankered

after simplicity. When night falls
don't come to light the candles and pour

the wine. There's not enough for two;
I cannot share my hunger.

THE GRUDGE

Strange that your image should occur to me
as I beat the grass for snakes in this

forsaken patch. It doesn't seem right to me.
I have always thought your manner somewhat

too correct, but your business dealings
are of good report. Or is it the woman

who shares my bed? She burns in the flesh
of many a man and I find it galling, I confess,

that you should never look at her that way.
It kind of blunts the sting of my pleasure.

Nor does the splendour of my house and fame
move you much. Yet there you are, my friend,

flushed out of grass by the scouting stick
amid the knotted vines, pleasant as ever,

tall in the haze a cut above the likes of me.
It bothers me. This is my brother's vineyard.

Alexander Craig

SEA AT PORTSEA

Blue/viridescent/with a cold edge
    against the biscuit
  hue the yellow and brown
  of this nude populated

rim: its light shifts with the light
    of sun moon stars
  shafts stabbing from a beacon
  night-beams on flounder-spears

We dared to slither from it once
    now revisit
  no longer than we need to
  Daylong its sunlit spray

is barely glimpsed the sheerest drape
    drawn over
  the sand across the shallows
  where the sharp-toothed prototype

of streamlined grace is driven in
    by hunger Why
  Do I seem baptised beneath
  my beach-umbrella landlocked

in that evangelistic tent
    (its congregation
  the cold-eyed gulls the sermon
  unspoken)? It's a dream

like others: it will pass I watch
    with a kind of awe
  the vestals in bikinis
  tending the sacred fire

Dorothy Hewett

FROM TESTAMENT

These have I lost, being too much beloved,
And having for their virtue only this—
That I have loved them.
That cold white wanton with the stiff-necked pride
Of centuries of narrow-minded squires,
Migrating to a strange, dark brutal country,
Where you met the convicts shackled on the roads,

And the hangman's rope cast shadows on the soil.
Sitting astride their horses, their two feet
Clamped coldly in the mud marsh;
Giving birth to sons; all with the dignity of Englishmen.
They carefully translated their whole way
And pride of living to a hangman's land,
Ploughed the dark soil, wrenched order from its chaos,
Its sullen, hostile hatred of their hands,
Subdued it, mixed their coldness with its hunger,
Never gave up, or ceased to plough and sow,
Because it was their only living passion,
These cold-eyed men with honour in their hearts:
The passion for the land, to feel the soil
Ache through their thin loins, it was like
Another man's hunger for a wanton woman:
Building their red board churches in the clearing,
Puritanical among the ringbarked gum trees,
Standing like a witches' sabbath on the sky;
Leading the flock, sending their thin, dark daughters
Home to England for their education;
Treating the sad-eyed blacks with kind contempt;
Shipping their pianos, portraits, rugs, from England;
Building their English houses by the rivers; and yet
All mad-eyed, lonely men with strange misgivings.
Your heritage, my love, these forefathers,
Who sit with white skulls nodding in the grass,
Holding you with their stiff-necked principles,
As if they were a council of old men
Crouching like stumps against the reddened sky.
Mad-eyed and lonely, riding your horse at dusk
Over the flats, the green and purple bogs,
The dark pools winking in the angry sunset,
Clinging with frightened knees against his ribs,
Galloping with your black head moving down
The fretwork of the skyline, the small
Dreadful smile of terror on your lips.
When you rode at sunset it always seemed
The dark old men rose, silent from their graves,
And walked, mumbling behind you down the hill,
Smiling and bending to the earth, and nodding
Their heads over the new green shoots of grass:
Turning their faces to the skyline where
Their mad descendant rode with white hands twisted
Round the reins, the light reflected on their lips
The same small smile of your self-mockery.

The Witnesses

This is the wide country
I lived in when I was young,
The great clouds over it,
The hawk in the high sky hung ...

Hung upside down like a metal bird,
Fixes time in his fatal eye.
The mice run circles, the plovers cry,
Till I hardly know in that hurtling sky
Which of the three wild things am I ...
Murderer, victim, recorded cry.

The hawk spins round like a weather vane.

The seed spills bitter, the hawk turns slow.
Under the rainbow arch will lie
The girl with the haystack hair awry,
Her legs outflung and her brief blood dry,
While the bumpkin boys go whistling by
with gravel rashed knees and weeping eye ...

And the hawk in the high sky hung.

Summer

This summer I will go back
to the country of sunburnt children
the lost country at the end of the world
where two oceans meet ...

I will walk up the moonlit path
between the peppermint bushes
to the little weatherboard house
with the rusty windows facing the bay

I will cross the porch
pushing open the flywire door
the room will be full
of the hush and pull of the sea
I will see the children
circling the oval table
with the dark blue inkstains
playing Rickety Kate
their earnest faces bend to their cards
they don't look up
even when I stand beside them
they will not know I am there
I will point and tell them
which card to play

but they won't hear me.
My father lies reading
under the lamp on the sofa
my mother washes up
in the tin dish on the kitchen table
the fuel stove burning behind her
the scrub closes round the house
and the sea listens
outside through the window
the light on Breaksea
flickers on and off.

I will turn quietly
leaving the way I came
tomorrow the children
will get up early
to swim in the sea
ringed with black crags
one with a glitter of sunlight
they will build their cubby houses
under the peppermint bushes
racing through the bush reserve
playing wild horses ...

one will be shot
out of his Kittyhawk
over the Owen Stanleys
one will give up his farm
and all his possessions
to the Jehovah Witnesses
one will lose his wife to cancer

one will lose her child
one will be unhappily married
my father will be buried
in the graveyard
on the edge of town
my mother will lose her wits
but none of them know it ...

nothing will stay in its place
except the sea   and the little house
and the black crags showing
above the line of the rip
that will not stop flowing.

B. R. Whiting

Our sad monarchies

Is there a structure that stands up to time
That whistles in the wind when we're away
With the same tune? Do details hold their line,
Do the proportions stay?
We have added ourselves to make reality,
The selves we add being dreams and being there;
Without the dream, things lose their credibility
In quite another order:
These familiar limbs,
The closest animal,
Turn into tombs,
Merge in the real—
Grown out of chaos to kill us, the linked teams
Of atoms have their iron priorities,
To claim the bodies and ignore the dreams,
Smoke from the pyre of our sad monarchies.

Splitting firewood

Splitting firewood I often found
Fat white grubs in the grain
And would toss them on the ground—
The fowls learned this, and a vain
Old crow who posed apart in liberty
Used to wait for me to throw
The juicy ones under his special tree,
Where he would stab them straight
Before the frantic fowls arrived—
Bird-brain, they were in such a state,
The brown contentious crowd that lived
In a clucking strain of imitation.
But then, a cackling hen, meanly
By cunning, running to look
Would try to beat the mob to it again,
Push up, put her head on the block,
Staring, arrogant, stupid, plain,
And I would cut it off, throw
It to the black and elegant crow
Who did not rely on my offering—
There was no change in the fowlyard cries,
They were indifferent to headless suffering,
And he would peck out its opal eyes.

BLIND CHESS

The squid behind his cloud of ink,
The actor in his tragic part,
The Council Chairman, make you think
How much is there, how much is art.

We had to make the God we made
Omniscient, and omnipotent,
Able to pierce the inky shade
To see which way the heart was bent.

But now that we have lost His glance,
We are abandoned to Blind Chess,
A game that gives us all a chance—
We can't see them, they can't see us.

David Rowbotham

THE RATTLE IN THE MARQUEE

The night I heard the soldier
with the death rattle, I knew the game was up
and over—no more banter
between beds about medicinal beer
prescribed to put an edge on appetite,
to slap fat on our jungled bones.
What a perfect pair of pyjama boys we were
with our perimeter diseases and malnutrition
in a marquee of temperature and rest—
full of hospital spirit, the kind to keep
away the creeps. Later, diagnosed,
I was stung by penicillin—mosquito of cure
with a proboscis no anopheles could match—
and shipped home numb, feeling out of touch.

Never diagnosed—except
perhaps post mortem—he grew dirigibly fat
and yellow as a warning, looked at himself
and joked watch out mate that beer's a pump,
and then began to yell
Get me out of here, I want to go home,
I want Mum. Hell came down on his bravado.
As I listened it did the same to me.
Like dice from a game of ludo
the rattle stuck in his throat, and hit the whole marquee.
We became a perfect bunch of huddling kids.

And the night the rattle stopped,
the war went so deep it was never removed.
And I know—from diagnosis—that the soldier lived
in what I did afterwards;
how I spoke, how I saw, as I versed being
urgently, from the landscape of great hope
where he was never buried
to more perimeters, waiting to be farmed.

With his death he laid down the law
like a legacy from birth to infancy
and fate. The game's up and over mate
for me ... and I lost
my appetite for beer. And whenever I've seen
a baby with a rattle, would it be true
to say I've been alarmed?

Vincent Buckley

NATURA NATURANS

Rilke said of her,
with the usual grand regretfulness,
'Nature knows nothing of us.'
But this pregnant mare with her low head
and propped legs, mooning by the electric pole,
tricked by her hormones,
knows me; and the gamebird knows me enough
to walk the few steps before me.
It is Rilke they know nothing of,
and nothing of Proust, either, or Sartre.
They hear the engines in the next paddock
run, shudder, crackle,
like a tree falling. They know
it is not a tree.

These new scarlet blotches
on the backs of my hands,
are they Nature? or some new
vellum-art of the skin?

SHEELA-NA-GIG

The wintry keen goes. He has cut a
scythe line through the dry berries
and scraped stone-dust from the *cunnus*.
Now two men, squatting in the rain,
are measuring her

with red rubber, saucy as latex
as though for a young bride's coffin.

ONE PUT DOWN HIS NOTEBOOK

One put down his notebook
on the sand, among the shells,
and walked into the sea
whose foam seemed kinder than,
yes whiter than, blossom. Another
swam to a climax of drowning in his hometown river.
One cut her wrists, expecting
a great flow of wine. One tried to die of no sleep.
We did it without the American fad
of the loony-bin, with its frisson
and all the stories and anecdotes
it would lead to, and the portraits
of oldtimers, and the poems
polished like an apple to rough shine.
We let down in private, in secret;
suicide is not an export commodity
and will not come alive on air.
It is just the ending of this affair.

INTROVERT AS HORSEMAN

The introvert as horseman.
Staring as if at your relations,
See him there
in sepia, hat cocked, leggings
tight as a Nazi's, and you can
place him, any way you like, a black stump,
for example, on the creek-bank,
the stick in his right fist
tapping at nothing,
the soil ghostlike as steam,
or full of nostalgia in the kitchen
keeping an eye out for
the last century, the century of lost marriages.

The money in the bank, the suits,
the pony-and-trap, the watch-and-watchchain,
the silver-dented sets of harness,
proxies for the land; and so were
the brick house he had almost started to build
for his bride-to-be
that nobody had met; and the smoke-browned portrait
of his mother swaddled to the neck.

He noticed these; but he kept love
for the great purebred shire horses,
with their plumed feet stamping, and their shoulders
rubbing the trees, the old blind one,
Sailor, still serving
his droves of mares in the dustbowl,
the sweat drops thick as wool scrapings
on the fence, the lintel brown with mugginess,
the crooked iron tanks, the ungrowing light.

Laurence Collinson

BEDMANSHIP

The undulating swans at first
were decorations of the bed
where you and I, under-rehearsed,
had fled.

The mathematics that I knew—
the one and one, the prac and pure,
the unknowns that are false and true—
were insecure.

The droll equation from the facts:
the u, the i; who's plus? who minus?—
to such infinities our acts
confine us.

The seaweed with its languid paw
scratches our ambiguity;
our bed chug-chugs beside the shore
of continuity.

Beds are seldom what they seem;
swans and seaweed never cease;
I beg of love its lesser scheme:
an x of peace.

NIGHT AND DAY

Father architects the earth,
Mother excavates the sky;
darkness sidles up the sky;
sun and moon bestow a birth.

Mother grins within a wreath,
Father humps her undersea;
brilliance scatters on the sea;
moon and sun deliver death.

J. R. Rowland

CHILDREN AT WEE JASPER

As rotting autumn spreads
In northern trees, and treacherous
Yellow fevers lift
Leaves down from twigs
That meet frosts naked,
Roaming shorthaired clouds
Blue as cattledogs
Muster and drive the soft
Stock from summer's acre.

The stringy country stirs
And lifts a sombre head
Its foreign clothing fallen,
Takes on its native air
In olive ochre dun;
A dark accurate gaze
Penetrates to where
Furthest hill and valley
Are silent in the sun.

There, mazes of dead-finish
Sway their brown clubs
Of light whispering metal:
Deep into the sky
A luminous random swarm
Appear and vanish
Wandering stars of day
Inconsequential, mortal
Angels of thistledown.

Mysterious and close
As the tiny sprinkling sound
Of seedheads, or the sight
Of those untimely stars
My son and daughter watch
With serious listening face
Cloud and season pause,
Learning land and light
As native to them each.

At night, in foreign towns,
May this, too deep for memory,
Yet comfort and secure;
Involuntary, profound,
Absorbed by vacant eyes
On vacant afternoons,

Be compass still to find
The north of who they are
And where their true soil lies.

Cicadas

Cicadas build boxes in air. Their intersections
Multiply in an overarching city
Of corridors, walled with minute corrugations
That file the nerves passing through.
Intensity! Yet the clear blue
Is depthless still—

Each sits invisible in its station
Wound tight, pulsing without movement,
As celestial tweezers make delicate adjustment
Over the whole field. The Greek notion
Was that they feed on air.
Their varying shrill

Lasts all day, burns out the summer.
At evening, wind and thunder
Collapse their complex shimmer
To bury them deep under.
They fade into black skies
Like webs when the dew dries.

Tomorrow again they will be there.
The multiple silence of their noise
Vibrates with glittering leaves, atoms of trees
Ranked up the enclosing hill, the restless glare
Of sea, the dazzling beach, and those who lie
Tranced like them, in thronging vacancy.

Francis Webb

Vase painter

Old grey-headed painter, why do you moon
In a tiny, close attic this long afternoon,
While heavy air flaps like a moth in the heat,
Dust slowly puffs down the length of the street
As a sweating wind fingers each yellow mud brick,
And a hawk breaks the sky like a black crooked stick?

You're hardly alive, shut away in your room,
Your beard like the tattered old ghost of a broom,
The whites of your eyes sadly gone in arrears

As they tremble above (with the flicker of years
Or possibly joy, or yet possibly grief)
Your Kamares vase with the whirlpool of leaf.

All the priests and the ladies, the little fat king,
Watch the bull-sports in the grand circus-ring
Where slender sheer women, curved shapely as thorns,
Vault over the sullenly glittering horns,
And, arms raised to the sun on the hill's highest fold,
Laughs a beautiful goddess in ivory, gold.

Miles out of hearing, though still within reach
Of those far-away cheers like surf on a beach,
Your holiday lost, how you toil to produce
With fingers too shaky almost for use
This black-and-white bauble, this chipped precious thing
For our eyes and our books and our reckoning!

$\mathcal{E}$ND OF THE PICNIC

When that humble-headed elder, the sea, gave his wide
Strenuous arm to a blasphemy, hauling the girth
And the sail and the black yard
Of unknown *Endeavour* towards this holy beach,
Heaven would be watching. And the two men. And the earth,
Immaculate, illuminant, out of reach.

It must break—on sacred water this swindle of a wave.
Thick canvas flogged the sticks. Hell lay hove-to.
Heaven did not move.
Two men stood safe: even when the prying, peering
Longboat, the devil's totem, cast off and grew,
No god shifted an inch to take a bearing.

It was Heaven-and-earth's jolting out of them shook the men.
It was uninitiate scurf and bone that fled.
Cook's column holds here.
Our ferry is homesick, whistling again and again;
But still I see how the myth of a daylight bled
Standing in ribbons, over our heads, for an hour.

$\mathcal{F}$IVE DAYS OLD

For Christopher John

Christmas is in the air.
You are given into my hands
Out of quietest, loneliest lands.
My trembling is all my prayer.
To blown straw was given
All the fullness of Heaven.

The tiny, not the immense,
Will teach our groping eyes.
So the absorbed skies
Bleed stars of innocence.
So cloud-voice in war and trouble
Is at last Christ in the stable.

Now wonderingly engrossed
In your fearless delicacies,
I am launched upon sacred seas,
Humbly and utterly lost
In the mystery of creation,
Bells, bells of ocean.

Too pure for my tongue to praise,
That sober, exquisite yawn
Or the gradual, generous dawn
At an eyelid, maker of days:
To shrive my thought for perfection
I must breathe old tempests of action

For the snowflake and face of love,
Windfall and word of truth,
Honour close to death.
O eternal truthfulness, Dove,
Tell me what I hold—
Myrrh? Frankincense? Gold?

If this is man, then the danger
And fear are as lights of the inn,
Faint and remote as sin
Out here by the manger.
In the sleeping, weeping weather
We shall all kneel down together.

*C*ANOBOLAS

Love best of all the hour of that grave Wish:

Colour elected, deposed: something is dying:
Galahs parade in their circuit cheering and crying,
Each flaunting his ruddied ceremonial sash.
The sun goes down as an ancient broad-mouthed fish
Whose blood asleep is alarum and defying
Bent pins of usage, all the worrying, trying.
It is now the unchevroned sentry puts on flesh.

His mother is this mountain. Athens and Troy,
Orange, her Son breathe in a welter, suck
The balanced single breast: she may not pluck
Destiny, nightfall from them: one destroy,
One be destroyed, one croon in a summer's joy,

One be fastened with nails, left hanging sick.
And all this houseless firmament, by strange luck,
Is sunset playing with dice and nipple and toy.

Because, rising above earth, she takes station
Upon eternity, between her two veined hands
Weaves dateless things from all the yellow strands
Of metronome, glances, memories, and commotion.
Pure hypostasis—all the inconsequent ocean
Of fading colours, all the grey towns and lands
and faces flock to her, rasping demands,
And drink, and settle and sink in her devotion.

If only we learn to pause and let her rise
Not steeply but as a gentle concave, all,
Towns, lands, faces, must nuzzle her tender swell
and learn from her the true Form and be wise.
Darkness? gesticulating memories?
There is raised a television aerial
Above her breast: low-flying aircraft tell
Of every darkness thwarted by her eyes.

Airliner

I am become a shell of delicate alleys
Stored with the bruit of the motors, resolute thunders
And unflagging dances of the nerves.
Beneath me the sad giant frescoes of the clouds:
Towerings and defiles through intense grey valleys,
Huge faces of kings, queens, castles—travelling cinders,
And monuments, and shrouds.
A fortress crammed with engines of warfare swerves

As we bank into it, and all the giant sad past
Clutches at me swimming through it: here
Is faith crumbling—here the engines of war
In sleek word and sad fresco of print,
Landscapes broken apart; and here at last
Is home all undulant, banners hanging drear
Or collapsing into chaos, burnt.
And now we are through, and now a barbarous shore

Grimaces in welcome, showing all its teeth
And now the elder sea all wrinkled with love
Sways tipsily up to us, and now the swing
Of the bridge; houses, islands, and many blue bushlands come.
Confine me in Pinchgut, bury me beneath
The bones of the old lag, analyse me above
The city lest I drunkenly sing
Of wattles, wars, childhoods, being at last home.

ℒEGIONARY ANTS

The world, the tranquil punctual gyroscope,
Is more or less at peace after her fashion,
Broad bowels work, creatures rejoice or mope,
There is clash of interests in all dogged creation,
When silence comes as at noiseless thwack of a drum,
And look! the warriors come.

First shudder away the birds, all flaking, wheeling
Out of range and all forgetful of their young,
Crying at the ominous shadowy floor stealing
Over their earth; and then not giving tongue.
Now all things hold silent, and the surf
Breaks on beleaguered turf.

They come. And whose ear can divine the awful waves,
Signals of command suspired by what demagogue?
They tumble in orgies of commitment, these black slaves,
All activity, but insensible as rotted log.
Their mad absorbed unity of hunger and mirth
Is the belly-heave of earth.

The wounded mammal whimpers and butts and runs,
Glazing, eaten alive. The three-days' chick
Shrills fear, and like a paradigm of guns
Anarchy gorges itself and life is sick.
Look close for a second, stranger, you will find
Blear paradigm also of our mind.

For this is our mind for today—never creation
But all nakedness. Odours and colours blent
And sounds and shapes, swivel throughout that ration
Of basic nerves, like darkness imminent;
But sometimes in moments of withdrawal one sees, feels
Certain subterranean wheels.

As their cloud progresses it may assume strange shapes:
Of devouring lover and organ, it may weep
Like mandibles of rain and whatever rapes
The fruit and flesh of life in very sleep.
Sleep is ever the enemy, it seems,
To all who dream these dreams.

But punctilious night now sweeps away all lust
On wheels, and another, a blessed, silence broods
Over many bones left twinkling in the dust.
Earth debates bitterly in these solitudes
Whether she dare replace, below, above,
The singings, ramblings of love.

Nessun Dorma

IN MEMORY OF JUSSI BJORLING

Past six o'clock. I have prayed. No one is sleeping.
I have wandered past the old maternity home's
Red stone fermented by centuries; and there comes
New light, new light; and the cries of the rooks sweeping
To their great nests are guerilla light in a fusion
—Murmurs, echoes, plainsong; and the night
Will be all an abyss and depth of light between
Two shorelines in labour: birth and death. O passion
(One light in the hospital window) of quickening light,
O foetus quaking towards light, sound the gaunt green,
Trawl Norfolk, and make shiver the window-blind,
Harass nebulae for Bjorling. Find him, find.

And now the bar, the feeble light, glissade
Of tables and glasses, and the mantal-set
Intoning his death. Broad tender sunlights fret
Our twilight, his remembered voice has laid
Cock-crow and noon upon harrowed palms of the sill.
O broad light and tender, lucent aria,
Lacerate my paling cheeklines with the steep
Bequest of light and tears, flood me until
The man is the dawning child; be anathema
To man-made darkness. No one, no one shall sleep
Till the cry of the infant emergent, lost and lame,
Is the cry of a death gone towering towards the Flame.

Bruce Beaver

Cow dance

I came across her browsing on a slope
Thatched with dry brown fern scythed in a day
Between milkings, the stones hid in each clump
Blunting the brush-hooks' blades, clanging back
Unhuman oaths over the hill's shoulder
In a noon crackling with summer's fierce wit.
There, mooning and nosing about the grass-tops
Chaffed with holocausts of laughing flame
Or full of chuckling juice mellow as mead,
With an inward jolt at sudden confrontation
She looked up fixedly with liquid eyes
Wide as the stretch of innocence that holds
Pellets of gamin treachery, eyes full of
Remorseless motherhood and blind foraging,

With her two stomachs quite outwitting love,
Lust even, in the common faith
Of bull and cowdom: tyranny of gut.
Being on the loose for laughs, I ran at her
And watched her bolt, all belly and backside
With teats like bagpipes slung beneath a bronco,
For she exploded then, a milk-filled grenade
Gone careering down the slope to the others
Watching her progress with the same wet eyes
Till off they all went, down the hill together,
Horns down, hoofs up, harridans gone dancing
Hell for leather; and, as much a part of the dance,
Centaur-wise I followed in the wake
Of the heifers, leaping down those summer slopes,
Laughing, shouting, mad with the fun of it all.

THE RED BALLOON

To those of us with irons in the fire
Of art, that hand upon the shoulder of
Our flexings at the forge comes with a clear
Summoning to pause and witness love
Wandering with our childhood through the narrow
Streets of bitterness beneath wide skies—
Love like a red balloon lifting our sorrow
Up and above itself into the ways
Of bright air and the singing birds of the sun
Until, so swiftly, the bleak heart of the street
Breaks in its bitterness, throws up its stone
Of envy, treads love down under its hate.
But still the rainbow bridge is built again
Out of imagination, out of pain.

DEATH'S DIRECTIVES III

Death offered me ecstacy or suffering,
one or the other at differing times.
It knew that what I really wanted
was neither but the lot of the half-being,
some happiness, some unhappiness, not this
heaven, this hell of genius, without
the making gifts of genius—at most
a moderate talent among other talents.

But the living of life, death told me, would be
at recurring times ecstatic or agonising
when all I wanted was peace or acceptance.
The middle way of the Buddhists denied me

because I believed in a divine mystery.
The way of non-attachment of the Hindu
impossible for me because I clung to desires.
The way of my Jewish forebears unattainable
because I accepted and rejected a pantheon
of gods and goddesses—yet I could not be
wholly pagan and at the most
in love with the earth, at the least healthy.

Neither could I worship the terrible tripartite
god of the Christians and its central figure,
the tortured scion—Not wholly accept the myriad
creeds of dualism, though I thought the cosmos
made by a god of more evil than good.
And when I found the ancient way of the Gnostics
reviving among the philosophers of this present
twentieth century I welcomed their writings and studied them
confusedly only to feel I was not one of them.

At last death drew me away from ecstasies and sufferings
and said *You are human, a middle-aged man—*
celebrate the brilliancies, the overshadowings,
of men and women for they have invented
all the gods and goddesses you ever knew
on earth. Interpret and show forth their thoughts
and emotions. And when you have done this
to the best of your ability I will show you
the way towards the way towards the way
towards the ways of the divine mystery.
It seemed then that death understood me
better than any angel of life on earth.

*S*ILO TREADING

At silo filling time the air was similarly wet
between the dense-packed, leaf-clustered corn rows, in the little
shed that housed the howling, belting, stalk-chopping silage-
making machine and in the empty silo, treading under
a rain of moist fragments the corn leaves, corn stalks, stray cobs
into a green pudding that would cook itself, beginning
the thermic process even while we trod that upright vintage.
But the whole process depended on corn. And corn is a truly magic
thing. As much a gift from the gods as the grape. It shares with the
        grape
religious rites and its history is linked with the dismembering
and rebirth of a god. I was nearly partially dismembered myself
one season, hacking at the heavy stalks and zipping swiftly upwards
with a saw-bladed reaping hook. It slipped from my grasp in

my sweat-slippery hand
and I mechanically hauled at it stuck in the base of a stalk and tore
a half inch gash in my second finger, nearly lifting off
the top of it, only the bone and the nail held things together until
about forty-eight hours had passed and my relatives said
            they needed more help.
But sometimes there was the picking of the fruit of the corn. I dimly
remember as a child it must have been picked in its husk because
there would be at the appropriate time get-togethers
            of neighbouring families
after tea and late into the night for little boys and girls.
After the fiendish games of pursuing the nesting mice to their deaths
from the barn's cornerfuls of unhusked corn we would at first
with enthusiasm gradually turned into lethargy run the finger
taloned with leatherheld three inch nail down the harsh cocoon
of the husk to disclose the gold, the betel-red, the milk-white grains,
until someone would carry us snoozing into a shadowy corner on top
            of
more corn (and mice) and fulsome sacks of sweet and foul smelling
            mixtures
of things that only adults understood the use of. But in
the later years my uncle husked the cobs on the standing stalk
and fed them to the cattle as an additive or prelude
to the plum-pudding silage that the cows went crazy over, screaming
like overweight adolescent girls to get at it as though
it were some edible pop-performer, another dismembered god
and would roll their eyes and bony hips and bump the stalls and belch
and shit while gorging. Cows are unmentionably crass and canny
at the same time. Bulls are bulls—that is, you keep out of their way
in and out of serving times. Sometimes they sing in Brahmsian
monotones, sometimes they shriek and kick up clods, sometimes
they even rupture their pizzles masturbating into a grassy
mound. But only cows really care for them. And only
they really care for cows as cows despite the farmer's habitual
endearments and namings. But corn—or the stalks thereof—and
            the sandpaper raspy
leaves. And the thick, wet air between the neverending rows.
One humid day after several hours of hacking, humping and dumping
those full green six feet and more stalks I fell down dead asleep
in a chocolate furrow and did not dream of anything for the first
and last time in my life. When I awoke an hour later
my disgusted cousin was half a dozen rows on having left mine
like gapped teeth in between. However, my uncle even stopped letting
the cobs grow on the green stalks and soon it was cut and hack
and stack on the sled and chop and stamp down, and that was it.
The neighbour's son upheld the Attis myth in the form of adding
three severed fingers to the silage pudding. Those machines
were gluttonous for everything choppable. But while there was
the neighbour's mutilated son, there were also the neighbour's

daughters to help stamp down the silage and in between
        loads there were
sessions of mutual inspection. Then, one sad afternoon
the good share-farmer's better daughter, sweet Laura of the warm,
wide face and narrow hips and feet like pizza plates came shyly
up to me as I stamped on and on under shower of fragrant,
tickling chips and looked at me from the ladder top and spoke
with eyes as large as curiosity, and I nodded, thinking
she was offering maximum assistance with her remarkably functional
feet, not knowing both of us may have been blessedly released
from virginity's yoke. So we glumly trod. And I kept wondering why
she looked and looked with sadder and sadder, if not wiser, blue eyes
towards me. And as I'd shrug heaps of the wet green chips from my
        shoulders she'd briefly
smile, and then there was a welcome pause and as I rolled
a cigarette with far from trembling hands she slowly crossed
without a word to the ladder, leaving as silently as she came.
And that no doubt is why her eldest child is one or two years
younger than it might have been. Then the roar and green rush
of relentless ensilage in the making all but drowned my donkey-
at-the-water-wheel treading, till I prayed like some mad catherine-
        wheeling
anchorite those masochistic prayers of pious-randy
youth, and trod and trod the green wheel of the neverending
hours, stained green and yellow, smelling like a sweaty stalk,
talking and singing songs of food and drink and love to myself
in the most innocuous words ever disassembled, the cowboy tunes
of the Thirties and Forties: 'San Antonio Rose',
'You are My Sunshine', 'Be Honest with Me',
'I'm Walkin' the Floor Over You', 'Goodbye Little Darlin',
'Old Shep', 'Cool Water'—delirious with weariness and love
unsatisfied while the Niagara of shredded stalks descended
upon my cropped head, down my neck, inside my khaki shirt,
even into my underpants. Deluged with god, the blood
and semen on the cornstalk deity, I trod and chanted,
always ascending like an apprentice shaman towards that last
hole in the concrete roof from whence I'd issue on leaf-green wings
and tread upon the air up to the glazed galactophil-
ideal heaven of Khamaduk, the celestial bovine with ever-
flowing teats and other accommodations—for bulls. Back to
the heavy-footed, the Frankensteinian monster's tread, Boris's
bandy, soulful plod. In several months we'd shovel off
the top muck and the chooks would gobble it, a solid cross
between Drambuie and mud, and lurch and flap drunkenly for
a few days. Then the silage would be ready. And ploughing begin.

Peter Porter

THE SADNESS OF THE CREATURES

We live in a third-floor flat
among gentle predators
and our food comes often
frozen but in its own shape
(for we hate euphemisms
as you would expect) and our cat's
food comes in tins, other than
scraps of the real thing and she
like a clever cat makes milk
of it for her kittens: we shout
of course but it's electric
like those phantom storms
in the tropics and we think of
the neighbours—I'm not writing
this to say how guilty
we are like some well-paid
theologian at an American
college on a lake
or even to congratulate
the greedy kittens who have
found their mittens and are up
to their eyes in pie—I know
lots of ways of upsetting
God's syllogisms, real
seminar-shakers some of them,
but I'm an historical cat
and I run on rails and so
I don't frame those little poems
which take three lines to
get under your feet—
you know the kind of thing—
*The water I boiled the lobster in
is cool enough to top
up the chrysanthemums.*
No, I'm acquisitive and have
one hundred and seven Bach
Cantatas at the last count,
but these are things of the spirit
and my wife and our children
and I are animals (biologically
speaking) which is how the world
talks to us, moving on the billiard
table of green London, the sun's
red eye and the cat's green eye

focusing for an end. I know
and you know and we all know
that the certain end of each of us
could be the end of all of us,
but if you asked me what
frightened me most, I wouldn't
say the total bang or even
the circling clot in the red drains
but the picture of a lit room
where two people not disposed
to quarrel have met so
oblique a slant of the dark
they can find no words for
their appalled hurt but only
ride the rearing greyness:
there is convalescence from this,
jokes and love and reassurance,
but never enough and never
convincing and when the cats
come brushing for food their soft
aggression is hateful;
the trees rob the earth and the earth
sucks the rain and the children
burgeon in a time of invalids—
it seems a trio sonata
is playing from a bullock's
skull and the God of Man
is born in a tub of entrails;
all man's regret is no more
than Attila with a cold
and no Saviour here or
in Science Fiction will come
without a Massacre of the Innocents
and a Rape of El Dorado.

An Australian garden

FOR SALLY LEHMANN

Here we enact the opening of the world
And everything that lives shall have a name
To show its heart; there shall be Migrants,
Old Believers, Sure Retainers; the cold rose
Exclaim perfection to the gangling weeds,
The path lead nowhere—this is like entering
One's self, to find the map of death
Laid out untidily, a satyr's grin
Signalling 'You are here': tomorrow
They are replanting the old court,
Puss may be banished from the sun-warmed stone.

See how our once-lived lives stay on to haunt us,
The flayed beautiful limbs of childhood
In the bole and branches of a great angophora—
Here we can climb and sit on memory
And hear the words which death was making ready
From the start. Such talking as the trees attempt
Is a lesson in perfectability. It stuns
The currawongs along the breaks of blue—
Their lookout cries have guarded Paradise
Since the expulsion of the heart, when man,
Bereft of joy, turned his red hand to gardens.

Spoiled Refugees nestle near Great Natives;
A chorus of winds stirs the pagoda'd stamens:
In this hierarchy of miniatures
Someone is always leaving for the mountains,
Civil servant ants are sure the universe
Stops at the hard hibiscus; the sun is drying
A beleaguered snail and the hydra-headed
Sunflowers wave like lights. If God were to plant
Out all His hopes, He'd have to make two more
Unknown Lovers, ready to find themselves
In innocence, under the weight of His green ban.

In the afternoon we change—an afterthought,
Those deeper greens which join the stalking shadows—
The lighter wattles look like men of taste
With a few well-tied leaves to brummel-up
Their poise. Berries dance in a southerly wind
And the garden tide has turned. Dark on dark.
Janus leaves are opening to the moon
Which makes its own grave roses. Old Man
Camellias root down to keep the sun intact,
The act is canopied with stars. A green sea
Rages through the landscape all the night.

We will not die at once. Nondescript pinks
Survive the death of light and over-refined
Japanese petals bear the weight of dawn's first
Insect. An eye makes damask on the dew.
Time for strangers to accustom themselves
To habitat. What should it be but love?
The transformations have been all to help
Unmagical creatures find their proper skins,
The virgin and the leonine. The past's a warning
That the force of joy is quite unswervable—
'Out of this wood do not desire to go'.

In the sun, which is the garden's moon, the barefoot
Girl espies her monster, all his lovely specialty
Like hairs about his heart. The dream is always

Midday and the two inheritors are made
Proprietors. They have multiplied the sky.
Where is the water, where the terraces, the Tritons
And the cataracts of moss? This is Australia
And the villas are laid out inside their eyes:
It would be easy to unimagine everything,
Only the pressure made by love and death
Holds up the bodies which this Eden grows.

$\mathcal{W}$ISH WE WERE THERE

It would be our garden of scents and Spitfires,
it would be our yard for exercise,
it would go on for ever (and ever),
it would, of course, be Paradise.

And be fitted like a German kitchen,
every pleasantness at eye-level,
the cats on their curly yellow cat-mat
unequivocally of the Devil.

Mother and Father in frayed straw hats
and swatches of angelic flannelette,
the nimbus of childhood spreading wider,
the milkman trying to place a bet.

Getting old would be growing younger
as the CDs turn at 78
and Haydn's No. 97
provides a coda for Beethoven's Eighth.

The pet dogs buried by the roses
should rise from the limed and clayey soil
and the Council steamroller-driver
bring belated tears to the boil.

The post come twice a day from Youville
with letters of triumphant love—
you and Joseph on the river,
you with Fyodor by the stove.

And there too Indestructible Man
would keep death lurking by each bush,
clipping and pruning tirelessly,
the old lawnmower hard to push.

The voice of friendship calling up,
can you come down today to play
so time shall not move round the dial
and after-breakfast last all day.

The macaronic air refresh us,
taking pity on a poor linguist
till it's Pentecost and Schubert's Miller
takes his withered flowers for grist.

The end is nigh but will not happen
as tea appears on the lawn—
the synchronicity of Heaven
is owed to us for being born.

R. A. Simpson

Evening

There is little to recommend this light
at evening as the tall men return
like undertakers from the railway station.

Children have moonstruck mouths—and wives
pour their clarity into saucepans
and watch themselves boil away for minutes.

There is a sharp moon in the pine-tree
where so many lines are credible
and where the answers are impossible to guess.

Tonight some wives will be unwrapped in rooms
and some may lie awake, hoping
no one has come to repossess the Milky Way.

All Friends Together

A SURVEY OF PRESENT-DAY AUSTRALIAN POETRY

Charles and Bruce, Geoff and Ron and Nancy
May publish books this year: some hope they won't.
Tom and Les, Robert, Nan and John—
We live our lives quietly using words
And write of dragons and birds: we are our critics.
Asia, of course, is waiting, but somewhere else.

Max and Rod and Les, and someone else,
Are writing well, and so are Charles and John.
Who would have thought they knew so many words.
Who would have thought this country had such critics.
Mary may come good some day—she won't,
Of course. And yet we may all hear from Nancy.

Nan and Don are better now than Nancy.
Robert, too, writes well for all the critics—
And did you see that latest thing by John?

Nothing queer—the 'queers' are somewhere else
Painting paintings. And all our poems won't
Be anything but normal. We know our words

And buy anthologies to read our words—
David, Robert, Ron and Alex and Nancy.
And did you choke upon that thing by John?
Wasps and grass, magpies and something else
Have often made us write: I'm sure they won't
Seem overdone; they always please the critics.

The critics know (of course, we are the critics)
The qualities of Max and Geoff and Nancy.
And so we carry on with Charles and John,
Tom and Alex, Robert, and someone else—
Big thoughts about a myth, and simple words.
Perhaps you think we'll stop, and yet we won't.

Sometimes I think we'll stop, and yet we won't—
John and David, Bruce and Ron and Nancy.
Robert and Les, Rod and someone else,
Who love the words of friends, and please the critics
With neat anthologies and simple words
Geoff and Max, Charles and Gwen and John.

Sometimes I think that Nancy, Don and John
And someone else are neither poets nor critics:
They won't like that. We only have our words.

My FUNERAL

I would like to be there
in a more active role;
no matter.

However, what I require
is the Roy Harris
Third Symphony, very loud:

that's one way
to drown the talking
in the backstalls.

You may not have heard
of that symphony;
I'm very esoteric.

Then, after the noise,
a sudden silence
for a poem—

Andrew Marvell's
The Garden
which is completely out of place.

Then I want this to happen:
the coffin should be opened
slowly

to show a wax-work model
of John Donne with hands on chest,
miming death and having a giggle.

Of course, the secret
is that I'm being burnt
elsewhere.

Bruce Dawe

CITY LOVERS

Every meeting seems a sort of miracle
They cannot bear to think about, as if
To think of it could only work them ill
In future when their arms must fall away
And each turn to his mortal prosody,
The muted happenstance of day-to-day.

Half in, half out of time love guarantees
Safe conduct for them as they venture out
Among the whistling knife-edged certainties,
Their vulnerability in times apart
Becomes unfailing talisman to these
Jaywalkers in the main street of the heart.

So in the lyric moments when they meet
Neither will give utterance to that care
Which is their fond familiar, the discreet
Unanswerable ghost they can't dismiss,
Who comforts and distracts them everywhere
And is their blindfold reason when they kiss.

THE ROCK-THROWER

Out in the suburbs I hear
trains rocketing to impossible destinations
cry out against the intolerable waste,
at 3.40 in the morning hear the dog-frost
bark over the dark backyards with their young trees
and tubular-steel swings where tomorrow's children
laughingly dangle their stockinged feet already
and the moon coats with white primer
the youthful lawns, the thirtyish expectations.

Midway between the hills and the sea
our house rocks quietly in the flow of time, each morning
we descend to sandy loam, the birds
pipe us ashore, on the rimed grass
someone has left four sets of footprints
as a sign to us that we are not alone
but likely to be visited
at some unearthly hour by a dear friend
who bears a love for us, wax-wrapped and sealed,
sliced, white, starch-reduced ...

Sometimes I wake at night, thinking:
Even now he may be at work,
the rock-thrower in the neighbouring suburb, turning
the particular street of his choice
back to an earlier settlement—the men armed,
mounting guard, eyeing the mysterious skies,
tasting the salt of siege, the cleansing sacrament
of bombardment, talking in whispers, breaking humbly
the bread of their small fame,
as the planes going north and south
wink conspiratorially overhead
and the stones rain down ...

And sometimes, too, dieselling homewards
when the bruised blue look of evening
prompts speculations upon the reasons for existence
and sets the apprehensive traveller to fingering thoughtfully
his weekly ticket, when the sun draws its bloody
knuckles back from the teeth of roof-tops
and the wounded commuter limps finally up the cement path
—I think of the rock-thrower, the glazier's benefactor,
raining down meaning from beyond the subdivisions,
proclaiming the everlasting evangel of vulnerability
—and the suburbs of men shrink to one short street
where voices are calling now from point to point:
'Is that you, Frank?'
     'Is that you, Les?'
         'Is that you, Harry?'
'See anything?'
     'Nup ...'
         'Nup ...'
            'Nup ...'

Teaching the Syllabus

Teaching lions to leap through flaming hoops
    Teaching baby elephants to waltz
Teaching dogs on bikes to loop-the-loop
    Teaching chimps to undo nuts and bolts

Teaching doves to pick out painted numbers
    Teaching hawks to sing
Teaching bears the latest Latin rhumbas
    Seals, the Highland fling

Teaching those with wings to walk up mountains
    Teaching those with feet of lead to fly
Tossing coins in intermittent fountains
    Calling in the plumber when they're dry

And lastly—when it seems that each performer
    Has learnt the lot—to teach them one thing more,
The thing that in the process they've forgotten:
    Dogs, to bark again; lions, to roar ...

Returned Men

At the Wonchip cross-roads
at 8 a.m., just as the whistles blow
and the first waves go over, shouting,
they return, little Billy,
the Watson boy, Cec Arkinstall ...
They lean a little against the light,
trying hard to conceal their weariness,
little Billy's moustache has grown, the Watson boy
is fatter (only to be expected, we all change),
Cec Arkinstall is silent, having forgotten
his habit of whistling, his mangled repertoire
of tunes where *The Rose of Tralee* would become
without warning *The Eriskay Love Lilt*, his lips
purse soundlessly.

They advance towards the cenotaph
in a painful silence. The mayor
fingers his tie, the band hold awkwardly
their bright instruments.
The three men read their names haltingly,
with wonder, on the memorial plaque,
then nudge each other and salute with sudden vigour
the concrete figure of their archetype.

At the base of the memorial
they pick up the wreaths and set them on one side.
They lower themselves onto the stone ledge.

They take off their hats and slide the sweat from around
        the hat-band,
adjust the chin-straps, tilt the broad brims forward
to shade them from the steadily rising sun
and fall asleep forever.

HENRY ARTENSHAW'S CANAAN

'Golden Lizard Liniment country, without a doubt ...'
His first enthusiastic report to head-office said,
'Gazing across the damp mist-bandaged valleys,
The experienced traveller can discern at least
One strained ligament in every pot-holed paddock,
To say nothing of the Wilson's Lightning Salve
Potential in the rickety ti-tree bridge
Across the creek and oh, what glowing testimonials
To the wondrous efficacy of Wilson's Sure-Fire
Throat and Chest Elixir lie concealed
From prying eyes in those bronchitic shacks!'

'Hot foments and red-flannel here abound,'
He later wrote, 'While round the children's necks,
Like some bulbous scapular announcing
A faith not of this world, may still be seen
The humble onion hung ...
        Here, tried and true
Remedies which a sadly idolatrous city
(Corrupted by hygiene and Vitamin C)
Has driven out, find refuge and a people consecrate.
And I, by Wilson's Products called to render
Service in the name of the Most High,
Have found at last belief to match my own.'

And, later still, 'Despite a growing tendency to cough,
And certain spasms in the lumbar region
(Which locally-grown herbs do much to alleviate)
I deem this territory too rich to be forsaken,
For this is truly Golden Lizard country,
Not a day passing but the liniment brings
Relief and solace to some one inhabitant
(I have been blessed a thousand times since coming).
Hearing the hoarse rooster croak at dawn
To clear the thick contagion from his throat,
I am reminded: "Here, where I was sent,
I must remain ...
This people needs me".'

ℱROM THE OUTSET

From the outset I think I thought it strange
that there were all these things into which I came,
which moved around me, flowed, and fled, and stood
like *anima* around my first bedstead,
peculiar, and open-eyed, and kind,
purposeful as clouds before the wind,
and it was many years before I knew
that this same oddity struck others too,
and that the broken song, the vanished race,
could tell as much of life as the long peace.
And now again the night sky with its stars,
the flowers, the voices, all particulars,
surprise me, just as if, on some vague shore,
a traveller from Atlantis were to hear
bells from undersea, and yet not know
whether hand or tide controlled their ebb and flow.

Evan Jones

ℐDDRESS TO THE PURE SCHOLARS

PHI BETA KAPPA POEM, STANFORD, 1959

Gentleman scholars in an age of violence,
Clear readers of the insensate and the past,
You are betrayed by your unbalanced calm
To the indifferent forces of destruction:
Scrupulous indeed has been your learning,
Inadequate indeed has been your vision.

For only in the context of a vision
Passionately opposed to mere destruction
Can you bring to its fruition your cold learning;
In the historic present, not the past,
Must you, facing its obscurity and violence,
Labour to build in time a juster calm.

Sheltered you are and should be by the calm
Conditions that are traditional to learning;
You are seduced by this until your vision
Loses its apprehension of old violence,
Gathering stillness from an unreal past:
Thus you betray the present to destruction.

Look westward to the remnants of destruction
Under the cone of Fuji; try to envision
People still crippled, dying from the violence

That blossomed from the physicists' new learning.
Remember the rain of fallout in that calm;
Envision it as present, not as past.

What man or men should answer for that past,
This present and whatever future violence?
All those, perhaps, indifferent to destruction,
Who wait impassive in impassive calm,
Failing to know or speak that juster vision
Which well might be concomitant with learning.

Teachers, you should have more to teach than learning;
Scientists, there is no mere natural calm;
Historians, you are not plighted to the past:
You are servants of society, your vision
Must fight at every point against destruction
Until perhaps our wisdom outweighs our violence.

An age of such great violence, such great learning
Dragging destruction with it from the past:
Who should be calm to see such lack of vision?

STUDY IN BLUE

In his blue suit, an Oxford Standard Authors
Caught in his hand, I watch him passing by:
Nothing could be more sober, more discreet.
It's me O Lord—or rather, it is I.

LANGUAGE, TALK TO ME

Language talk to me, language
tell me what I know
after forty years—
language, will you show
the way out of the labyrinth
to me, myopic, slow
and singular as when
I fell in love with you
twenty odd years ago?

Language talk to me, language,
while I listen for
the wheezing snuffling clumping
of the Minotaur:
now from your endless store
recruit a devotee who
on this illegible shore
lost, without a clue,
turns as ever to you.

Language talk to me, language
teach me what to say
in the face of disaster,
in the height of hope,
as things fall away.
Mother-tongue, lingua franca,
all that anyone knows,
bring me, kindly bring me
to a perfect close.

INSTRUCTIONS TO A SERVANT

FOR DON GUNNER

Since I'm retiring late again, dear Smith,
please try not to disturb me when you come.
The nest of papers and the books on myth

might best be left untouched. The bath shows scum:
the pantry needs more rat-bait: clear the sink:
there are some cob-webs in the living-room—

but otherwise, proceed just as you think.
After the dusting, washing-up and mopping
don't hesitate to give yourself a drink

if you can find one (I missed out on shopping).
That's almost all, but you might like to look
at some things in the garden before stopping:

there's a dark weed I rather think is hemlock
which chokes the parsley; and the pile of bones
in the far corner might with care and luck

submit to being cairned beneath the stones
from last year's digging. Little else to say.
I hope you and the world are well. Yours, Jones.

INSOMNIA

FOR ALAN DAVIES

There are two kinds of sleeplessness. One is mean:
you lie there with your eyes shut, and things war
in endless repetition, racing, in dull white.
Or you might lie there, patient, wide-eyed in the dark,
thinking the same things over and over with a dull peace,
resigned to the resolution of day-break.

Grace save us from racing thoughts: they always break
down to one question: *what did she (or he, or it,
     even they) really mean?*

Dialogues are remembered, dismembered piece by piece,
yielding nothing but the sense of a last sad war
where all you want is to wave a flag of white,
to have it stop, to be gone into simple dark.

Insomniacs, bless them, are never afraid of the dark:
bad nights are called 'white nights' for that dull white
which lurks behind their eye-lids, dingy, mean,
nothing at all like innocence, purity or peace,
signalling that all the nerves would like to break.
Something in the whole being is at war,

but whatever war it is, it's an undeclared war,
and whatever might ensue, it won't be peace
unless with the clarity of saintliness or heart-break,
whatever either or both of those words might mean,
someone or something from another and certain dark
is able somehow to offer a glimpse of unsullied white.

I lie at ease these nights in fields of white,
thinking of this and that, murmuring in the dark,
convalescent perhaps from a younger war:
I think of gain and loss, of how things grow and break:
I think of meanings, what my meanings mean,
and counting words can almost count myself at peace.

But who else asks no more than singular peace?
All the bright strainers yearning towards day-break
are coining messages, slogans against the dark
to break into the rainbow that they want from white.
Some will make love: they and others will make war:
generous, self-seeking, high-minded, vague, and mean.

There will be no golden mean, however things might break:
there is going to be more war, much of it in the dark:
there will also be unsullied white and drifts of peace.

Philip Martin

DUNE SHIP

It was there when the first settlers came. The sea
Hurled three men from their boat against that coastline.
One was drowned. The others tramping the beach
Towards Port Fairy stumbled across it: a ship,
Inland, beyond the reach of any tide.
Dark form among pale dunes. The masts gone,

The prow driving into a wave of sand,
The timbers weathered by wind and spray. One man
Took his knife to them, and it glanced off.

A ship sailing the dunes. For forty years
Whalers, farmers glimpse it, talk of it briefly,
Busy with other things.
      A girl out riding,
Thinking of a young man back in Ireland,
Dismounts, looks down from the deck, watches
A spill of sand falling into the hull,
Building grain on grain. The hourglass motion.

Forty years, and then no sign of it.
But it's remembered. Now, year after year,
Men bring steel rods to probe the hummocks, probe
And turn away defeated. It's there still,
Far from its first sea. Dark image
Of a surfer poised inside his cresting wave.

A CERTAIN LOVE

There's no gainsaying this:
We're blessed. We know it.
And if God came to me today and said
'You must give her up', I'd answer
'Ridiculous. Why contradict yourself?'

DREAM POEM

I hear a voice coming out of sleep, and I
Am there still, I hear its joy ring out,
This voice, and I must get up quickly, catch it,

Write, knowing that I dreamt of her, that she
Has once again renewed me, just before sleep
In words, and still in sleep itself and through it,

The voice speaks in thankfulness and praise
This is a marvellous house, made by women,
The good are welcomed here,

      And I look up,
A grey building heaping itself towards
Trees growing high and dark and dense, what is it,
Some kind of mills? and now I am inside it,
I am almost at the other side of it,
It is dark, goodly, ample, and it smells of
Wheat and hay which it holds with other plenty,

Praise, praise this house, the voice exults,

The wide door open to a harvest landscape

Like Brueghel but without figures, land
Sloping away towards perhaps the sea,
And sunny, all of the colour of ripe wheat,
Some of the harvest cut back sheer already,
Everything bright and basking, while in here
Shadowed by walls and rafters it is cooler,
And yet still warm, smelling of gathered country,

And the voice goes on *Here those come who have travelled*
Straight from their mothers to their first good love,
I know this love is a deep woman, fruitful,
Wise whatever her age,

     And the voice, *They come*
Here to tell their secrets in their joy,
Trusted and safe-kept here,

     And towards the door
I see a figure hurrying, small and dark
Against the sunlit and the golden landscape,
Almost running, he is coming to tell ...

Keith Harrison

THE ISLAND WEATHER OF THE NEWLY BETROTHED

'The winds are more predictable in summer;
Not like that January one that banged
Off walls and clutched a cold hand at your groin
When you were forced outside. Now you can walk
With the sun firm across your shoulders
Not waiting to be shaken, or spun, flapping
Like a scarecrow. There's merely
A wavering, at dusk, in the lemon leaves,
A light lifting—and the strong one that
Drives from the sea and spins the mill-blades fast.

If it is anyone's weather it is yours—
Or part of the kindness that is yours.
Elsewhere the sun might mean silence of anger,
But today we are pleased to walk in it,
Sea all around.
     And it will stay like this.
Unless the other thing comes, like a shock
Of impotence at noon, as when a friend
Whose words you've long admired, stares at you and

Stares, forgetting your name, dribbling
The same crude sound over and over.

Against which sudden changes we have learned
Our loving's fallible. Though not entirely.'
'Speaking of winds, I think the saddest one
Is that broad breeze in the afternoon that lifts
The gorse for thirty miles, and slides warmly
Up the face. I have been studying
Why it should sadden me: something to do
With bones, or the sense of age it carries.
Hearing September rain against the window
Or fizzing in leaves, others are moved
By something similar. All that leaves me indifferent.
Still, we are too fond of metaphor.
Such moods are personal, inexplicable;
The weather has no connexion with you or me.

And as for loving, I've chosen you
Because you know your stances are ridiculous.
And if one night you also lose your reason,
Or puff yourself, confounding metaphor
With fact; or, when grey weather comes,
Slump, world-rejecting in your favourite chair—
Or if my body lose its tang for you,

Against those sudden changes I would say
Our loving's fallible. Perhaps entirely.'

Here

The day was still as honey in a bowl;
the maple-sap came fast, with winter gone
the cattle stood beside the bright snow-pool
their dung packed down and steaming in the barn.
No help for it—go get your fork and spade
for even those who serve the world with wit
are trundling down into the deep barn-shade
and blocking up their nose, and shoveling it.
You hacked and grunted all day at my side;
and then we heaped it, drove it up and flung
great cartloads on the cornfield, near and wide,
breathing new air rich with earth and dung.
Then stood a little while, single and whole.
And the day still as honey in a bowl.

Vivian Smith

SUMMER SKETCHES: SYDNEY

I
City of yachts and underwater green
with blue hydrangeas fading in between
the walls of sloping gardens full of sails,
as sudden as a heart the sunlight fails
and over all the city falls again
a change of light, the neon's coloured rain.

II
Tourists in their lives of sudden ease
stare through dark glasses at the coral trees
and know at once that only colour's true:
the red in green: within the green, the blue.

III
At night the cool precision of the stars,
the neon glitter and the sexy cars,
the easy pick-up in the close green bars.

IV
A holiday like some smooth magazine;
how photos can improve the simplest scene.
They isolate the image that endures;
beyond the margins is the life that cures.
But when the surface gloss is thought away
some images survive through common day
and linger with a touch of tenderness:
the way you brushed your hair, your summer dress.

THERE IS NO SLEIGHT OF HAND

There is no sleight of hand
not caught by art's reflection.
Poetry which can't pretend
is perfect lie-detection.

Who knows what echoes then
the song of chaos finds?
A self-intoxicated tune
dazzles, confounds, and blinds.

Dismay is all its load,
it has no way to take;
but words on their proper road
dance for the spirit's sake.

Let candour be your guide
and may your words rejoice

in art's only reward
to speak in one's own voice.

Tasmania

Water colour country. Here the hills
rot like rugs beneath enormous skies
and all day long the shadows of the clouds
stain the paddocks with their running dyes.

In the small valleys and along the coast,
the land untamed between the scattered farms,
deconsecrated churches lose their paint
and failing pubs their fading coats of arms.

Beyond the beach the pine trees creak and moan,
in the long valley poplars in a row,
the hills breathing like a horse's flank
with grasses combed and clean of the last snow.

At the Parrot House, Taronga Park

What images could yet suggest their range
of tender colours, thick as old brocade,
or shot silk or flowers on a dress
where black and rose and lime seem to caress
the red that starts to shimmer as they fade?

Like something half-remembered from a dream
they come from places we have never seen.

They chatter and they squawk and sometimes scream.

Here the macaw clings at the rings to show
the young galahs talking as they feed
with feathers soft and pink as dawn on snow
that it too has a dry and dusky tongue.
Their murmuring embraces every need
from languid vanity to wildest greed.

In the far corner sit two smoky crones
their heads together in a kind of love.
One cleans the other's feathers while it moans.
The others seem to whisper behind fans
while noble dandies gamble in a room
asserting values everyone rejects.

A lidded eye observes, and it reflects.

The peacocks still pretend they own the yard.

For all the softness, how the beaks are hard.

Jennifer Strauss

AUBADE

Daybreak-waking
Curled still in sleep's habitual posture
(Back to the womb)
I find you subscribe to the opposite camp
(On to the tomb):
A crusading original, purely profiled,
Hands tidily
Clasped upon sculptural midriff. Feet?
Ah, vulnerable,
Resting not virtuous on some trampled beast
Of lust or wrath
But on the covers passion thrust away.

Quiet like the world
You sleep, while sunlight at the window
Entering equably
Perceives no need to call up husbands, fathers,
And not a bird
Cries out in either consolation or alarm,
Nor yet a car
Revs up its engine for the busy day—
Only my mind
Plays truant, makes my faithless fingers itch
For typewriter keys
To try the combination of experience, sounding out
'Complementary?—incompatible?'

WHAT WOMEN WANT

Without in any way wanting
to drop names or big-note
the heaviest heavies,
I've news for Freud
and for Pontius Pilate:
even in jest,
they were much too abstract.
Here is something
that women want
specifically, truly:
to lie with a lover
a whole afternoon
so close that the skin
knows boundaries only

by knowing contact
and the mind surrenders
managerial fuss,
until to murmur
'What are you thinking?'
is only a game, words
breaking light
and unimpressive
as the quietest of waves
on tide-washed sand.
It is a truth:
time and desire can stand still
although it is also true
that clocks tick faster
than the light's slow glide
across floor and walls
and that sometimes the tongue
does not touch tenderly
but flares into speech
to set division
sharper than any sword
between sleeping bodies.
Perhaps separation's essential,
like sleep, or like sex,
but women want
sometimes still to lie
truly together
a whole afternoon
awake, without wanting.

TIERRA DEL FUEGO

Love is the territory of fire.

Sea-travellers,
becalmed by indifference
or driven past
on winds of ambitious trade
or turbulence from the icy south,
have glimpsed through misty clouds
a flicker, a glow,
a lightning flash.

See, says one,
the land where firewalkers go
passion-tranced,
dancing unscathed through flames
until the faltering moment
(mistrust, boredom)

wakes them—
to scream, clutching charred soles.

No, no, says another, those
are the fires of home,
beacons to draw the wayfarer
havenward
to a safe landfall,
a final discovery—
that love is whatever
survives sex.

There was time for all that
when travellers went by ship,
lovers by metaphor.

Leaving you behind,
not certain
whether you'll follow,
when the plane stops
at your continent's most remote tip
I write a postcard:

Didn't expect to be here:
believe we're only refuelling,
but it's cold and dark
and all I'm wanting
is one clear view
of Tierra del Fuego.

Fay Zwicky

Waking

My young sister last egg of all thought
She safely black enough to mimic ethnic
Affliction, cried Lawd have mercy
Spare mah soul, hallelujahed all over
The house (a musical family) paining
Me, a prickish twelve, no jew nor black
Neither but whiter than Persil.

And the Lord let her caper, smiled on
Childhood dreamtime, me forgave not, bent
Himself double to push pride, ambition,
*Rugos' inflavit pellem,** flushed my greedy
Pellets down the wind till fit to puzzle
Pieces back, praised Him, woke
Monochromatic, pointed as Kafka.

* 'it [the frog] inflated its wrinkled skin'—from Aesop's fable,
'The Frog and the Ox'

Reading a letter in Amsterdam

Under chestnut clusters looped in light,
a firm clean-painted bench.
I'm remembering you as you were before
we met, before I sat here with your letter,
waiting, watching children, joggers, lovers
pass, a blurred and broken line.

You've been away a long time
through all our pointless winters.
I've found you now in tenderness
like something lost in childhood,
remembering you as you were before
we met again, before I sat here waiting
on a bench in Amsterdam.

Like distant ghosts, older men and women
slowly pass the bench in silence. I watch unseeing
what's closer to me now than you,
remembering you as you were before,
as you might be now,
before your bright green spring
cut short our winter,
swam us into flower.

Your voice, a longing subterranean stream
has shaped our story, and your words,
those *words*, shake out like rain
in my cupped hands.

You are not with me.
I've come a long way to tell you
this reminds me of some other time,
some other place, but not the same
as what was lost in childhood.

Your letter's shaking in my green-veined hand.
I open it. Not open—
tear is closer to the truth, my hand
still trembling on a firm clean-painted bench
in sun-struck Amsterdam.

TALKING MERMAID

Doing my posthumous glide, I left the amber windows
of the sea, my father's granary all Bible-black. The land
above cerulean in autumn, sun plum in a mist
so beautiful my eyelids prickled like a wounded

child outsmarting tenderness. Below, the plangent
chords, deep-sunk cathedrals tolling benedictions
to the drowned. I felt myself rising through translucent
green high on the wordless surge, once a connoisseur

of loss, stressed syllables and self-reproach,
big for my boots, myopic. Legless now
invisible to love, I'm free to circle silently.
The waterfront is murmurous with attention.

Look, dolphins! cries the waitress to her Sunday
table, Bower Lane corner café. All eyes widen,
blond heads swivel over croissants, oranges and—
there, there, look there! two three four five

dark cleavers barrelling, soft surfers curling high
round shallow turquoise circles laced with foam
to darken, vanish, leap again in light.
No family ever moved more gently.

Close to shore they skim and roll up glistening,
morning's anthem swelling out their wake. In play
no choice, responsibility, vocation. So why
the single human head that bobs and pushes

outward, seeks to join their widening arcs?
They tease and lollop close in chorus file: his path's
presumptuous, chancy, stretching things beyond
his lineage. There is no lyric in the human stride.

See the silent watchers on the promenade leaning
outward to the shining host, the blundering head,
the flash and glide. They stand so still, suspended calm
like innocence hushed before a cortège or a ghosted

hero's speech. The young ones perch like pelicans on rocks,
crane plump over cliff and boulder, hair etched on the wind.
Their hearts are flying with the dolphins, briefly
tender, unashamed, gripped in beauty's stress,

the bobbing head irrelevant, its course imperfect.
Pure play is for the feudal few. I knew a woman in New York,
a man in France, who laughed and dolphins leapt
heaving for the open seas. Were they ever trouble!

She was a cleric's daughter, told my fortune
by the Tarot fraught with wily morose mountain men

afraid of water. Pray for a good death, always the
worry, she added kindly (still her father's child),

calling up planets lightly as you'd pick a daisy.
He was a dreadlocked *colon*, black as bronze in starlight,
slippery coaxer sprouting his burnished hydra heads
to pace each catch of breath. They lit my life,

laid nothing on me but a moment's play.
Pliant now and pruned, I trail a clownish tail,
their secret legacy, across the knives of memory.
Whoever watches creatures of the sea cavorting

with a happy eye remember those
who made us what we might have been.
Look on this world with underwater eyes, tell
tall tales to the tongueless, take in the hiss

of water-snakes and worms sidling the skull's gape,
cruise the waterfront for song and monkey business.
Learn to breathe on land, feed tears to whales and
forecast, if you can, the grace of dolphin weather.

William Grono

THE WAY WE LIVE NOW

' ... *at the end of the earth*
where existence is most easy.
Snow never falls there and no wild storms
disturb the sweetly flowing days;
only the soothing breezes of the West Wind
drift in each day from Ocean, bearing
constant refreshment for the inhabitants ...'
            The Odyssey, Book IV

1
Here the talk's of flowering annuals,
investments.

Ah, the *richness* of our soil!

Each morning automatic sprinklers bless
all that's governable and nice;
sleek insects fatten on our ceaseless flowers;
glistening motors roam the land.

In our desirable brick-and-tiles
we dream of real estate.

2
Pursued by industrial suburbs—
'the concrete evidence of our progress'—
the bush has fled to the hills. Those hills are alive
with machines, developers, dust. Beyond,
our country lies, wide
and open.

We are, we often feel, living
on the edge of something good.

3
Nothing disturbs us.

Winds from Africa and Indian waves
bear each day to our long white shore
only what we most admire: fashions,
technology, and rich strangers as neat as
beetles who smile at our
simple friendliness.

4
Yes, we like it here.

Sometimes the shrewdest of us find the time,
after the gardening, before television,
sipping beer on enclosed verandahs,
to speculate on the future.

THE CRITIC

My slow step-father
boorish and ignorant,
used (often) to say:
'What's a bloody uni student
know about life? Eh? Nothing!
Absolutely fucking nothing! And
I'll tell you something else,
you bloody little pisswit,
you never bloody will either.'

How does one cope with crudity?
I realized of course
that reasoning was useless, yet
I could not help but point out
that understanding did not necessarily
accompany experience; indeed
one could say (I would say)
that one could as it were achieve
a greater a more viable
understanding of life by discussing it
in a spirit of rational disinterest—But

he would always interrupt: 'Ah, shit!'
and stagger off to get
another bottle.

He died of course drunk
whilst swimming with a Mrs Montgomery
in the surf below the Ocean View Hotel
at one o'clock in the morning.
He was sixty-seven, penniless,
and probably tubercular.

I, on the other hand,
am now an assistant professor
of English literature, and
a not insignificant critic.

Barry Humphries

THRENODY FOR PATRICK WHITE

FOR GEOFFREY DUTTON

In a Federation bungalow beside Centennial Park,
With its joggers in the daytime, perves and muggers after dark,
Lived a famous author hostesses pretend that they have read;
A querulous curmudgeon with a tea-cosy on his head.

He had a vulnerable hauteur, he was arrogant and shy
He had the visage of a dowager with a beady light blue eye,
He wrote at least two masterpieces, his correspondence flowed in
        torrents
With Firbank in one pocket, in the other D. H. Lawrence.

He was generous to young artists; often petty, never mean,
He was a typical high-minded, interbellum, stage-struck queen.
Before the War he would have queued to hear Bea Lillie sing,
One imagined him in private dragging up like Douggie Byng.

He had a few friends (mostly female), whom he wrote to all their lives,
And he loved his male friends too until they traded in their wives.
Then he cut them and he dropped them and defamed them on the page
You felt he'd once been dropped so cruelly he had to share the pain and
        rage.

He dropped Sid and Geoff and Lawrence, he dropped Bruce and Brett
        and me
He preferred those lisping toadies who wouldn't dare to disagree.
With lickspittles round his table he was the Venerated Crank
But the malady was in his bones and he shrank and shrank and
        shrank …

Now his writing light is switched off, though his wall-eyed dogs still
    bark
In that Federation garden beside Centennial Park,
Home of the family picnic and the jogger and the mugger;
Oh I pray God doesn't drop *you*, you miserable old bugger.

David Malouf

ETERNAL CITY

Always coming here
is like coming back home:
pale crocus burn, watery
blue marble floats
its miraculous dome,
bridges with wings
transport us from red velvet
snowbound thoroughfares
to wherever saints aspire to
when they go leaving the Church
a cut-glass spire to house their collar-bones.
Even water leaps upward—
a City of Signs,

though where they point is anyone's
guess. The Campagna
flowers: aqueducts
and hilltop villages, a sky
cerulean, dust-powdered,
the eyelid of a god.
But mostly they direct us
one way to another
part of the town;
real man-holes lead,
SPQR,* to drains; power poles
are for cars to be wrecked on.
Heat prickles. Traffic snarls.

Unhallowed! What I like
about it is the dust,
which is sharp enough to smart
in the eyes of visionaries,
small change in fishbowls feeds
the goldfish, silence
echoes in canvases;
eternal it is not,

* SPQR: Senatus Populusque Romanus: the Senate and People of Rome

with its nine-digit numbers
and children's games, graffiti
chipped from the ruins of a third declension.
The New Jerusalem—
Rome-Babylon.

Which is what we should expect
of course. Lake water
was warm but temporary,
fire blistered. It is earth
we long for, and air—
a location of variable
weathers and lovers,
of pigeons levitating
over bald heads. Double agents
unfaithful to both worlds,
we watch a red Ferrari, hellbent, scream
through four gears, careering
off, coasting home.

THE CRAB FEAST

I
There is no getting closer
than this. My tongue slips into
the furthest, sweetest corner
of you. I know all

now all your secrets.
When the shell
cracked there was nothing
between us. I taste moonlight

transformed into flesh
and the gas bubbles rising
off sewage. I go down
under mangrove roots and berries, under the moon's

ashes; it is cool
down there. I always knew that there was more
to the Bay than its glitters,
knew if you existed

I could also
enter it; I'd caught so deeply all
your habits, knowing the ways
we differ I'd come to think we must be one.

I took you
to me. Prepared
a new habitat under the coral
reef of my ribs. You hang there, broken like the sun.

II

Noon that blinding glass did not reveal us
as we were. It cast up variant selves
more real than
reflections, forms

with a life of their own,
stalk eye a periscope
that determined horizons, Doulton claws
that could snap off a thumb.

I liked that. Hence the deep afternoons
with pole and net, the deeper
nights when I went down after the tropic
sun. Hence too the Latin

names, a dangerous clawhold. I wanted the whole of you, raw
        poundage
in defiance of breathlessness
or the power of verbal charms,
on my palm, on my tongue.

III

This the Place. I come back
nightly to find it
—still, sleepy, sunlit, presided over

by old-timers, waterbirds whose one
thin leg props up clouds,
the ruck of open water

ahead, and the hours
of deepening blue on blue the land wades into afternoon.
These then the perspectives:

matchwood pier, a brackish estuary
that flows on into
the sun, a rip of light over the dunes.

I enter. It is all
around me, the wash
of air, clear-spirit country. It goes on

all day like this. The tide
hovers and withdraws. Under the sun, under the moon's
cross-currents, shadows

fall into place
and are gathered to the dark. This hunt
is ritual, all the parties to it lost. Even the breaths

we draw between cries
are fixed terms in what is celebrated,
the spaces in a net.

Among mangrove trunks the fire
-flies like small hot love-crazed
planets switch on,

switch off. They too
have caught something. A chunk of solid midnight
thrashes in the star-knots of their mesh.

IV
You scared me with your stillness and I scared
myself. Knowing
that everything, even the footsoles of the dead, where your small
        mouths
nudged them, would feed

the airy process of it.
The back of my head
was open to the dream
dark your body moves in. I hunted you

like a favourite colour,
indigo, to learn
how changeable we are, what rainbows
we harbour with us

and how I should die, cast wheezing into
a cauldron of fog.
That was the plan:
to push on through

the spectrum to that perfect
primary death colour, out
into silence and a landscape
of endings, with the brute sky pumping red.

V
I watch at a distance
of centuries, in the morning
light of another planet
or the earliest gloom

of this one, your backward
submarine retreat,
as hoovering across
the seabed—courtly,

elate, iron-plated—
you practice the Dance.
I watch and am shut out.
The terrible privacies!

You move slow motion sideways,
an unsteady astronaut:
step and counter
step, then the clash,

soundless, of tank engagement;
you might be angels
in the only condition
our senses reach them in. I observe

your weightless, clumsy-tender
release. I observe
the rules; cut off
here in the dimension

of pure humanity, my need for air
a limiting factor,
I look through into
your life. Its mysteries

disarm me. Turning
away a second time
to earth, to air, I leave you
to your slow-fangled order,

taking with me
more than I came for
and less. You move back into
my head. No, it does not finish here.

VI
We were horizons
of each other's consciousness. All transactions
at this distance are small,
blurred, uninsistent. Drawn

by unlikeness, I grew
like you, or dreamed I did, sharing your cautious
sideways grip on things, not to be broken,
your smokiness of blood, as kin

to dragons we guarded
in the gloom of mangrove trunks
our hoard. I crossed the limits
into alien territory. One of us

will die of this, I told myself; and one of us
did. The other
swam off to lick warm stones and sulk with clouds along a shoreline,
regretting the deep

shelves and downward spaces,
breathing easy,
but knowing something more
was owed and would take place. I go down

in the dark to that encounter, the sun
at my back. On the sea-bed

your eyes on their sticks
click white in the flattened shadow of my head.

VII
A dreamy phosphorescence
paddles towards me. The moon drowses,
feeds, its belly white, its tough shell
black. We are afloat

together. You are
my counterweight there, I hang above you
in sunlight and a balance
is struck. No, the end

will not be like this.
We belong to different orders, and are trapped
by what we chose. Our kinship
is metaphorical, but no less deadly for all that,

old Dreadnought; as if I wore
black and carried death clenched in my fist. I do
wear black. My hand is open. It is my teeth
that seek you in the dark. And I approach bearing a death.

VIII
It was always like this: you
broken before me,
beautiful in all
the order of your parts, an anatomy lesson,

the simple continent
our bodies broke away from.
Because you are so open, because
the whole of your life

is laid out here, a chamber
to be entered and stripped. You have nothing
to hide. That sort of power
kills us, for whom

moonlight, the concept blue,
is intolerably complex as
our cells are, each an open universe
expanding beyond us, the tug

of immortality.
We shall reach it and still die.
I will be
broken after you, that was the bargain,

all this
a compact between us, who love
our privacies. I play
my part. Bent over you I dip my hand

in the bowl, I shake my cuffs, out in the open
and lost. Deep down
I am with you in the dark. The secret flesh of
my tongue enters a claw.

Because you are so open. Because you are.

IX
It is your weight
that hangs upon me. How
to deal with it. Hooded, claws locked
to your body like star

you drag me under
the light of this occasion
to others. I've dreamed you once
too often. So this

is what it is to drown, this suffocating
torpor, giving up to
the drug of, the drag of
the moon. Here in your kingdom

I feel night harden over
my skull. That we should have come
so far out of the dark
together. I try to drown

well, I hold my breath,
no thrashing. Blue, majestic,
you blaze in my thoughts. Displacing more
than your real weight, making less

than the usual disturbance,
you plunge and take me with you.
I go out
in silence, in full view

of waiters; having learned
this much at least; to die true
to my kind—upright, smiling—
and like you, beyond speech.

X
No I am not ashamed
of our likeness, of what is in it that betrays me,
a smell of salt

backwaters, a native
grasp on the gist
of things, our local patch

of not-quite-solid earth from which the vast swing of the sky
is trackable. Night
comes on and I am caught

with a whole life on my hands,
in my mouth raw words,
the taste of so much air, so much water,

flesh. It was never to be weighed,
this dull shore and its landscape, water
poised above water

and all its swarming creatures, against the kingdom of cloud castles
we build with our breath.
But words made you

a fact in my head. You were
myself in another species, brute
blue, a bolt of lightning, maybe God.

Now all has been made plain
between us, the weights are equal, though the sky
tilts, and the sun

with a splash I do not hear breaks into
the dark. We are one at last. Assembled here
out of earth, water, air

to a love feast. You lie open
before me. I am ready.
Begin.

Chris Wallace-Crabbe

INTROSPECTION

Have you ever seen a mind
thinking?
It is like an old cow
trying to get through the pub door
carrying a guitar in its mouth;
old habits keep breaking in
on the job in hand;
it keeps wanting
to do something else:
like having a bit of a graze
for example,
or galumphing round the paddock
or being a café musician
with a beret and a moustache.
But if she just keeps trying
the old cow, avec guitar,
will be through that door

as easy as pie
but she won't know how it was done.
It's harder with a piano.

Have you ever heard the havoc
of remembering?
It is like asking
the local plumber
in to explore a disused well;
down he goes on a twisting rope,
his cloddy boots
bumping against
that slimed brickwork,
and when he arrives at bottom
in the smell of darkness,
with a splash of jet black water
he grasps a huge fish,
slices it open
with his clasp-knife
and finds a gold coin inside
which slips
out of his fingers
back through the unformed unseeing,
never to be found again.

THE FALL OF THE WEST

Jig, barbarian, over these
machicolated ruins;
question your soothsayers what they mean,
these bricky brac geometries
and bushland scene.

You are standing, marauder, on a college—
a kind of, sort of barracks
plus public house where the gone pale folk
laid claim to worship knowledge.
See, where that mouse

scurries through rubble was inscription-barn
in which they stacked their lore.
Why did they vamoose and let the bush take over?
Why leave this extended pinkish cairn
without dish or door?

Ah, that would be telling. The gods have not replied
but let us say this wing
was named for Boog who devised the manila folder ...
    Just looking at such ruinous things
    I feel abruptly older ...

This middle part for Kogo, inventor of scissors,
that mound beneath low trees
for Pipp who first designed the bike and the bra,
and so on; its deeply graven logo
is too arcane by far.

Right, I was coming to that pointy-crested minaret;
no doubt proconsul or priest
bawled from its holes his awesome guttural words ...
    Look, in the shrubbery, that odd beast.
    And what are these bright green birds?

THE HOME CONVEYANCING KIT

Michael and Trish have bet their bottom dollar
on getting the house paid off, it is so sweet
they just fell in love with it from the start

so bought it, or began to, from Mario
still paying it off himself
who had a malignant growth removed before Xmas.

He it was planted the vegie garden
after handing over the deposit to Hugh and Min
who went overseas to try and save their marriage:

it failed, of course. The paint job and the sleepout
were the work nine years ago of dotty Trevor Platt
out of whose estate the balance was paid.

He had snapped up the then-quite-newish cottage
from a wolfish pig of a landscape painter
who mainly cared for what was under skirts

and collected it—till he suffered an amputation.
The place was originally sold by a dairy farmer
who never made it back from Armentières

as a building block within cooee of the station
before the city sprawled and gobbled it up.
Under the lemon are the bones of somebody's dog.

GOD

That is the world down there.
It appears that I made it
but that was way back,
donkey's years ago, children,
when I spoke like a solar lion
beguiling physics out of chaos.

I spun my brilliant ball in air.
Such thought was new to me
though I had not guessed at my lack
in the old indigo days,
children, before you fell—
to use a technical verb.

It is full of beautiful flair,
a jewel and a garden at once,
bluish-green with the track
of silver engraving its veins ...
Shit, but it's lovely
and no end of trouble at all.

Children, it once was bare
of all salacious language,
of goats and bladderwrack,
of banksia trees and wrens.
I endeavoured to bring it up rich.
I reckon it's my museum.

I gave a big party
and the name of the party
kept slipping clean away
from my wooden tongue
but I reckon it was
called history.

Some honoured guests
took off their names
or left them impaled like scarecrow rags
on my staggy front hedge.
I thought of it as being
a party for my son.

For crying out loud

Here
quite as much as there
in the dead straight street
or snailed and breathing gardenplot

time,
that sarcastic medium,
ran silvery through my fingers
like sand, or bonemarrow.

It
leaches through every life
which steps gingerly into it
under and over again.

We
were set down on moist earth
as though to train for some Grand Final
which is never going to take place.

Such
living as you greenly had
flowered and fruited boldly after all
but you misread what it meant.

Now
there's a torrent in the blood,
a sense of arabesques fanning out
across their shining enormous mudbrown delta.

In
the sepia vision, daily, diagonally,
you are walking in mufti backward
through yourself.

AND THE WORLD WAS CALM

Sandbags of sugar cannot conceal the gloomy fact
That we are inserted headlong into life
As a new pen is dipped in lavender ink.
We take up a space amid the comings and goings
Haphazardly, wanly. Velvet wrappings of eternal night
Contain our small blink, pitiless in their Logos.
Powderblue through gentle distance, lyrical mountains
Look at our passing span with incomprehension:
We never read their huge minds, and we die.

Why was the serpent given access to language and stuff?
Awareness becomes a different kettle of fish when eked
Out in a long line: the clipped image gives over
Until your modulation from rambunctiousness to grief
Is felt as a matter of slow brown flow, all river
And no cute islands. Remember, grace yields to Valium
Down on this late-in-the-century flood plain
Where even the fodder and grain crops are postmodern;
That is to say, containing no vitamins.

I'd like to build a cabin or humpy for awareness,
Something rustic like the Bothie of Tober-na-Vuolich
Where I could hum and tootle against the wind,
That long grey stranger skirling through everything.
Grammar is always complete, but the world is not,
Shrugging and folding, surely hatching out of magma.
'You see what you are dreaming, but not with your eyes',
Said a chap who met little sailors down in the park

But grew austere as the case went on wearing him down.

Light is more mysterious than anything else—
That is, except for having to shit and for loving,
Categories you could not have invented, supposing
You were God for a while.
                              Am I alive or dead?
A question basalt or sandstone could never ask.
Awareness becomes a different kettle of herrings
When it's applied to the psyche of a whole country,
Something quite rosy, hydra-headed and fat:
Public opinion did a jig on the carpet of madness.

In the beginning green verbs went bobbing in space
Which was pearly or golden in its painterly turn
And we do not think about gales in the Garden of Eden
Nor about any distinction between plants and weeds
So that Adam is constantly doing something with roses.
Rubric, baldric, erotic, I brood on these terms,
He could have reflected, leaving his pruning aside
While he rolled the well-made words on his tongue like stone:
For the main thing then was learning how to think crudely.

Subtle as ivory handles, we think we are now
Umpteen years on from that scene in the Olduvai Gorge,
Outside the gates of which St Michael struts with his sword.
Pining, we find paragraphs in which to lament
That we are inserted headlong into life;
Poetry survives with its coppery glint of gnosis
Along one edge.
                    It is a drug that endures
Riding atop the bubbles of evanescence.
The river we step in will burn us off at the knees.

TRACE ELEMENTS

... but surely the dead must walk again.
They stroll most oddly in and out of
small corners of your being, optical blips.
They go with an awkward gait, like foreign changelings
through the edges of a crowd or down the block.

It is at random seasons when the mind
is full at ease that my father, roundshouldered,
shuffles along to wait for lights to change
or my tall son shambles down the footpath
in a woollen cap, relentlessly unfashionable
and quiet as a cloud.
                        What do they want?
Can they be translated?

Space-time is no longer their medium;
                              they inhabit
antipodes of the radiant fair dinkum,
post-Heisenberg, transphysical, post-Planck,
taunting us all with quips of antimatter.
They are black holes punched in the modern world.
They have been resurrection.
                        They are Dreaming
and we the dream they paint their names across
in grey and lavender and thunderblue,
photocopies of Krishna passing
by Lasseter's reef; or somebody
behind us on the back road to Emmaus,
footsteps in the dust.
                    I would not have it
any other way.
              They walk on by.

Katherine Gallagher

IT IS WRITTEN

FOR SHAHNAZ WHO TOLD ME THE STORY

She died in seconds
her chador catching fire
    burning its envelope,
closing on her screams.

None of the men there
dared touch her
    for under the law
only a husband
    may touch his woman's body ...

Their reason
    for hesitating.

POEM FOR THE EXECUTIONERS

This is a blinding-place.
Only the hangmen see
fixing the knot of shame
upon their chosen tree.

Moments of waiting shrill,
finally echo out
past the creak of startled wood
and a soon-muffled shout.

Slowly the air recoils
on another unheard plea
and light is locked upon
a desolate, marked tree.

Rodney Hall

*M*ADAM'S MUSIC

An Ancient, puckered like a prune
—virtuoso on bassoon.
Virgin at the virginals.
    pavane

Cellist a rapacious tart
—couldn't play but looked the part.
Harlot on harmonium.
    gavotte

Madam's favourite prostitute
—love affair with transverse flute.
Spinster to spinet.
    minuet

Glaring through peroxide curls
—the surly hurdy-gurdy girls.
Bawd with clavichord.
    lavolta

All the time a breastless crone
fondled her sarrusophone.
Gorgon on organ.
    hornpipe

*H*YDRA

A whitewashed church is now my neighbour,
whose cloisters arching fine and shy
outwit the fingers of my olivetree.

Midwinter: through this bitter morning
customers stamp the market quay,
the cold leaps up like a fish from the slab,

while trombone mules protest against
the load of this, as of any day,
and puzzle out the terraces.

Roofs the lightning combs and scratches
tilt their aqueducts for wells,

and water booms beneath our floor.

Freestone walls assert their texture
floating with apples round the harbour
like children's kites to a lonely flute,

as vendors cry their catalogue.
Unrehearsed from winter sea
the sun fruits in my olivetree.

THE PUBLIC TURNS TO ITS HERO

It was his feet we mostly saw,
gigantic boots with rumpled uppers—
muffled drums upon our conscience;
or else the skirts of his overcoat
kniving like iron against his gaiters;
or else the muzzle of his carbine
casually against our temples.
Who could escape the fear of giants?
His shoulders tapered, almost lost
to view.

But worse was to hear our prayers,
confessions, and our coward cries
whispering around his metal,
begging him to bend his face
smile and approve our emulation.
He never did. And so we kept
our secret hope that long ago
some vaster hero had sliced his neck
and rolled away our single greatness.

Antigone Kefala

PRODIGAL SON

He spent his life abroad
in noble houses, as the lesser one,
eating with ghosts from silver plates
in ancient dining rooms where
stained glass windows looked on
lawns that stretched up to the lakes.

He waited for the time when
things would give themselves.

When he came back, Father had died,
they had already laid him in full

dress between the lighted candles,
as stubborn as before.
He never moved when the thin silver
needle struck the heart, up to the end
in quest of certainties.

ULTIMO BRIDGE

By six the bridge was empty,
soot raining on warehouses,
railyards, the hotel
where we were waiting for the fixer.

The light fell gilded through
the stained glass leaving them
absorbed, all worshippers, he knew,
as he danced lightly past their beers,
his voice—echoes of strange birds,
milk stones, salt flowers, bone trees,
earth—ochre to the touch.

The gutters full of onions,
blue dusted porcelain the sky,
above the railway clock
the new translucent moon was flying.

Thomas Shapcott

LIGHT ON THE WATER

How ridiculous that the first moon
should repeat itself through water
changing and incontestably nervous.
This local water, so ancient,
so re-cycled, is the most trapped image we have.
We have taste of water and it does not recover the moon.
We have the floating splashing diving
accompaniment of water
(think how earth bumps our heels, after)
—it does not remember us at all, none of us.
How simple we are, declaring our cities
on the rocks, and in sunshine.
We do not even have a way
to believe perfect darkness.
We plant flags on the moon.
When you say 'forget the past'
you are denying what water was

always sure to be,
before it entered your throat.

ADVICE TO A POLITICIAN

Do not answer any questions: ask them.
Do not forget your friends: use them.
Do not forget your enemies: use their mistakes.
Do not forget yourself: if you do, deny it.
Have an Enemy. That is essential.
If you cannot find an Enemy of the People
find an Enemy of the Law. Change the Law,
if necessary, to do it (the law has been acquired,
piecemeal, by politicians other than in Queensland).
There is a lot of prejudice waiting to be harvested:
remember—bigotry is only indefensible
when it is apologetic.
Hitler showed the political strength of bigotry,
Mussolini showed the voting power of prejudice.
Learn from them. Of course you do not go so far
as that (of course)
        Got things done, though;
    the Electorate was contented, dissidents
    could always leave. Trains were on time.

You will find enemies easily enough.

This is a wealthy place, waiting to be exploited.
Are you the one to do it? Slip through an Amendment
to the Companies Act and use nominees. Brazen it out.
And remember: justify nothing.

People who live by the open sewer
        forget it was once a shaded creek.
People who drive the bare road between Bulimba and the airport
        forget is was once shade rainforest.
People who live in development brick-veneer bungalows
        have forgotten entirely whatever was once meant by
        words like 'community'
You will go far
        taking us all with you.

ELEGY FOR GERTRUDE LANGER

Gaunt Gertrude Langer, grand and aggrieved,
improbable exile in Brisbane, you were loved and unloved
and became in the end an ikon. That's what I believed.

There was that day back ten years
when we drove to Caboolture

to see (improbable exile) an old canvas
claimed as Bellini—*Deposition*
in a galvo-roof church. With keen eyes
you searched out patina, form, texture.
You stood back and sighed: 'Ach! Darling,
in this place of cyclones and mildew
yes. Yes, these dead flesh tints. Unerring:
there is a master's hand.'
And with surprise I found myself thinking:
Why impossible? You grunted and shook your head
and all Europe came to your summoning.

But I first met you in print—
researching early reviews
of a young painter called Blackman
'52, '53. Here in Brisbane you saw
more than the others, and your eye
led us all in to share
the raw tenderness of the new artist's power.
Gertrude Langer, art reviewer, priestess
and follower, in the hot Brisbane of my teens
you were sure of art's certainty.
You were making this city possible, opulent,
inhabited, a community.

Then your grief when Karl died.
We winced and avoided you. This was not
Vienna, we had no heart
for such complete widowhood,
mid-European, effusive, claiming
some part of our own hoard
asking return, desperate
in a way altogether too visible,
theatrical. 'Darleenk!'
we would parody, 'Darleenk, without Karl
ach the desolation! Unendurable!
How can I go on? Now there is no one.
Ach darleenk. Impossible.'

You were part of the scene,
fixed, immutable—galleries, concerts,
openings. Theatre was possible, larger than life
as you were, you were larger than our lives were
and your belief in the possible opened the screen.
I cannot believe Brisbane without you, gaunt,
grand Queen of the parquet. I still spring
with a kind of mad joy as you enter the foyer
of my mind, grieving, aggrieved, and again
there. With a hug and a kiss on both cheeks
as is proper, I enquire

of your cousins in Budapest, last year
in Vienna—you are there, Gertrude, still there
in hot thundery Brisbane, forty years there
and the town, for your memory,
will not be the same.

THE CITY OF HOME

The City of Home is reached only in dreams.
It has a town centre, a river with curved bridges

and the famous clocktower. There are always pigeons
which signify abundance not overpopulation.

There are no walls, no toll gates, no ribbon developments
full of hoardings, carpet Emporia or used car allotments.

The City of Home has retained only stone monuments and spires
and the shady maze of the Municipal Gardens

or perhaps secret childhood wildernesses of bramble
—the smell of lantana still clings to an old pullover.

You approach from the air, it is a plan, a totality.
It is worthy of all your best secrets and the secrets of others

Like all great cities, the City of Home reaches back
into all the generations, all the inheritances

though you have your own special associations
and insist on the second seat outside for your coffee.

There is no other coffee, no taste in all the world
to compare with that coffee! Yes, you insist, the second chair

the one under the awning where you can glimpse the fountain
and the bronze angel. The City of Home is like no other city

not even the City of Remembering or the Cities of the Plain.
The City of Home has only one drawback, but that is terrible:

The City of Home is empty of people.
All its songs are the songs of exile.

Randolph Stow

SEASHELLS AND SANDALWOOD

My childhood was seashells and sandalwood, windmills
and yachts in the southerly, ploughshares and keels,
fostered by hills and by waves on the breakwater,
sunflowers and ant-orchids, surfboards and wheels,

gulls and green parakeets, sandhills and haystacks, and
brief subtle things that a child does not realise,
horses and porpoises, aloes and clematis—
Do I idealise?
      Then—I idealise.

As he lay dying

As he lay dying, two fat crows
  sat perched above in a strangling vine,
    and one crow called to the other:
      'Brother,
  harvest his eyes, his tongue is mine.'

As he lay dying, two lithe hawks
  caressed the wind and spied two crows;
    and one hawk hissed to the other:
      'Brother,
  mine is the sleekest one of those.'

As he lay dying, two eagles passed
  and saw two hawks that hung in flying,
    and one said soft to the other:
      'Brother,
  mark your prey.' As he lay dying.

Jimmy Woodsers

Remembering. Pools. Remembering. Eyes. Remembering
(my eyes in the mirror, my eyes among the bottles)
my eyes: dry pools, in the waterless country.

The pool is empty now beneath the olives,
drained for the safety of the little cousins,
who are now tall men, and safe, in the waterless country.

My grandmother's long white hair wept in the basin.
Gumtrees stooped and crippled by the southerly
were ladies washing their long green hair, remembering.

Green: the green explosions of May, the August fires.
Rampaging radish ambushed a sleeping train
and held it, for a season, hooting through flowers,
wreathed, leaved, unheard, remembering.

The olives drizzled; green petals, abortive fruit
on the undrained pool. Then, like a storm, November,
and among the sunflowers, behind the oleander,
gulls assembled to mock my calamitous birth.

The bitter wind bent all my trees to northward.
The sea at each end of the street advanced to meet me.

On a morning in March I said goodday to time,
and doves and all went down in the blowing dunes.

In the white smoke of the sand remembering
today and the grey smoke of my lips on the glass
I set out again for the clay-pans of my eyes,

crying: 'My friend. You must drove your sheep elsewhere.
My dams are dry. You must leave this waterless country.'

The singing bones

'Out where the dead men lie.'
     Barcroft Boake

Out there, beyond the boundary fence, beyond
the scrub-dark flat horizon that the crows
returned from, evenings, days of rusty wind
raised from the bones a stiff lament, whose sound
netted my childhood round, and even here still blows.

My country's heart is ash in the market-place,
is aftermath of martyrdom. Out there
its sand-enshrined lay saints lie piece by piece,
Leichhardt by Gibson, stealing the wind's voice,
and Lawson's tramps, by choice made mummia and air.

No pilgrims leave, no holy-days are kept
for these who died of landscape. Who can find,
even, the camp-sites where the saints last slept?
Out there their place is, where the charts are gapped,
unreachable, unmapped, and mainly in the mind.

They were all poets, so the poets said,
who kept their end in mind in all they wrote
and hymned their bones, and joined them. Gordon died
happy, one surf-loud dawn, shot through the head,
and Boake astonished, dead, his stockwhip round his throat.

Time, time and time again, when the inland wind
beats over myall from the dunes, I hear
the singing bones, their glum Victorian strain.
A ritual manliness, embracing pain
to know; to taste terrain their heirs need not draw near.

Judith Rodriguez

FAMILY

In my mother's family
We have no ancestors
only the long silence
between pogroms.

In my father's family
we have little tradition—
lands, legends, powers
passed us by.

In my country
we have no grandparents
no continuing song
no dances. Silence

feeds music,
father's our legend.
Husband and wife, estuary
into a continent,

we open our arms:
touch peaks, touch breakers.
Forest and white water
our children dance.

ESKIMO OCCASION

I am in my Eskimo-hunting-song-mood,
Aha!
The lawn is tundra   the car will not start
the sunlight is an avalanche   we are avalanche-struck at our breakfast
struck with sunlight through glass   me and my spoonfed daughters
out of this world in our kitchen.

I will sing the song of my daughter-hunting,
Oho!
The waves lay down   the ice grew strong
I sang the song   of dark water under ice
the song of winter fishing   the magic for seal rising
among the ancestor-masks.

I waited by water to dream new spirits,
Hoo!
The water spoke   the ice shouted
the sea opened   the sun made young shadows
they breathed my breathing   I took them from deep water
I brought them fur-warmed home.

I am dancing the years of the two great hunts,
Ya-hay!

It was I who waited   cold in the wind-break
I stamp like the bear   I call like the wind of the thaw
I leap like the sea spring-running.   My sunstruck daughters splutter
and chuckle and bang their spoons:

Mummy is singing at breakfast and dancing!
So big!

THE MAHOGANY SHIP

IN MEMORY OF JOHN MANIFOLD

How I would have the poem rest:
that European circumstance, the ship
storm-blind
and unaccompanied
beating along by shelved cliffs, gulfs, west
under the gales' whip,
the length of her
urged at the last ashore
prow abutted on hummocks
to sift, to burrow like a burr.

And the passionate connection to begin:
thrown once for all too far up to be manned,
sea-jarrings
and the speaking charts
of sea-roads stilled, their known ports shunned to earn
a pilgrimage in sand—
the timbers weigh,
sailors run crouching, bayed
by fears, and snatch at brush
for watch-fires in her lee—

night-long at the flickering edge
of their race and language. Fires sicken. The dark
land dawns,
dunes packed by rain
mass, shoulder aside Europe. At the ridge
a face flares, turning last
from sand-bloated breakers
after water, timber, game.

Un-history cancels them. The Yangery
like the long wind hurling and raking

take them, unravel and stow
their genes between the dark thighs of the tribe.

Coast songs
and the wry cross
possess their children, the songless ship-ropes go
for nets that childbearing wives
three centuries on
re-knot for fishing—Jim Cain's
black Kitty and yellow Nellie—in their flesh.
Captain Mills notes the strain

surfacing, a legend's landfall,
even while the wind-grey panels of the hull
knives slip on
and farmers pillage
wear out of sight like the Great Expedition, founder
in wastes, and bearings fail.
The poem, consigned
and claimed, deepening in sand,
shifting, reaches among layers
to a beginning, to ends ...

The long stain in the mind.

This wreck lay among the sand dunes near Warrnambool, in the tribal land of
the Yangery. No remains have been seen since the 1890s. The Portuguese Grand
Expedition of 1536 has been suggested as the origin of the wreck.

Les Murray

THE BROAD BEAN SERMON

Beanstalks, in any breeze, are a slack church parade
without belief, saying *trespass against us* in unison,
recruits in mint Air Force dacron, with unbuttoned leaves.

Upright with water like men, square in stem-section
they grow to great lengths, drink rain, keel over all ways,
kink down and grow up afresh, with proffered new greenstuff.

Above the cat-and-mouse floor of a thin bean forest
snails hang rapt in their food, ants hurry through Escher's three worlds,
spiders tense and sag like little black flags in their cordage.

Going out to pick beans with the sun high as fence-tops, you find
plenty, and fetch them. An hour or a cloud later
you find shirtfulls more. At every hour of daylight

appear more that you missed: ripe, knobbly ones, fleshy-sided,
thin-straight, thin-crescent, frown-shaped, bird-shouldered, boat-
          keeled ones,
beans knuckled and single-bulged, minute green dolphins at suck,

beans upright like lecturing, outstretched like blessing fingers
in the incident light, and more still, oblique to your notice
that the noon glare or cloud-light or afternoon slants will uncover

till you ask yourself Could I have overlooked so many, or
do they form in an hour? unfolding into reality
like templates for subtly broad grins, like unique caught expressions,

like edible meanings, each sealed around with a string
and affixed to its moment, an unceasing colloquial assembly,
the portly, the stiff, and those lolling in pointed green slippers ...

Wondering who'll take the spare bagfulls, you grin with happiness
—it is your health—you vow to pick them all
even the last few, weeks off yet, misshapen as toes.

THE MITCHELLS

I am seeing this: two men are sitting on a pole
they have dug a hole for and will, after dinner, raise
I think for wires. Water boils in a prune tin.
Bees hum their shift in unthinning mists of white.

bursaria blossom, under the noon of wattles.
The men eat big meat sandwiches out of a styrofoam
box with a handle. One is overheard saying:
drought that year. Yes. Like trying to farm the road.

The first man, if asked, would say *I'm one of the Mitchells.*
The other would gaze for a while, dried leaves in his palm,
and looking up, with pain and subtle amusement,

say *I'm one of the Mitchells.* Of the pair, one has been rich
but never stopped wearing his oil-stained felt hat. Nearly everything
they say is ritual. Sometimes the scene is an avenue.

LACONICS: THE FORTY ACRES

We have bought the Forty Acres,
prime brush land.

If Bunyah is a fillet
this paddock is the eye.

The creek half-moons it,
log-deep, or parting rocks.

The corn-ground by now
has had forty years' grassed spell.

Up in the swamp
are paperbarks, coin-sized frogs—

The forty, at last,
our beautiful deep land

it was Jim's, it was Allan's,
it was Reg's, it is Dad's—

Brett wanted it next
but he'd evicted Dad

for bitter porridge
many cold returns.

That interior machinegun,
my chainsaw, drops dead timber

where we burn the heaps
we'll plant kikuyu grass.

Ecology? Sure.
But also husbandry.

And the orchard will go there
and we'll re-roof the bare pole barn.

Our croft, our Downs,
our sober, shining land.

THE FUTURE

There is nothing about it. Much science fiction is set there
but is not about it. Prophecy is not about it.
It sways no yarrow stalks. And crystal is a mirror.
Even the man we nailed on a tree for a lookout
said little about it; he told us evil would come.
We see, by convention, a small living distance into it
but even that's a projection. And all our projections
fail to curve where it curves.
        It is the black hole
out of which no radiation escapes to us.
The commonplace and magnificent roads of our lives
go on some way through cityscape and landscape
or steeply sloping, or scree, into that sheer fall
where everything will be that we have ever sent there,
compacted, spinning—except perhaps us, to see it.
It is said we see the start.
        But, from here, there's a blindness.
The *gouffre Avenir* that will swallow all our present
blinds us to the normal sun that may be imagined
shining calmly away on the far side of it, for others
in their ordinary day. A day to which all our portraits,
ideals, revolutions, denim and deshabille
are quaintly heartrending. To see those people is impossible,

to greet them, mawkish. Nonetheless, I begin:
'When I was alive—'
     and I am turned around
to find myself looking at a cheerful picnic party,
the women decently legless, in muslin and gloves,
the men in beards and westkits, with the long
cheroots and duck trousers of the better sort,
relaxing on a stone veranda. Ceylon, or Sydney.
And as I look, I know they are utterly gone,
each one on his day, with pillow, small bottles, mist,
with all the futures they dreamed or dealt in, going
down to that engulfment everything approaches;
with the man on the tree, they have vanished into the Future.

Rainwater Tank

Empty rings when tapped give tongue,
rings that are tense with water talk:
as he sounds them, ring by rung,
Joe Mitchell's reddened knuckles walk.

The cattledog's head sinks down a notch
and another notch, beside the tank,
and Mitchell's boy, with an old jack-plane,
lifts moustaches from a plank.

From the puddle that the tank has dripped
hens peck glimmerings and uptilt
their heads to shape the quickness down;
petunias live on what gets spilt.

The tankstand spider adds a spittle
thread to her portrait of her soul.
Pencil-grey and stacked like shillings
out of a banker's paper roll

stands the tank, roof-water drinker.
The downpipe stares drought into it.
Briefly the kitchen tap turns on
then off. But the tank says Debit, Debit.

Poetry and Religion

Religions are poems. They concert
our daylight and dreaming mind, our
emotions, instinct, breath and native gesture

into the only whole thinking: poetry.
Nothing's said till it's dreamed out in words
and nothing's true that figures in words only.

A poem, compared with an arrayed religion,
may be like a soldier's one short marriage night
to die and live by. But that is a small religion.

Full religion is the large poem in loving repetition;
like any poem, it must be inexhaustible and complete
with turns where we ask Now why did the poet do that?

You can't pray a lie, said Huckleberry Finn;
you can't poe one either. It is the same mirror:
mobile, glancing, we call it poetry,

fixed centrally, we call it a religion,
and God is the poetry caught in any religion,
caught, not imprisoned. Caught as in a mirror

that he attracted, being in the world as poetry
is in the poem, a law against its closure.
There'll always be religion around while there is poetry

or a lack of it. Both are given, and intermittent,
as the action of those birds—crested pigeon, rosella parrot—
who fly with wings shut, then beating, and again shut.

THE TIN WASH DISH

Lank poverty, dank poverty,
its pants wear through at fork and knee.
It warms its hands over burning shames,
refers to its fate as Them and He
and delights in things by their hard names:
rag and toejam, feed and paw—
don't guts that down, there ain't no more!
Dank poverty, rank poverty,
it hums with a grim fidelity
like wood-rot with a hint of orifice,
wet newspaper jammed in the gaps of artifice,
and disgusts us into fierce loyalty.
It's never the fault of those you love:
poverty comes down from above.
Let it dance chairs and smash the door,
it arises from all that went before
and every outsider's the enemy—
Jesus Christ turned this over with his stick
and knights and philosophers turned it back.
Rank poverty, lank poverty,
chafe in its crotch and sores in its hair,
still a window's clean if it's made of air
and not webbed silver like a sleeve.
Watch out if this does well at school
and has to leave and longs to leave:

someone, sometime, will have to pay.
Lank poverty, dank poverty,
the cornbag quilt breeds such loyalty.
Shave with toilet soap, run to flesh,
astound the nation, run the army,
still you wait for the day you'll be sent back
where books or toys on the floor are rubbish
and no one's allowed to come and play
because home calls itself a shack
and hot water crinkles in the tin wash dish.

Ariel

Upward, cheeping, on huddling wings,
these small brown mynas have gained
a keener height than their kind ever sustained
but whichever of them fails first
falls to the hawk circling under
who drove them up.
Nothing's free when it is explained.

Pigs

Us all on sore cement was we.
Not warmed then with glares. Not glutting mush
under that pole the lightning's tied to.
No farrow-shit in milk to make us randy.
Us back in cool god-shit. We ate crisp.
We nosed up good rank in the tunnelled bush.
Us all fuckers then. And Big, huh? Tusked
the balls-biting dog and gutsed him wet.
Us shoved down the soft cement of rivers.
Us snored the earth hollow, filled farrow, grunted.
Never stopped growing. We sloughed, we soughed
and balked no weird till the high ridgebacks was us
with weight-buried hooves. Or bristly, with milk.
Us never knowed like slitting nor hose-biff then.
Not the terrible sheet-cutting screams up ahead.
The burnt water kicking. This gone-already feeling
here in no place with our heads on upside down.

Eagle pair

We shell down on the sleeping-branch. All night
the limitless Up digests its meats of light.

The circle-winged Egg then emerging from long pink and brown
re-inverts life, and meats move or are still on the Down.

Irritably we unshell, into feathers; we lean open and rise
and magnify this meat, then that, with the eyes of our eyes.

Meat is light, it is power and Up, as we free it from load
and our mainstay, the cunningest hunter, is the human road

but all the Down is heavy and tangled. Only meat is good there
and the rebound heat ribbing up vertical rivers of air.

J. S. Harry

One, in the motel

One, in the motel,
bleeds, and cannot be stopped.
Endlessly, the flow
saps, reduces the span.
Across the highway
hessian-coloured sheep
drift, halt,   drift and eat.
Neon-green paddocks' long-grassed spring
augurs well for summer.

It is the Abattoirs' paddock.
The sheep put their heads down and eat.

Coming and going: peripatetic poet

It is not
        that what you see
when travelling around the world
is significantly different
from the land you are leaving,
rather, that what you observe, returning,
although seeming the same as when you left
in itself,
is viewed altogether differently.

Having realised you cannot depict the world
in which you are travelling—
its guns, nails and cash-registers
turning you blindly back into yourself—
you realise, now,
shut in your own state,
you cannot see that, clearly.

To make the agony of the condition
real, you must accept

the full weight of the pressure out—
the torn flesh, the cries, the hostilities;
in order to return,
with a traveller's eyes,
to the miserable hearth you left.

$\mathcal{I}$F ... & THE MOVABLE GROUND

If
you see
'modernity'
as a bridge
between the past & the future
on which the troops
of those countries
fight a war

you will need
to go to classes
in destruction

every house that is built on it
every support it is arched upon

even those twigs
your words lay   as if rough mat/ over a moving pit
for a moment
to stand to fight from

a contiguous moment
will call you out
to knock down

you   will be a newer/ demolition expert/
existing/ in the field of that instant/
as instant follows instant
each with its instant's fighter

as the war goes on ...

$\mathcal{A}$N IMPRESSION OF MINIMALIST ART IN THE LATE TWENTIETH CENTURY

A yellow
semi-deflated balloon
floats trapped
on a small
green circle
of water surrounded

by white
water lilies. Jagged
reeds fence the outer
water circle of it,
making palisade. Wind
would stretch
this balloon's rubber luck
thin as a condom
around nothing, pressing it up
against the submerged
pricks of the
flattened
fallen palm fronds.
It breaks with a soft
plosive,
sign or an exhalation,
leaving no children.
The burst balloon's rubber
drifts slowly
down centuries of water
past the forms
of the swirling eels
and the sucking mouths
of their skinny offspring.
Going down without a self
through the centuries
it is seen as a yellow flower
or a floating petal
on a water lily garden
at Giverny. In the late
twentieth century,
it's ok, don't cry;
it is rubber!
Perfectly hygienic
to wear against the skin
to suck
or to throw away.
Ego leaves a mark on it
redundant as the whorls
of the first,
artist's finger prints.

Clive James

THE CRYING NEED FOR SNOW

It's cold without the softness of a fall
Of snow to give these scenes a common bond
And though, besotted on a viewless rime,
The ducks can do their standing-on-the-pond
Routine that leaves you howling, all in all
We need some snow to hush the whole thing up.

The ducks can do their flatfoot-waterfool
Mad act that leaves you helpless, but in fine
We need their footprints in a higher field
Made pure powder, need their wig-wag line
Of little kites pressed in around the pool:
An afternoon of snow should cover that.

Some crystalline precipitate should throw
Its multifarious weightlessness around
For half a day and paint the whole place out,
Bring back a soft regime to bitter ground:
An instant plebiscite would vote for snow
So overwhelmingly if we could call it now.

An afternoon of snow should cover that
Milk-bottle neck bolt upright in the slime
Fast frozen at the pond's edge, brutal there:
We need to see junk muffled, whitewashed grime,
Lean brittle ice grown comfortably fat,
A world prepared to take our footprints in.

A world prepared to take our footprints in
Needs painting out, needs to be a finer field:
So overwhelmingly, if we could call it now,
The fluffy stuff would prime it: it would yield
To lightest step, be webbed and toed and heeled,
Pushed flat, smoothed off, heaped high, pinched anyhow,
Yet be inviolable. Put like that,
Gently, the cold makes sense. Snow links things up.

THE BOOK OF MY ENEMY HAS BEEN REMAINDERED

The book of my enemy has been remaindered
And I am pleased.
In vast quantities it has been remaindered.
Like a van-load of counterfeit that has been seized
And sits in piles in a police warehouse,

My enemy's much-praised effort sits in piles
In the kind of bookshop where remaindering occurs.
Great, square stacks of rejected books and, between them, aisles
One passes down reflecting on life's vanities,
Pausing to remember all those thoughtful reviews
Lavished to no avail upon one's enemy's book—
For behold, here is that book
Among these ranks and banks of duds,
These ponderous and seemingly irreducible cairns
Of complete stiffs.

The book of my enemy has been remaindered
And I rejoice.
It has gone with bowed head like a defeated legion
Beneath the yoke.
What avail him now his awards and prizes,
The praise expended upon his meticulous technique,
His individual voice?
Knocked into the middle of next week
His brainchild now consorts with the bad buys,
The sinkers, clinkers, dogs and dregs,
The Edsels of the world of movable type,
The bummers that no amount of hype could shift,
The unbudgeable turkeys.

Yea, his slim volume with its understated wrapper
Bathes in the glare of the brightly jacketed *Hitler's War Machine*,
His unmistakably individual new voice
Shares the same scrapyard with a forlorn skyscraper
Of *The Kung-Fu Cookbook*,
His renowned abhorrence of all posturing and pretence,
Is there with *Pertwee's Promenades and Pierrots—*
One Hundred Years of Seaside Entertainment,
And (oh, this above all) his sensibility,
His sensibility and its hair-like filaments,
His delicate, quivering sensibility is now as one
With *Barbara Windsor's Book of Boobs*,
A volume graced by the descriptive rubric
'My boobs will give everyone hours of fun.'

Soon now a book of mine could be remaindered also,
Though not to the monumental extent
In which the chastisement of remaindering has been meted out
To the book of my enemy,
Since in the case of my own book it will be due
To a miscalculated print run, a marketing error—
Nothing to do with merit.
But just supposing that such an event should hold
Some slight element of sadness, it will be offset
By the memory of this sweet moment.

Chill the champagne and polish the crystal goblets!
The book of my enemy has been remaindered
And I am glad.

REFLECTIONS IN AN EXTENDED KITCHEN

Late summer charms the birds out of the trees
Onto our lawn, where the cat gets them.
Aware of this but not unmanned, Matisse
Makes the whole room as sexy as the girl.

'Distributed voluptuousness,' he said,
Matching the décor to her lazy gaze.
Just book me on the first flight to Morocco.
You see what I see? Feathers on the grass.

Nothing so sordid in Henri's backyard
Where colored shapes may touch, but not to crush.
Look at that death trap out there, lined with roses!
We grew a free-fire zone with fertilizer.

Caught on the ground like the Egyptian Air Force
A wrecked bird on its back appears outraged:
It could have been a contender. What a world
Of slam-bang stuff to float one fantasy

Amongst her figured curtains, blobs for flowers,
Lolling unlocked in filmy harem pants!
Where did we see her first? That place they called
Leningrad. She looked like History's cure,

And even he could use that. When he turned
An artful blank back on his wife and child
They were arrested, leaving him to paint
In peace a world with no Gestapo in it—

A dream that came true. Agonies recede,
And if his vision hid harsh facts from him
It sharpens them for us. Best to believe
He served an indispensable ideal:

Douceur de vivre on a heroic scale—
Heaven on Earth, the Land of Oobladee,
Cloud Nine and Shangri-la hooked to the wall
As bolt holes for the brain, square wishing wells.

Suppose that like his brush my pen could speak
Volumes, our cat might stay in shape to pounce,
But only on the arm of that soft chair
You sit in now and where you would lie lulled,

An ageless, in-house *odalisque couchée*
Never to be less langorous than this,
Always dissolving in the air around you
Reality's cruel purr with your sweet whisper—

And nothing would be terrible again,
Nor ever was. The fear that we once felt
For daughters fallen ill or just an hour
Late home: it never happened. That dumb bird
Stayed in its tree and I was true to you.

Mudrooroo

I'VE MET THEM ALL

I've met them all, green and black and white.
The greeny said that he had come from earth
And had overshot the stars,
But the metho had turned his body bad,
He struck a match and went out as a fire.

The black one was a woman urgent with loves and hates,
She cried over the sins of all humankind,
Sang a female song in keeping with these times,
Then tried to convert me to a faith red with menstrual blood.

The white bloke knew every answer,
To every question I never asked,
I winked at him and grinned a drunken grin,
And said I was off to see a childhood friend.

I've met them all, green and black and white,
And all of them talked and none of them thought,
That I had the answer I never sought
In sitting and waiting as the billy boiled,
Watching the flames flickering with a thousand forms
Of soft life whispering in the scrub around,
As my mate passed the smoke over to me.

OLDERING

The not quite right suit, the not quite right trousers,
The not quite right times of oldering out the seasons.
Now clinging desperately, now greedy, now a psychic drooling
At what has been missed. Private eyes drop away from the video
Images forming a hooded cliché figure with a sickle.
Essaying to believe that death comes like the man in the mask,
Like Yama riding on his black buffalo plodding towards—
You won't believe it even when you're there in the ruins;
You won't believe it when the old man beckons to you from
The dark tunnel of his wurley. You won't believe and doubt
That this is your last home. You defy the death brutal attack.

Killed by train, killed by plane, killed by car, killed by home
Tragedies, done in, fallen in towards the water hole bracken
Surrounded by the pitiful aching years of rubbish self
You clean and clear these rancid waters for the death jump.
Oldering, clinging, greedy, a thousand thousand year lotus
Closes over the grey head in sleep expelling times of later on.
Oldering, the light flickers, grows stronger, blazes in mists.
Oldering, Jack Davis's dancer dances towards you his face,
Old Worru mutters in his fitful sleep, then quietens down.
Oldering, fervid fancies turn tolerance-laden towards earth things,
Love tears relieve as you fall beneath the surface of the water,
As you mount the buffalo, as you evade the sickle for the lotus
Covering you for an eternity of sleep, or nothingness,
Or what might have been as a vacancy not even signed with your name.

Peter Steele

ᖴUTURIBLES

FOR CHRIS WALLACE-CRABBE

Low-lit, off-hand, up-staging what happens to be,
    The postulata gleam:
The hirsute King of France; the constancy
    Of Heraclitus' stream;
Inebrius Severus' mistress Festina Lente;
    The Happax Legomena Team.

They're there, or not there, to stay. The wide black yonder
    Brings them out of its bag
Innumerably for the pragmatist to ponder:
    Michelangelo's David in drag;
Mount Tuscarora; Chaucerian fowls called Wanda;
    Diogenes banking the swag.

Maieutic, mimetic, mitotic, they shuffle their shapes,
    While the Band of the Spheres plays low:
The garrulous Marcel Marceau; Houdini's escapes
    Recycled as Sartre's *Huit Clos*;
Victoria's 'How we all laughed with Sir Robert Peel' tapes;
    The last round of Gandhi/Thoreau.

The author not answering, management dining away,
    The noise and the people, my dear,
Look set for the longest of runs: and we, half distrait,
    Half diverted, contribute a cheer,
Admiring the buckram and motley by night. For the day,
    Our heads and our hearts are the gear.

WEDNESDAY

Safe from the katabatic wind
And the mooching bear, we've still known
The rake of a claw from the north rescind
Some things we thought our own—

As, chiefly, movement. Roads glaze.
The pallid croupier leans and spins
Our frosted wheels to a locked phase.
Today though, for our sins

We're here in this gothic house, first
And last time for a year perhaps.
Carnal hunger, mortal thirst,
The shadowed slow collapse

Of lungs and apprehended sphere,
The blank of memory's board, the clash
Of each gear in the breast—they're here.
Quiet, we wait for the ash.

Forty-nine years ago today
Dresden was put to the torch. We start
The service. Ashen-faced, I pray
For less ice at the heart.

THE ACADEMY OF CONTEMPT

In the beginning there is no requirement
To establish prior accomplishment; indeed,
Parents are urged to enrol their children while
They are no more than a spark in the eye. Special
Arrangements can be made for the more deserving
And for those of unusual promise. Our tuition
Is in the nature of things a bargain, granted
The scope, rewards and future open to graduates.

Faculty has been recruited from
A wide array of backgrounds. All are skilled
In choosing targets for contempt, including
Ugly ducklings, old hands, the too
Familiar or too novel, the poor, the rich,
And other versions of oneself. Professors
Have expertise in advanced remedial work
For those delayed by residual charity.

Emphasis is given to workshops and
Practical work. Analogies are established
Between the work of the mouth, the mind, and the hands.
Freshmen will study films which focus on killing,

With particular stress on self-congratulation.
Electives deal with the history of cant
And the morphology of scorn. Seniors
Will contrive their own supervised forms of study.

Rumours that the Academy is lacking
In real standing were only to be expected:
As we point out, self-interest governs all.
Those, however, concerned to become proficient
In the ways of the higher deturpation or
Demotic reductivity will know
Where the truth of the matter lies. History
Is on our side, and what more can we say?

Syd Harrex

ATLANTIS

He came too close to finding Atlantis;
stranger, friend, other me. On old Thera.
Entangling time in his mind, fishing myth
with the nets and tackle of afflatus,
perhaps he went mad, as the saying is.
He disturbs me now here in this other
island, where stone speech and architecture
preserve the class-system through all weather;
where garden cats (their energies expended
in teasing mice, rippling along pickets)
lick the sugary sunlight off their fur,
and curl like petals now summer's ended.
So it is my memory encloses
Atlantis and the purring of roses.

LIBRAN BIRTHDAY

In ivory winds like these, whip-handled,
off the shining flanks of the bucking mare
(pun: honour of Baudin), this chopped
crystal of waters given the sinister
map name *Backstairs Passage*;

these breezes threshing into Hog Bay by
bouncing trawlers tethered to the pier,
this blue tremor in ear-shaped shells
some fancy is a sea-soul's pain;
this gale of mixed seasons green

now as it fuses with the island Spring,
convulsion or tantrum of a dark angel's

symphony, its paper score torn
into scraps of seagulls; this crush of air,
this writhing botany planted or

uprooted; froth of wild-flowers
in a surf of grasses (bluewinged
Comesperma; Epacris impressa
cathedral bells; purple
sneezing spasms of *Swainsona*);

this air-borne honey of fertility
spilling cells of seeds wherever,
this fever fore and aft history
that blew the burnt Europeans here
in their moth-winged match-stick ships—

Investigator, Le Geographe, Casuarina—
and us long-weekending on this shore
white-laced with foam: we charge
these winds to enfold in tissue of gold
your first birthday here in Penneshaw.

Elizabeth Lawson

Valentia Street wharf

Poet casting in light, remember:
when you looked back, it was
Eurydice, your love, who died.
Daily, through morning glory, purple rumination,
racked on the minute hand of your momently
stoppable clock,
latch-shy, reeled in like film, you watched for a ferry.

And she sailed serenely in
dutiful as religion at a distance
—Lady Woodward. Edeline ... —
and the birds in singing trees you stilled
(one instant of sung
Avernus) were only soldier birds, the quick
grey slash of butchers.

Memorable for me too, since I was 'happy' there
treading the same asphalt sticky with wild figs,
sandstock walls sounding a harbour wash
of murk, resilient jelly-fish,
resilient schoolkids fishing murky life,
the same path silk with creeping sun
to the same sunlit darkening wharf; I

remember the houses, improbably
lovely, as if of dreams or
memory. Did you know the other poet?
older, sheaved in paper, collar up,
who daily hazarded a deck heaving
cutthroat business, plunged Quayward,
ferry-commuting to the clock, to words?

Yes, I remember Onions,
benignly charitable to Cockatoo,
so sensitive to Long Nose Point.
I made it daily to the squat boat
that rocked my early corner in the sun,
as you, dead-stopped at haunted
windows, caterpillar slow,

(you say) could not. I remember
incense of jacaranda, singing loquat trees,
dead still: remember. And now remember misremembering:
this, for instance: this soft-ware stupidity
that tries to make your real ferry real.
untwines your metaphor of vines
that trumpeted clear purple:

'morning glory', 'morning only'.
We are then, cold as stopped hands,
in the real wash, for real.
Rushing downhill however slow we cannot miss—
She's always—I remember now—
punctilious to the finest fault
with time. On deck,

casting a last time, poet, for love,
it is always Eurydice
who (happily) will not die
on the path young with flowers, sex
and houses sweet with art.
Spinnakers snatch an evening gust in red,
Looking back soon we *will* fail to see the point.

Geoffrey Lehmann

BIRD-WATCHING WITH MR LONG

'What's that bird, Mr Long?'
'That's a chipper.'
'What's that small bird over there?'
'That's a fly-bird.'

There's a forest I'll never see again
where birds with exotic names
whistle to each other,
flashing blue and scarlet
as they dart and fan their wings.

'What will you have for breakfast, Mr Long?'
asked my father.
'I could eat the leg of the Holy Ghost,'
replied Mr Long (meaning toast).
'I would *not* have expected that of *you*!'
said my father with ice.
But Mr Long was rarely put out.

On a wooden chair by my bed
there's hot cocoa I'll drain fast
because these autumn nights
are taking the warmth out of things
as they loosen the poplars' yellow leaves.

Then I'm going on that journey
Mr Long always promised
through the spinifex
with a covered wagon and cockatoo,
cooking fish on river stones,
to Palm Valley and its wild blacks.
'What's that bird, Mr Long?'
'That's a parson bird with the white collar.'
'And that one over there?'
'That's a grey hopper.'

Walking all day
out on the western plains, Mr Long
could sustain himself
with a line of trees on the horizon.

The Spring Forest

Each year we get further away
from the Spring Forest,
the original text.

'Drinking straws' we say,
sipping a milkshake of imitation vanilla
through a thin plastic tube.
My children in summer
used stubble from paddocks
for sipping crushed strawberry water.
These days you don't find tadpoles
boiled up in the washing.

Each year
there are more gaps in the text,
privet in creekbeds
chokes out she-oak,
weeds blot the lettering.

Each place spoke through its plants
and fauna, until we came.

Not yet found

I chose the name Spring Forest
and I've yet to find the spring.

Some unfinished equations
are the closest I've come
to the puzzle of why I'm here.

There is a book before our eyes—
the night sky of the universe.
Galileo saw its language was mathematics.
A cricket's encrypted love song,
light from an ancient star
are mathematical messages
arriving in sultry air.

Imaginary and complex numbers
allow life to reproduce itself
endlessly and intricately
without repetition—
the elusive algorithms of a summer night.

The golden wall

Don't ask Uncle Pat why the night sky is dark—
in hot weather
taking his mattress out on the grass
inside his dog-proof fence to sleep.
When Pat lifts his face up to the night—
propped on a pillow
of kapok stuffed in mattress ticking—
he'd fix you with sheep drench if you told him
that his line of sight
should intersect at every point
with a near or distant star
glimmering in the transparency of space
so the whole sky
should be ablaze from end to end
like 'a golden wall'.

Pat's golden wall was his orange tree.
Like Uncle Pat it had never borne fruit
until I dumped five tons of chicken manure
on its roots.
His line of sight
from the cane lounge where he sprawled
intersected at every point with oranges
twenty feet up in the sky,
a Utopia of fruit
which the district came to visit and eat,
oranges with no ending
like the return veranda
around the four sides of his house
where nephews and nieces ran forever
and their children after them.

Pat forgot his promise to pay for the manure
and the oranges didn't come back.
But he didn't miss them,
so don't ask Pat why the night sky is dark.

Olbers' riddle has hung around
for centuries.
You can't explain it by absorption.
Gas and dust heat up and glow.
Nor by absences or voids.
Every square inch has its galaxies.

Ask the cells inside your head
the same riddle,
why don't they all blaze at once
a golden wall of noise,
each neuron singing its own note
deafening your mind with light.
Political and religious visionaries
promise us this,
every cell singing in unison,
a mass of indistinguishable stars.

But something in the universe denies
the golden wall,
some structure which became Uncle Pat
calling to his nephews from his cane lounge,
'Now don't trample them tomahawk plants!'
(meaning hollyhock plants).

Pat prefers his own company on hot nights
leaving Auntie Bridge inside
with pictures of saints on the bedroom wall.
He takes his bedding
and lies in a darkness
where each star can broadcast as a soloist.

The universe
is a composition of unique bodies
on display,
and the night sky of the mind
allows a single file of thoughts
to light up as a sentence.

Kate Llewellyn

THE AUNTS

All my aunts are dying
their bones
in the tissue paper parcels
of their hands
pleat the past
into the edges
of their sheets

they don't flirt now
or pelt each other
with fruit
or toss their heads
at cheeky boys

their red hair
or black
'Straight as a yard of pumpwater'
as Granny used to say
is grey now
permanently
curled on their pillows
they lie
gesturing vaguely
at their future
which is as clear
as the water
in the glass jug

O

O is blonde
a pale egg
the shape of arms and legs around you
it is what we say
when we hear of death
or love

but we say it silently of love
because then it is the shape of a bullet
it is too oval to utter

it is a bubble when we must make a sound
but do not really wish to
yes it is fragile
but it is also strong as a stone
the sound a woman makes
when she remembers centuries of men
or a particular man
it can be sung up and down the scale
with love

it is the shape of the cave's entrance
and of the rock at the tomb
the trail of the earth round the sun
spinning O around O
it is perfect
it is the sound made when the arrow strikes
it's the bullseye
the death rattle
and while we are living
the sound and shape of love

*P*RISON WITHOUT WALLS

When every woman
fears every woman
life seems good for men

fear
that rat in the eye
flicks over the knot
of another's scarf
her boots or hair or brooch
and lashes

there are no witch hunts now
when every woman
fears every woman
who needs them

and every woman
who fears other women
is any woman
plotting to steal power

and any woman
fearing other women
knows that if by association
she showed she didn't

she'd be either
slut tart scrubber
or conversely
a tattered posted parcel
lacking an address

and in this hell
men do well
and women try
with the knot of a scarf
to lasso power

and wisdom talent
and perception

are hung nightly with the scarves
and blinded with the brooches

Summer

There we are six at tea
at the black oval table
I later sold for a lot.
The man at one end,
the woman at the other.

The boys are fighting over
the custard skin
and we are putting cream
on the icecream on the custard.
No wonder the man died young.

An austere abundance fills the house.
All things are polished—
our shoes, our hair,
our noses too,
which are peeling.

Outside on the mallee roots
in the wheelbarrow
the dishpan is warm from the sun
and beyond that
tomatoes are hanging red and green.

We don't know anyone
who doesn't speak English
except Eraldo the prisoner of war.

We have never seen our mother cry
and we don't know men can.

After the meal,
one at a time,

not changing the water,
we were bathed,
then the woman, then the man
used it.
I always felt sorry for him
as the water was cooler by then,
but he said he didn't mind.

Last to bath,
first to die.
Who will be next?

Jan Owen

TWILIGHT

Suddenly they arrive,
flung to a six o'clock sky
of Brisbane mauve
like the ultimate trick—
the lining ripped from Mandrake's hat.
He and she, I'd say,
writing themselves on air—
brief pictograms of here,
cursives of where.
Off-cuts from Lucifer's wings
or Dracula's cloak?
No, op-shop scraps
with a boutique flair.
Or this one—a false moustache,
and that—a quizzical pair of eyebrows.
Some black joke.
I call them the persuaders,
the go-betweens,
tacking day to night
with a shudder like sex or pain.
Both swerve in close
and then again:
each ultra-violet voice
affirms I am.
(Some minor co-ordinate
of un-flight.)
Zut! Instantly out of sight
over the darkening railway line,
where the poinciana pods and fronds
make a soft aspiration of down.

On Stradbroke

After the eclipse,
round 2 a.m.,
going out into the pearly light
and squatting in shadow
under the frangipani to pee.
Sweetness of face-down flowers
around my feet.
Between the paperbarks,
a sector of sea,
its purple implosion of sound.
A flash at the rim of the world,
and another:
Danger—Go Back.
The crickets' Clamour in G.
Touching across the path,
the female grasses'
rose-brown pungence;
clouds herded east;
star stragglers in paddocks of sky.
Above all,
mother of images,
the moon,
pierced ovum in a ring of gold.
And the chromosomes
aligned to dance.
Standing and stretching:
next door's glowing window—the hush
of someone suckling a child.
And now the clouds are lower and fining out,
shawl-white,
like a very old woman's hair
brushing the moon.
Nearby, a sleepy butcher bird
clears its throat.

Window

Like is mauve for love,
the faint horizon, the friend:
love touches a child with green,
dreams dazzling white,
looks for an amethyst embrace,
finds a red barn.
As for the blue room
at the heart of the flame,

gothic, uninhabitable,
sometimes a wavering
clarity opens there,
a window on a legend
tiny and desolate,
props for a one-act play—
a cloak, a lock of hair,
a sleepy monster, a sword,
and silver below the arras,
a skeleton key.

THE TRANSMUTATION

We are the moment's vertical:
sine, cosine, tangent, space—
faire trigonometrie.
Or, say, the alchemists of now:
that dazzle of being flown from,
this soft dross of dark.
See, you could pan for gold
and silver in this room:
sequins and synapse sparks,
scales from the eyes of angels,
and our alembic, merest aire.
You want us up to date?
We are an affair
of more than fusion,
taste me—selenium, cobalt, zinc,
born of ten^{10} degrees
at the supernova's heart,
light as an afterthought.
And us a subtiler bodie yet,
a virtual particle,
'the tried intent'.
No, let's get megalomanic—
Venus conjunct Mars.
Why not exaggerate,
high on figures of speech—
our hands are stroking stars,
we are the metaphors.

Geoff Page

MY MOTHER'S GOD

My mother's God
Has written the best
Of the protestant proverbs:

You make your bed
You lie in it;
God helps him

Who helps himself.
He tends to stay away from churches,
Is more to be found in

Phone calls to daughters
Or rain clouds over rusty grass.
The Catholics

Have got him wrong entirely—
Too much waving the arms about,
The incense and caftan, that rainbow light.

He's leaner than that,
Lean as a pair of
Grocer's scales.

Hard as a hammer at cattle sales
That third and final
Time of asking.

His face is most clear
In a scrubbed wooden table
Or deep in the shine of a

Laminex bench
He's also observed at weddings and funerals
By strict invitation, not knowing quite

Which side to sit on.
His second book, my mother says,
Is always somewhat overrated;

The first is where the centre is,
Tooth for claw and eye for tooth—
Whoever tried the other cheek?

(Well Christ maybe,
But that's another story.)
God, like her, by dint of coursework

Has earned his degree in predestination.
Immortal, omniscient, no doubt of that,
He nevertheless keeps regular hours

And wipes his feet clean on the mat,
Is not to be seen at three in the morning.
His portrait done in a vigorous charcoal

Is fixed on the inner
Curve of her forehead.
Omnipotent there

In broad black strokes,
He does not move.
It is not easy, she'd confess,

To be my mother's God.

*I*MMOVABLE FEASTS

Twenty-first and twenty-second,
twenty-third and twenty-fourth,
December's birthdays ran in rows
but always fell a fraction short.

The Reverend W. Bracingham
back before the first world war
with his good wife between the sheets
knew what the end of March was for.

Other seasons passed them by
circling through the Christian year.
The Reverend W. Bracingham
was always notably severe

if tenderly his wife in bed
(most often in the early spring)
might gently push herself against him.
She'd feel the sharp and sudden sting

of his rebuke. 'My dear,' he'd say,
'All in good time; you need not fear.
We tried it at the end of March.
It's not that special time of year.'

Yes, late March and autumn fires,
she had them often in her head:
the Reverend W. Bracingham
so warmly vigorous in bed.

Rebecca on the twenty-first,
Samuel on the twenty-second,
Rachel on the twenty-third
and James, more accurately reckoned,

appearing on the twenty-fourth—
just a fraction short of six.

Reactions downstairs in the hall,
though pious still, were brief and mixed.

'Four will be enough,' he said
and looked up sternly at the sky—
and never quite could understand
his wife as March went drifting by.

Rebecca, Rachel, Sam and Jim,
each child, she thought, is like a gift—
but God, for reasons of His own,
has kept from us the twenty-fifth.

'Self-discipline,' the Reverend said,
'is like the stiffness in the starch.'
'Yes, dear,' said his lovely wife,
remembering the end of March.

*U*LCER

The acids of dissatisfaction
turn themselves about;
they focus and begin to scour.

A fibre-optic in the throat
is checking for the wounds.
The sourness here

is excess to requirements,
a metal taste of 3 a.m.
as sleep drifts out the window

and chemistry attempts its Greek,
a capping of the peptic holes
to start the healing underneath

until the days prescribed are gone
and everything returns,
a minor twinge at first

and then
the steady hydrochlorics.
The stomach is a kind of life,

a widening in something longer,
a simple gourd, a metaphor,
a universe within itself.

The ulcers are its painful stars.

Andrew Taylor

THE BELL BIRDS

1 MORNING

The bellbirds pip behind the tractor shed
like echo-sounders in a depth of cool.
The rising wind behind the rising sun
sluices their thin precision from the trees
to where my hot-eyed cat glares at the sun.
You never see the bellbirds in the trees.
A kookaburra rattles into sound,
a distant rooster stretches, a car starts,
the first flies, heavy with sleep, bang at the glass
and my cat stares, sleepily alert. Beyond,
the sea's all shine and holiday and glitter,
a fish-bright, fish-scale flash of fins and fire.
Then sun breaks from the trees, the wind subsides:
it's yet another summer, sweltering;
the sea turns blue, turns deep, undiveable.
Sadly the echo-sounders in the gully,
like tiny submarines, unseen, unfound,
repeat their morse or message or mere sound:
they do it each day. My cat moves to the shade;
heat glazes his eyes—he'd rather sleep than prey.

2 AFTER LUNCH

Hanging like leaves or washing or parched peel
in gullies where the whir of the flies is thick
as the lowest tide fixed farthest at its retreat,
fixed farthest and fast, the bellbirds are not seen,
their morning signals silenced before the flies,
their utter notes not uttered nor signalised.
Somewhere under the fence my cat's gone off
into the scrub, the titree wilderness,
the tall trunks of the eucalypts, the litter
of fallen bark, the twigs, the ants, the flies;
most probably it sleeps, its nose pressed close
to small torn animals, the prey of dreams.
The distant town's gone fishing, or dozes too.
Even the distant mutter of a pump
continuous in the sullen heat of the day,
hefting the tinsel water to the frail
deliberate thirst of cattle along the hill,
is muted, succumbing to the heat.
Only the sea winds lazily at the beach,
persistent as a fly drones in the heat.

3   *EVENING*
The rising tide of shade in the thin gullies
broadens and brims. Darkness deepens, filling
the slotted gulf behind the machinery shed.
Further below the hill, beside the water,
shadow encroaches from the road and floods
the titree tangles and the mangrove swamps,
the long-legged jetties, the lean power-boats nosed
indolently at the mud, the fishing smack
heavy with age, anachronism and dusk.
The note of the bellbirds rises as the dark
settles and rises, a thin stick, a twig,
a pip of meaning in the rising gloom,
a shoot, a shot, insistent, echoing
from a deeper, earlier sunset, back
from the road by the water, from the retired boats.
After the day's drought they're voyaging,
after the day's drought, the heat, they're sending
radar doves beyond their dormitory arcs,
beyond my cat's glazed satisfactory purr,
beyond his claws, into the night, out there.

THE OLD COLONIST

1
Our old tomcat, with his weak heart,
anything over eighty, though once
menace of the whole district, prefers
to piss in the sink, in the frypan,
on the vegetables.
Anything but go out in the rain
and cold. Anything
than go at all. We house him
now in the laundry, on an old cushion
on the antique copper. He pisses
on the soap, finally on the cushion.
The laundry was a hazard of stale shit. Yet
when we scrubbed it with disinfectant,
hosed out the stink, encouraged clean air in,
he was neither grateful nor malcontent,
but with ravelled, unwashed dignity,
intelligent eyes, and ears alert,
from great age and its obscurity
pissed on the ironing with deliberate intent.

2   *SIX DAYS LATER*
Too old at last even to wash himself
his only thought was to be comfortable.

Mostly on the table under the vine
he lay on his side, watching all his years
slip quietly from him, kittens prowl
backyard and lane that had been once his pride.
His tail was a tattered skipping-rope,
his haunches rejects of an Op-Shop coat:
you almost thought the moths would pass him by
he was so tattered. Hardly weighed a pound.
He had stopped eating, would sniff milk, take
barely a bite to eat then turn away,
content that we had offered him the choice,
would purr when we coaxed him, but still turn away.
And yet he had his spirit to the end.
We used his table for our lunch, and found
him comfortable among the cutlery
minutes before the guests arrived—not once
but three times. Lunchtime yesterday. Our last
sight of him was a scornful rickety leap
over the fence, tail raised in a vague
vanishing salute. This afternoon
we found him, dead, ants beginning to swarm,
stretched in the sun, warrior to the last,
sprawled like an insult on the mayor's front path.

Alan Alexander

NORTHLINE

1
Alone today. But how familiar the scene
As round by water
Our three old dogs come on,

Dion, Patroklos, Stanislav—
All three abreast, on the hour,
Tap-tapping, politicking among the leaves.

And the voice again, heard clearly,
As if in the depths of its own village
Clotting the dusk with the melody,

And the faces going from the pond.
I touch the little streets and conversations,
The doors adhering to this round

While missing the wisdom and fun
You draw from this locus of life;
The language of our shared attention

As I follow these old ones we know
Setting a course down the familiar ways
Into the Northline archipelago.

2
Sometimes I go wandering
As if to prove how wet is was:
Lake Street and Water Lane—

Imagining, out of the wet,
The black roots of green things
Marketed in James Street.

But tonight the restaurants
Put out home smells,
Trailings of condiment;

And you put your arm in mine
Before the chosen door,
Armed with your bottle of wine.

Tonight, on a late corner,
Testy domesticity;
The Latin eyes appear.

Nodding, we walk on
Into our own zone.

STREET PARADE

Pudding-faced, offering the world
The accompaniment of her spring cleaning,
Mrs Poncini, in her headscarf, stands
By her little gate with its scroll top.
She has been caught on the hop by the parade
And her lips, like her feather duster, have moved:
'O Lord, tie my soul in the bundle of life.'
A clown in top hat and tartan trews
Blows her a kiss from his one-wheeler.
And, switching as far as the Moreton Bay
In the scraggy park opposite:
What a strength showing from the purlieu
Embracing the man with his half-empty flagon;
Tucked in the roots, he is part of the tree,
And his lips, just come off, have made an appeal:
'Please tie my soul with Mrs Poncini's.'
And our neglected lanes—alas,
Not one as yet to be seen!
Ah, there's a mouth in declamation:
'We are driven by love, despite our dejection;
Mere lanes, but the antics of the human

Keep us running with Alpha Centauri';
And yes, here's the crowd in the picture
Trading its delight around the band:
We will take these souls, one by one,
And tie them firmly with Mrs Poncini's.

Julian Croft

TIMETABLE

I caught the train each afternoon from Waratah to Civic,
each morning from Civic to Waratah;
twenty-five years later standing here at the end/beginning?
of a palindrome of years waiting for an engine
wide-eyed and smokestack high, or getting off
from one bluff-bummed, third-eyed, and dripping coal
you wonder where all those things were put in motion—
circles and ellipses, points of departure, trailing and facing
along the years, and you ask yourself if all leaving
is really a coming, and departures arrivals, whether
getting off at Civic was better than going right in,
or, letting the overbridge at Waratah flash past
and sitting tight, hanging on like grim death until
the train grinds slowly into that ultimate terminus
high in the northern tablelands, was what you really wanted?

AMICA

As the flower blooms without the bee,
the wave can break without a beach.
The tree can bend without the wind,
yet the apple stay forever out of reach.

The lamp may burn without the moth,
and my hand need never touch your hair;
my mouth gives body to your name,
but my lips kiss nothing but the air.

Like someone watching from a cliff
the thousand smiling ocean sprawl,
I see the light play in your eyes,
but know, this time, I need not fall.

So friendship is another kind of love,
engrafted to that ancient root,
unworried by the chafing bee,
or the bruised tongue on salty fruit.

DARKIE POINT

You see it from the Park across protected wilderness;
you approach through old runs mortgaged and lost;
you lose your way in fern and sclerophyll.

What seemed so certain from across the way is gone.
I never found the escarpment, never got to the point,
I lost myself in moss-bound southern darkness.

No matter how bright the sun at Ebor burns, here
darkness starts, and what the Irby brothers did
is a century-old eclipse that holds today.

Yet white Australia is all I'll ever know—
locked in the antipodes of my skin, my whiteness
is the dark side of this continent and I wear it now.

There is the crime—I recognise it, saw those shadows
falling from the cliff this morning, bodies, arms and legs,
a fall of light and dark across that adamantine southern face.

It's mine. I drove them there, and I stand here
among mortgages and drought. Who owns the darkness?
In Africa I swam in it, but I was glad to come to shore.

Yet here, home, and lost seeing things from a distance
I know that winter south throws light on Darkie Point:
I feel the balance tip between one man's rights and another's wrongs.

Roger McDonald

PROBABLY JACK

The chainsaw lurches, dragging delinquent teeth
down through the bones of his wrist.
He binds what is left
with a leather lace, and sets off,
aware that the sacrificed boot
is wearing a hole in his foot.

He walks ten miles to the town,
steps through the drone of the bar,
asks for a beer, and drops like a stone to the floor.

His name was probably Jack, nobody knows,
it happened a while back, and besides
the tale might almost be told
of anyone here—
somebody blunders a lift, or the truck breaks down—

anyone here would have walked to the pub
dying of a thirst.

The details of blood, and subsequent death,
is rolled like a stone between beers, a careful excuse
for drinks on the stranger, or to muse
without thinking, for the sake of the words.

MANGALORE

Windows are nailed tight. Blue sky
is wasted. Wind flattens the grass.
Smoke from improvident chimneys
dissolves on improvident farms.

The community hall is pierced
by blackberry thorns. Rust
gnaws at old cars. An ash-furred dog
lies dead among rosehips.

Nothing is new. Mangalore crouches
beneath peeled paint, cracked wood,
potato leaves and dry pines. It is harbour
for oil slick, black teeth and yellow eyes.

For twenty-five years there has been
no shop, no commerce with children.
The ice of an age of wind
spills its loose rivers.

Once tropical, once glacial, now this.
Geology only can spell
the history of Mangalore. Its young residents
are balanced on walking-sticks.

Those who are old merely trip
on the gravel of grave-holes.
Once down, their bones hold them up
as they did on the earth.

What warmth in a word can be spared
for Mangalore? Blunt ridges and wind
are its harvests. A blue face
is glimpsed at a window, and is gone.

RECENT ARCHAEOLOGY

At the end of the pit,
stacked upright as arrows,
precisely large as life,
they peer into daylight at the tip of my spade:

the retired man and his clay-haired wife.
Their eyes are curved
hard as Vegemite jars,
and their ears clipped back by rust
are pointedly waiting.

They want to know
if somebody stitches together
the long years of purchasing.
The answer lies within reach:

Brown soup tins foggy with webs,
shredded inner tubes,
hubcaps, the torn tread of a tyre,
a two pint milk can,
geometry instruments, soap savers,
green-bearded copper wire,
dinner plates plain as calico,
nails, wooden chocks, buckled oilskin,
old black macadamia nuts, scaly worms,
forty-five years altogether of bottles, of Aspros, of Dunlop
glue for setting soles, springs for slow doors,
a bicycle pedal and chain, the inkwell from school
still wearing its guilty eyeshadow, and one
and a half generations of lightglobes exploded
and poured like stars
down the same hole.

The wooden house, kiss, work
and chop-smoke life
has darkened.
God rules the far side of retirement,
but now from His paradise of teacups and azaleas
He's not telling.

The suburban king and queen in their burial mound
        of waste
cry out as they never dared while living.

Jennifer Rankin

DRAGON VEINS

Four birds fall over the sea.

Blue sky is lidding my after-day.

On a new-made southern beach
I search for a line
through hillside. Sand. Flat reef.

Trees gnarl down to sea-pull
tree-roots wrangle in wet coarse sand.

Gulls are whitening my daughter's eyes.

The line slips.

My iris sun bleeds at its edge.

Then over the sea. A thin shadow.
I find cloud

pick up the line

follow it into this poem.

I AM CHASING THE END OF THAT SHADOW

I am chasing the end of that shadow
drawn out now for the last days of summer
filtering down the needles of she-oak
into the gully and the laughing of my brother
who chases me around and around this paddock
smaller in day's light
spinning now
until I trip on that old gnarled stump
crash down into this crumbling earth
hot and sweating with my brother entangled
crying now digging in with my nails earth cold in my hands
clawing my way in my way out my way back
and the air is leaving my chest
hit hard in my back his fists thumping again and again
my voice lies in my lungs
I rasp at the air full of his laughter and the sun
and the smell of crushed and rotting grass
I know she is watching
knitting under the corrugated roof
I feel her steel needles nick sharp into my gasp.

*L*OVE AFFAIR 36

On the seventh day

in the late afternoon
with shadow already entering the valley

I watched your biceps.

They were flashing and beeping.
They were signaling confidence.

And I knew that my eyes were darkening
I knew that my eyes were slits when I glanced

as you walked on the balls of your feet through that house

your hips quite taut below your brain
and your lips too sweet by far.

And I stayed behind in the bedroom.

I was tossing and turning
I was considering the stars
I was laconically flicking a page
I was reading the dictionary
I was brushing my hair
I was wrapping myself in a shroud.

I lay on the bed with my terrible eye
and you strutted outside the door.

I ate a crisp apple
bursting the skin with my teeth.

You whistled so lightly in the bathroom
I very nearly stabbed you there
blood all over the green-tiled floor

toothpaste in your beard
a smile on your lips
apple between my teeth.

Instead I slowly turned the page
and the paper smelt of ink and a summer breeze.

Storms

So this is the time for a different kind of poetry?

It is as though the storm has passed
and now I must write

only the drip, drip, dripping
the soft-smacking onto dead leaves
the memory of storm
time-lapsing
perhaps, at most, the soaking-up of the earth.

Never mind I comfort myself
no storm has continued forever

without this space, this interlude of slow and simple words
we would never develop storm-hunger.

Nigel Roberts

DIALOGUE WITH JOHN FORBES

Nige—
why / at your age
do you still
play football?

a test of self
physical fitness / &
a matter
of / duende

jesus—
then wait
until / you discover
the private
& existential / terror
of golf.

THE GULLS' FLIGHT

The gulls' flight
is low
flat
& hard

they go
to sea
to the edge / where
the day's fire
is lit

they go
as shiftworkers
to the dawn.

Sylvana Gardner

FRIENDSHIP WITH BENITO

We have nothing in common, the carpenter
and I, nor wish particularly to commence
sharing beyond the required civilities;
we are as naturalised as the Oysters
after the walk but that's not enough,

our lives having run different courses
like the varicose rivers in the map
of our homeland, in their intricacy
never reaching the sea. But over a cup
of coffee (you've forgotten how
to make it, he says) and the progress
of his work (for someone who has been
a sailor, you're a good landlubber, I reply)
he tells me the name of his birthplace,
the mythical town I came from,
the one that changes its name
with each change of government. All I know
is that a certain breed of dogs
originated there, too highly strung
to be tamed, but he remembers everything
in the seniority of his years
and for this he becomes the messenger
long-awaited, the traveller who will tell
me where I was born. I listen reverently
to the half-truths offered under byzantine
icons 'and Moroccan arches?' No. It was
like Venice ... 'but the history books
claim the East met the West there!'
I don't care what is written! And he casts
the spell of the ancient story-teller
to the innocents of his tribe. Overlooking
discrepancies of architecture
and the eccentricity of time, we become friends
in the bondage of our inexplicable past
and day by day I wait for him to remember
the name of the street I lived in,
at the very beginning.

John Tranter

Sonnets nos 5, 13, 35

5
They burn the radio and listen to the blues. They
saunter through the cultivated gardens like giraffes
and whisper to each other, they are clever,
they build and revel in a culture shock,
they have an easy beauty and a multiple
limp. I suppose they stock religion in a
Frigidaire, and their prayers for the well-being
of the inhabitants of South America are touching.

We should leave them soon, for their dangerous magic
is a cheat, and none can explain its delicate
attraction: they reach a height of ecstasy by breathing
hydrogen and soft playmates endure them. Their minds
are woolly, loud; their speech is full of gaffes. Yet
they are almost lovely because of their beliefs.

13

FAMOUS POET JETS HOME TO USA!
How lucky to live in America, where
supermarkets stock up heavily on writers!
Thinking of the famous poets floating home
to that luxurious and splendid place
inhabited by living legends like an old movie
you blush with a sudden flush of Romanticism
and your false teeth chatter and shake loose!

How it spoils the magic! In America no writers
have false teeth, they are too beautiful!
Imagine meeting Duncan in your laundromat—
in America it happens all the time—you say
Hi, Robert!—and your teeth fall out!
And you can't write a poem about that!

35

To solve the problem of art and artefact
will you go down to the river
to paint a 'painting'? Will you 'paint'?
Will you paint the girl by the river?
Will you make a painting of the girl?
The light is Grecian, is adequate, et cetera.
He is sitting by the water. No,
he will not paint the girl by the river.

The girl is an artefact, the problem
of the painting is an artefact, is art,
the making of the painting is a problem.
Will you paint a painting of the artefact?
The scenery is well composed, the light
is Greek, is adequate, et cetera.

COUNTRY VERANDA

1 DRY WEATHER
This country veranda's a box for storing the sky—
    slopes, acres of air
        bleached and adrift there.

From outside, a shade-filled stage, from inside
   a quiet cinema, empty
   but for the rustling view

where a parrot scribbles a crooked scrawl of crayon
   and off-stage a crow
   laments his loneliness

and six neat magpies, relaxed but quite soon
   off to a General Meeting
   stroll, chortle and yarn.

When the summer sun cracks the thermometer, laze
   there in a deck chair,
   shake out the paper

and relax with the local news: who won the cake
   in the Ambulance raffle;
   what the Council did

about the gravel concession down at the creek, who
   suffered a nasty fall
   but should be well in a week.

2   *RAIN*
From that open room where sheets hang out to dry—
   cool, wet pages
   whose verses evaporate—

you stare out at the trees semaphoring their sophistry:
   their tangled, pointless plots
   and obsessive paraphernalia,

drenched among the spacious palaces of vertical rain
   where no phone rings
   and neighbours are distant.

Behind that ridge of mist and blowing eucalypt tops
   the world waited once:
   exotic, inexhaustible.

You've been there now, and found that it's not much fun.
   On the verandah, silence
   fills the long afternoon.

THE GUIDES

They used to be cheap and monochrome, explaining
how all Sydney was a target for the Jap subs. Like
rock'n'roll they started out in black-and-white,
   then stated the obvious—

that the Harbour was always blue, the parks army green,
and the stop lights were spreading in a scattered rash
out past the paddocks pocked by tussocks and riddled
    with pylons and power lines.

They grow a little each year, sprawling beyond
hectares of raw housing estates with extravagant names
bedecked with Bretts and Brendas and pramfuls of young
    Deborahs and Darrens.

When I was pushing at adulthood, on the painful side
of twenty, one took me to my father's funeral
in a blond building of brick in a strange suburb
    I never wanted to see

then guided me back to my city friends. Our journeys then
were measured in miles, we spoke the Queen's English
but shouted jazz in American every night above the
    living rumble of traffic.

They're brothers, Robinson and Gregory, but you never
see them together much, except in the newsagent's.
One of them's always going somewhere in a car. They say
    life's an open book.

OLD EUROPE

Turn from these old men sobbing on the sand;
turn from the waves, their iodine-perfumed shocks.
In that bowl of hot silence behind the dunes
recall the way their lives rose up to havoc
and prayer; and then we hear the visiting angels
rustle down the towpath to the bridge.
At noon, a young man slumbers under the hedge,
dreaming in its thick, unspeaking shade.
Through the afternoon they watch the sun
sail over France, and beneath the fiery sky
engines roaring, and the sound of tank-treads
clattering beyond the shoulder of the road:
they slump in the heat, sick with fatigue,
the eyeball dazed with rapid glimpses,
a blaze of fetid light, shook foil shining
on the mirror of the flooded field. Blackbird,
dart out from the shattered window,
cease your psychic striving, with your
blue-black feather and your orange eye:
in the whirling murmur of your chatter

how frivolous this frightened youth appears, grunting and bursting
with energy on the attack and then soaked with wild tears afterwards,
hearing his own memories creep and stumble from one wounded

denial to another. He'll end up sobbing in some veterans' home, slumped on a mattress, his scented spark of life quite quenched. Now the goddess Europa descends on the wrecked and smoking town, and heaps up the abandoned square with cobalt-coloured grapes and purple figs. See her roam the cool weed-covered bank with shreds of sun caught in her hair.

Robert Adamson

A FINAL SPRING

Outside, the garden's blown about
by a westerly, the jacaranda's
in flower—the world is full of doubt.
Mauve petals hit the verandah.

It's twenty years since we first met,
and this is the final spring
of the Seventies—Debra I regret
nothing, not a single thing.

(I say that perhaps too quickly
though with purpose) A silver-eye
darts through the hedge, thick
with ornamental vine—let's never deny

ourselves the memory of a year
so fecund we didn't notice spring—
We loved and talked our way clear
through a war, everything

seemed possible to us, even poetry.
The street beyond our Mosman garden
is alive with indian myna birds—We
don't see, these days, a blue wren

let alone a native dove or falcon.
The decade ends. We know the night parrot
is finally extinct—we live on,
passions wrestle with the thought.

HOLDING

Take the first step on the unmarked sand
gulls wait on the whistling wires
I am hunched into the gusty afternoon
you follow me from the road
I wonder how to touch your shirt how to

move beside you awhile
We have not spoken first words
we have no histories
no way of telling where we are
what we are doing
The land is stark and hard on us
only birds and fish live in these parts
even the gnarled vegetation behind the dunes
will not survive
The surf has the only voice
worth listening to its volume garbles the others
Out along the horizon the weather
gathers itself up
a great steel shuttle its wings touching the peaks
of the Continental Shelf

BLUE FEATHERED SONNET

They were there in all things I remember,
on bay shores and beaches, down lanes
and the streets, the eaves and gutters
under ceilings at home in school or at work,
pigeons, roadpecking and fanning through
dream pockets, at the edges of nightmares—
checker, flightly, fantail and tumbler.

Now I stand in a zoo with a broken winged
blue-bar, flapping ten yards back
in a cage of cats, lynxes, these sleek
rememberers of stealth and sheer viciousness,
creatures whose lithe power runs electric
blood in veins channeled to the stars,
striped and beautiful, killers of flight.

Caroline Caddy

KING GEORGE SOUND

Shoals of cloud diffuse the moon
crest and fade behind charcoal bluffs.
Mosquito mists mouth   skin warm.
The sea is a solid plane   slate of light.
Navigation buoys prick and shift away
from known channels to some more complex schema
articulating out from imagination's flare.
Familiar elements of earth air and water

have been transmuted   twice   to chiaroscuro
to metal. The scene is a pewter shield
nave-plate no one knows the use of
dredged from the grip of wrecks.
Hit with a mallet it would ring with its own name.

The Snow Queen

I have no power
though we play the three-legged beast—
my foot to the ledge
while I have you against
the blank wall of your youth.
Don't want my life done with that fiasco
but you
and your like are my lens—
I feel the world come
deep inside.
It's not me that's ice
but your body
cased in youth
so young you are giving birth to yourself.
I feel the butt and thrust
inside your chest.
I am the fire of lost control.
Force against my will
far away from me my walls
entice.
It makes you big to take my weight—
less than a feather!
Yet we both may make a living of
that nothing will come
of our union
for I have let myself be spoken for
by the natural palace
and that splinter in your eye—
such a tiny thing
you can remove at will—
all it does is not
let you hate.
But you won't.
It's not me that gets made younger
(so weak and you so strong)
I am going to let you drop.
Soon you will be born.

Tim Thorne

Reds

FOR S. P. H.

Autumn again: our hopes are melting down.
The weather turns Orcadian. You paint
in wind and watercolours, tidal forms,
the art of exile. This has always been
an island of artists-not-quite-in-residence.
Teachers are exiles. Our message bobs across
a sea to fellow-humans who resist,
know us as alien, cannot trust our fierce
enthusiasms. Old affirmatives,
cheerful as leaves, no stronger, fall, still bright.

Our colleague's dying where the hospital
looks out on rusty trees and murrey rain.
That culture's dying, too, 's a rumour we've
dismissed for decades. Our class enemies,
authoritative as surgeons, just can't wait
to excise vigorous tissue. Only, now,
April and May, I feel their victory,
who have been both doctors and disease.
This is the season for being patient while
malignant cells are breeding at the core.

But let's apply old remedies, fight the flames
of burning books with scarlet fire brigades,
rage red against the danger signs. Our health
is stronger than self-pity. We must build.
A century of scientific love
built Chernobyl. The cancer spreads. What next?
Surely some random active particle
will lodge where it can work a rational,
materialist miracle. After winter, spring.
Artists were always mutants. Working class
kids will baulk at Kulchur, will create
their own responses. Love and hope lie deep.
A sixteen-year-old I'd almost given up on
writes a superb poem—on suicide.

Alison Clark

Breathless

The expensive sadness of the suburbs.
The sweet thick domestic cloud
exhaled like the breath of orchids.

Yes, the babes look like cherubim—
charmingly naked for comfort
in the semi-tropical summer

which menaces with thick vines.
The glass doors must remain shut
to keep the warm air out.

In fact, the breeze is in the garden
caressing the midriff (all we can see)
of the dreaming giants.

Something wants to get in.
Something wants to get out.
Something's locked, begging
to be allowed to breathe.

It's the sweet ripe smell of nappies.
It's the old dark vegetation
moving to reclaim the house.

You paint to encourage light.
The tall trees waiting
at the window—do they notice?

Gestures muffled in cottonwool.
Words that don't break through.
Swamped in sadness,
you seem to breathe warm glass.

Reclaiming the feminine

At the Catholic conference
a soupy lady sang a chorus
and the one thanking the speaker
had to wait for two more verses ...

Meanwhile back at the opera
the big virgin in her satin tent
(paradigm for the sex that loves
and trills) grieves for her little tenor

who's fled, helping the captive queen
disguised in his love's

bridal veil. Brain fever!
She—trailing posies, left

like a large white wedding cake
no one will eat, mound
of obsessive flesh in a male
world of swords and rhetoric—

needs the quiet figure on the rostrum
urging her congregation
to bring the dark, feeling god
forward into the light.

Robert Gray

THE MEAT WORKS

Most of them worked around the slaughtering
out the back, where concrete gutters
crawled off
heavily, and the hot, fertilizer-thick,
sticky stench of blood
sent flies mad,
but I settled for one of the low-paid jobs, making mince
right the furthest end from those bellowing,
sloppy yards. There, the pigs' fear
made them mount one another
at the last minute. I stood all day
by a shaking metal box
that had a chute in, and a spout,
snatching steaks from a bin they kept refilling
pushing them through
arm-thick corkscrews, grinding around inside it, meat or not—
chomping, bloody mouth—
using a greasy stick
shaped into a penis.
When I grabbed it first time
it slipped, slippery as soap, out of my hand
in the machine
that gnawed it hysterically a few moments
louder and louder, then, shuddering, stopped;
fused every light in the shop.
Too soon to sack me—
it was the first thing I'd done.
I had to lug gutted pigs
white as swedes
and with straight stick tails

to the ice rooms, hang them by their heads
on hooks. Or fill a long intestine
with sausage meat.
You got meat to take home—
bags of blood;
red plastic with the fat showing through.
We'd wash, then
on the blue metal
towards town; but after sticking your hands all day
in snail-sheened flesh,
you found, around the nails, there was still blood.
I didn't usually take the meat.
I'd walk home on
the shiny, white-bruising beach, in mauve light,
past the town.
The beach, and those startling, storm-cloud mountains, high
beyond furthest fibro houses, I'd come
to be with. (The only work
was at this Works.)—My wife
carried her sandals, in the sand and beach grass,
to meet me. I'd scoop up shell-grit
and scrub my hands,
treading about
through the icy ledges of the surf
as she came along. We said that working with meat was like
burning-off the live bush
and fertilising with rottenness,
for this frail green money.
There was a flaw to the analogy
you felt, but one
I didn't look at, then—
the way those pigs stuck there, clinging onto each other.

A DAY AT BELLINGEN

I come rowing back on the mauve creek, and there's a daylight moon
among the shabby trees,
above the scratchy swamp oaks
and through the wrecked houses of the paperbarks;
a half moon
drifting up beside me like a jellyfish.
Now the reflected shapes are fading in the darkened rooms of the water.
And the water becomes, momentarily, white—magnesium burning.
My oars
have paused, held in their hailing
stance—
are melting;
and all the long water is a dove-grey rippled sand.

A dark bird hurries
low in a straight line silently overhead.
The navy-blue air, with faint underlighting,
has a gauze veil hung up within it, or a moist fresh smoke.
I land in the bottom of an empty paddock,
at a dark palisade
of saplings.
Among the ferns, dead leaves, fresh leaves, dry lightning-shaped twigs,
a cold breeze
comes up, rattling shreds all around.
A wind-blown star
is being drawn forth like a distant note.
The house I am the soul of lies,
hollow, on a ridge across the paddocks, although long occupied already
by the scouts of night.
I drag up the rowing boat, its rusty water slopping,
and start off, loosely in boots,
across the spongy, frog-bubbling undulations
of these coarse-bitten flats,
in a sharpened cow-dung smell.
After a day of sitting about,
spent reading and scribbling on margins
or bits of windy paper, and in remembrances,
the hours of which have passed
the way that water-drops fill at the downwards tip
of a twig,
I took the rowing boat out.
Rowed miles,
into the river, and downstream, over an ale-coloured brackishness—
through the societies of midges, in their visual uproar
(bronze-lit, like Caesar come to the Forum),
right out, equidistant from shore;
saw the birds swing on long trapezes across the green alcoves;
and followed all the notations of the tree-line
to those at dusk like flaking rust.
I came back with the slow-motion strides of a water spider over
    fluttered water.
As always, it has worked.
Now the mind is turned down low, like a gas flame
in a dark kitchen,
where the wind and all the night sounds can again be heard.
It lies once more beneath the truth of the body.
All of my demanding
has become, crossing these paddocks, and watching the other stars
    appear, delicate
as the first mould
on black bread, simply to take an axe and go on
up to the end of the cleared land, underneath a hooded eucalyptus
    forest,
to crack some firewood
from a weather-tightened grey log,
for a hot, deep bath, that I can draw out through the evening.

Karl Marx

Karl Marx was playing a parlour game
with his daughters. To their question
What is the quality one should most abhor?
he wrote: Servility.

This was found—a scrap of paper
amongst the family albums and letters;
it is the most essential of all
the Complete Works.

Aubade

The cold night that was clamped on the land
falls loose, an unwound
vise, and is lifted off.

Light rises on the spider's web,
the way a needle-drawn thread
is pulled through, to arm's length.

The room is a bush clearing,
a bale of light. A professional's grooming
these curtains, as in their youth.

And your long bright hair is like
the first paint-loaded brush stroke
that wanders before me over the white cloth.

The girls

All those unbalanced galaxies—
their rivets splayed,
the gas-blue constrictions.

And across the playing fields
lies a blue-white mist
of arc-lamps.

There are girls at practice,
implacable strike
of their hockey sticks,

whose limbs surpass
anything we have contrived
in wood, for shapeliness.

Wandering the pavements,
I watch with the separate men
through wire-netting

the girls play exactly
where they may, within a silent
roaring, and fangs of light.

Nothing seems so marvellous
as a small white ball
exchanged among their sticks.

Mark O'Connor

THE CUTTLE BONE

The cuttlefish bone
is like lard solidified
in a stippled mould.
She picks it up, knowing it floats,
expecting white styrofoam strength,
tough but fluffy-light.
She finds it dense as a white stone-axe
—a live foundation-stone
that a flesh-house was built around
by the nervous colour-changing
ink-squirting ten-tentacled swimmer.

Its delicate gristle edges
are not yet ground away.
She scrapes them with enamelled nail.
The airfoil top
has a sharp nose and duck-billed tail;
the underside is a boat,
hollow, with streamlined hull.
She feels its two curves,
each perfect but different
like a high-heeled shoe,
then discards it to him:
'The smartest fish in the sea.'

'Why does it wear its shell inside?'
—he senses the weak mollusc-thing
shrinking round its inner base of rock,
sphincters squeezing,
juicy flesh wanting to go inside
when the barracuta swirled.
In his hand it tapers, smooth
as a mannequin's back.
But air-cells and muscle-hooks

prove it was engineered;
a precise object for tendons to work on.
Strange!
so perfect a shape inside another.
She says, 'We mammals know—
we need thin skin, large brains,
and something hard within.'

Peter Skrzynecki

WALLAMUMBI

FOR JUDITH WRIGHT

Seasons of inheritance and shadows of voices
Haunt its hills like a recurring dream.
From the eastern sea a wind vanishes in snowflake,
Lyre's note and the green geometry of a man's eyes—
But how does a man choose the name
That will accompany him faithfully to the grave:
Become a witness to years of loss and joy,
Then survive him through eternity?

In the ancient forest of gorges
He listened to the whisper of birds:
Heard the chant of midnight prophecies
And a name spelt out into the darkness of gullies;
Saw the migration of men and wings
Along the frozen river in the Kingdom of the Dead:
The begin-all, end-all landscape
From which no one before him had returned,
Where all mists rise, frost hardens bone,
And each granite boulder, like a stationary planet,
Becomes a landmark under a galaxy of tableland stars.
Inanimate or living, he knew the migration
Must continue beyond the hills he had built upon
And the slopes of his own years.

Acres of stubble became the tracks over which
His mind and heart wandered—outposts of journeys
He made, settled before sons and daughters
Grew to know the poison of nettles and bull ants.
Acres he ploughed became chapters in a book
He never wrote.
          Grandfather and father, remembered
From an old time, old country where it rained all summer
And native bees carried the smudge of fires
From the black honey of stumps and hollows.

Grandfather and father—man I never knew—
The name falls softly across the ranges
And paddocks that once were part of your flesh:
Falls like my shadow did before the sun
On the winter morning of your death.
The chapters are still not finished
But a page is written in the Book of Change.

Lily Brett

THE FIRST JOB

The
first
job

of
every
Sonderkommando
unit

was
to
kill

the
unit

they
were

replacing

the
unit

they
were

replacing

mostly
went

willingly.

THE GUARANTEE

In
the
Sonderkommando

you
were
guaranteed

three
months
work

milk
bread
clean sheets

chocolate
cake
cognac

and
three
months
life.

Gary Catalano

A POEM IS NOT

A young but gloomy man
I'll never understand
that true poetic art
of writing from the heart.

A telegraphic line
is like a skinny vine
unweighed by any fruit.
I don't like poems which bruit

the heart's convulsions, or
put signs above the door
inviting all to peek
at what went on last week.

Poets must do more
than note their fondness for
the human species; if,
demurring, they insist

on passion or the like
and so uncaulk that dyke
no ogre's chilblained eye
shall water when they die.

The art, in poetry,
is not, like therapy,

an existential rub:
a poem is not a pub.

Slow tennis

FOR MEREDITH

There is a tree
at the far end
of my thoughts. It appears now

as a vague
irregular blob, no larger
than a tennis ball

and just clips
the sagging net
of the horizon.

How can I be sure
it is really a tree
—and not, say, a grey

frayed and unstitched ball
propelled
by an opponent

on the other side
of the world? Slow tennis
could well be the name

of this game: the object of it
is to whack these
battered, deflated trees

from one half
of the brain
to the other.

Dennis Haskell

No one ever found you

No one ever found you self-seeking or dishonest.
Giving is your gift. When you stand
on the spotted tiles, peeler in hand,
large-eyed, intent
on pontiacs, carrots and all the care
for yet another meal, you think yourself
ordinary, like the magpies

that march about outside the windows
while the afternoon light
drifts across geraniums, daisies, lawn,
but nothing and no one could be more distinct.
Living never came easily to you. You take everything hard.
All that we have ever said and done

seems less than what we meant
but to know this without saying
is love's bequest, the silent embodiment
that gives our every word its meaning.
We have shifted cities, our shift
into each other's lives so complete
that any other we could scarcely know.
Though your eyes are tired, my shoulders bony,
it matters little where we go,
how little we know
and how much our lives have passed,
our days will be filled with green
and we grow together like the grass.

ONE CLEAR CALL

Holidays, the bush, dusty Coonabarabran
and out of the blue your friend has rung
you, caught on the hop; an engineer
who never looks at a book, whose father's died;

the service is soon; and he wants to read
something—not scriptural—literature perhaps:
the skilled academic that you are,
you suggest—a good choice—'Crossing the Bar.'

'Where can I buy it?' he asks, 'and quickly?'
'I know it,' you say, down the glistening, impersonal wires,
'I'll repeat it, slowly.' He waits, still, fingers
at the ready, for the first poem he's heard since school.

So you start, inexpressively, enunciating each syllable,
'"Sunset and evening star, / And one clear call for me"',
into a vast tide of silence at the end of the line,
the unmoving pen you cannot see, foaming at the words

until his wife picks up the mouthpiece, and the pen,
and you are Tennyson's mouthpiece, shaken a little
and wondering now, as you begin again
before a face you cannot see: '"Sunset and evening star ... "'

until she is choking too, and her wrist falters
across the lines, registering the scatter of words
as they lift from Tennyson's dead mouth and your own voice
where they have lain like subject matter of no one's choice,

that past sensation of syllables sweeping you and your friends
across the bar of technique, of grieving, of consolation.

Martin Johnston

FROM *U*NCERTAIN SONNETS

FOR JULIE

5 DIRECTIONS FOR DREAMFISHING

First you must blow a bottle round your sleep
in concave bottle-greens of drifting seas
around dreams' hot vermilions, where unease
will abrogate its fishing rights to deep
seas where your Dreamfish, bred and interbred
to swim upnight with what you most desire,
slides through the streaming cellstrands in your head
stippled with swirling wet St Elmo's fire
and surfacing flutters on the midnight wind,
as fish can't, as you know. The night is green
with loss. In fading dictionaries you find
'the sea-green beryl, or aquamarine'.
You wake in billingsgate, haggling for a drab
dead slice of Dreamfish on a beryl slab.

*G*OYA'S 'COLOSSUS'

CYCLOPS SONG 3

If my verses seem conventional
this is because I live inside a pastoral
convention. I break it up
every morning when I clump down to the beach, a ram in each hand
for good companionship, practising Braille,
studying the cave-bats' knack of radar. Nor am I
Emily Post. I squat enormous at the edge of things
and breathe heavily, Gnarrh, at the frightened villages. Yet
the flock trails tapestries of brass bells, the ship
in my head bucks, elegant and sleepy, against
my long-suffering skull, and I skim ducks-and-drakes
across the numb inlet.
          It makes itself whole again; I'm sewn
again, each coolly synthesised evening,
rocks flocks and all, into my seamless formal chrysalis.

FROM *In* TRANSIT: A SONNET SQUARE

FOR ROSEANNE

2   *BIOGRAPHY*
About love and hate and boredom they were equally
barracudas, took an arm or leg quick as winking,
their totem Monkey Aware-of-Vacuity.
Empedocles added to the four elements
Love and Strife to set them spinning, Aeschylus
invented tragedy by adding the second actor.
Back past the sold houses in the lost domains
down in the midden-humus
grows the rotting trelliswork of 'family',
odd slug-coloured tubers wince at the touch
with feigned unanthropomorphic shyness,
naked pink tendrils explore holes. It is all
tentative, and these days the Island supports
a 'Jungian sandlot therapist'.

6   *THE CAFÉ OF SITUATIONS*

FOR GRACE EDWARDS
In this café they have solved the problem of names.
Orders go to the bar: 'Coffee for Calendar,
two cognacs for Backgammon Board and Football Poster.'
You are where you are. They know names must be revealed
most cautiously and that numbers only serve numbers.
In the café of situations they have found the golden mean:
sit there often enough and you'll win a table and name,
Clock, say, or Air Vent, which feeds not on you but you,
drop in occasionally and you're still gifted
while you're here with just that identity-in-place
you've been so long in quest of. Wherever I go
I wear the café walls around me, and the shuffling step
of the invisible waiters brings subtly misconstrued orders
to Broke or Loving or Drunk or wherever I happen to be.

11   *OF TIME AND TYPING*
I sit here writing you letters that always cross
and thinking about time and typing.
Those 'effortless' lyrical tropes, how drearily long they gestated,
'beauty, that unicorn'—fourteen years younger,
proud of how much I knew, how hard I revised.
The terms of the problem have changed: how to answer your last
when your next is on its way without warping both
how to fit the machine with seismograph paper
so as to write the honest poem that's mainly white space
to denote all the hours of just smoking and staring at crosswords,
reading and trying not to

auguries in what's not in your letter, drinking
and hopelessly masturbating, knowing the room smells,
the cleaning lady is at the door, the toilet will never flush.

Rhyll McMaster

FLYING THE COOP

When death approaches
the faint hum
of the body disappears,
the way the fan in the freezer space
cuts out as you reach for the ice-tray
quietly but unambiguously
the suddenness of inaction
implacable absence,
the leave taking
that doesn't take long
the walking off
without drawn-out explanations.

When death approached me
I felt levitated with fever.
I was in an oil-filled capsule,
my snug hospital bed.
I did not tell anyone I was dying
or not for a while.
I let myself die a bit.
I sank down.
I was never so relaxed
comatose as a scarab grub
in the ruby glow of dirt-underground.

It was as if the ultimate fusion
had occurred on my father's lap,
my armpit to his chest
my cheek to the curve of his neck.
Death cuddled me, detached
and read a book
smelling of cigarettes and whisky.

Death was bottomless
as the black basalt swimming hole
above Nerang
but without the fear of cold.
It was warm as a rock pool
late afternoon on Snapper Rocks.

Death shaped me like an ear,
curled up, cleaned out as a dried apricot
waiting for the tongue
of something like a mouth
someone like a god.

SET TO MUSIC

What's the song?
Be good
to me

baby
whatever I do
whoever I am
be true
to me.

The great names in history
had the same refrain
as you.
The sound of a body submerging
in a bubble.
the three b's
bay-bee be
good

don't interrupt
don't question me
put up
put up with my anger till eternity
acclaim
my idiosyncrasy.

I'm a babe in the wood
or is it dyed in the wool?
Baby close your eyes
and give up
to me.

THE LOST JACKAROOS

In the smash of ten-pin bowling we met the jackaroos
and spent an evening of small error
cruising the backblocks.
Such well-behaved boys.
My mother quite approved.
With little expectation
we made our plans, my girlfriend and I.
She the dark one, I the blond.
A few kisses, a fond goodbye.

Months passed.
They mended fences, we attended school.
On leave again, but my mother shut the door
firmly in eager faces.
I was not home.
Oh, Steve, Harry, Brian, what was your name?
I was behind the door!
One adult gesture from the future
could have changed our meagre histories
now lost to time.

Graham Rowlands

Elusive

You are too elusive for them, snake
slithering out of last year's fashions,
your cellophane self crinkled on the ground.

You slide so easily out of clothes for them.
Is it a rite, a ritual
this search for yourself
curving under them, coiling round, corded
together in strands of a rope?

Is your nerve of being sinewed in your flesh,
fibred too deep for men to unravel?
All you can do is ease sinuously
through yourself
and slough them off.

Marking secondary school papers

Surfies paddle out their boards,
furrow down a breaker
waving their last good-bye to rules, to me,
thumbing a nose or two.
They're off to groove their way, their waves.
They're different but they're through.
How just I am.

Forty, fifty, sixty papers mirror me
as I pass a former self a hundred times,
precocious, pithy, full of spite.
Good on them, good marks.

What can I do, though, with one word-hater
unable to hate in words?

Down back streets with hard knuckles,
broken bottles, drunken breath,
he'd teach teacher more than school.
Rape for women, scars for men, for me,
I imagine the perfection of his muscles' style.

I fail him as he stutters out
his impotence and rage.

Michael Dransfield

PURCELL

Archaic morning—
the wind furtively
came by night from the south
I hear it in the avenue of elms
moving through green vaults
as a rider who, tiring,
would falter and drop reins,
letting his steed walk at its own
pensive pace. Within the house
tapestries shiver like
reeds and moorland grasses; I hear
viol and spinet, etching
the story of the storm. Now
rain darkens the wilful air.
One could believe
autumn disobediently
regretted Priam's death.
I who wearily
chronicle the final days
cannot think that seasons merely
succeed as pages in a calendar
follow. Does not the wind
sometimes turn pages, as though reading them?

GOLIARD

Going south
Sydney two hours behind is less than a memory.
I walked down the highway after a while
a truck stopped and by morning
Melbourne will be all around. Of that city
I'd save only the paintings and Como House.
The suburbs could be dumped into the Yarra
as Melbourne's garbage is. Next I'll go

either to gloomy Launceston to visit
Hofmannsthal's friend, my publisher,
or west to wildflowers and the nickel hills.
The driver wonders what I'm writing
but with the superb manners of an Australian
merely asks, 'Got enough light there, mate?'
We stop for beers at the Surveyor General,
night fills the wheelruts left by Cobb and Co,
the people in the bar have foreign voices.
Progress erodes tradition. When that's gone
nothing is left but fashionable landmarks
marooned by emptiness, and carved into
a vandal's library of huge initials.

*F*IX

It is waking in the night,
after the theatres and before the milkman,
alerted by some signal from the golden drug tapeworm
that eats your flesh and drinks your peace;
you reach for the needle and busy yourself
preparing the utopia substance in a blackened
spoon held in candle flame
by now your thumb and finger are leathery
being so often burned this way
it hurts much less than withdrawal and the hand
is needed for little else now anyway.
Then cordon off the arm with a belt,
probe for a vein, send the dream transfusion out
on a voyage among your body machinery. Hits you like sleep—
sweet, illusory, fast, with a semblance of forever.
For a while the fires die down in you,
until you die down in the fires.
Once you have become a drug addict
you will never want to be anything else.

*M*INSTREL

The road unravels as I go,
walking into the sun, the anaemic
sun that lights Van Diemen's land.
This week I have sung for my supper in seven towns.
I sleep in haysheds and corners
out of the wind, wrapped in a wagga rug.
In the mornings pools of mist fragment the country,
bits of field are visible higher up on ridges,
treetops appear, the mist hangs about for hours.

A drink at a valley river coming down
out of Mount Ossa; climb back to the road,
start walking, a song to warm these lips
white-bitten with cold.
In the hedges live tiny birds
who sing in bright colours you would not hear
in your fast vehicles. They sing for minstrels
and the sheep. The wires sing too, with the wind;
also the leaves, it is not lonely.

No, BUT I SAW THE MOVIE

cat plays with a cottonreel
rolls down a passageway for miles

passage and cotton disappear

on the floor
girl shooting up

the girl dies beyond sleep
a mouse runs past with
cat in its mouth

the house burns down
ties your mind in cotton

you don't lose things
they lose you

PSYCHED OUT

I
longer we cannot
stay in such a place

the staff is unconcerned
what if the patients cry

stumble from Group in tears
at the end of their tether

what if the patients die
Shock continues

only the sun-damned minority
the biblical perish

our treatment is the salem
witchhunt

the sun shuffles
over the sky of our day

farmers might call this
midas weather   gold brilliant

actor
hanging about

waiting for tips when
longer we cannot stay

II
the lake bridge is
too low to jump
fall thirty feet
and swim for shore

designed for such
eventualities   the suicide capital

if i seem obsessed
with death
its just that
death shadows me

i don't need suicide
to finish me off and friends

the body
worked too hard
destroys its cancerous self
all i need do

is walk the floors
and watch and to expect

   i'm not dead
   sure of the poems

   life seems
   to suffer a bit

   in the translation

John A. Scott

CATULLUS 63

Below him there was darkness gathering.
Attis come to Phrygia, to yew-woods
and to wreaths, to shrouds of this dark centre.
First the sea. Then as he ran, the shadow
draining from him until darker moons
of heat were spat on dust, and padded feet
that fell to earth. But always darknesses.

Still within his palm, the flint whose razor-
edge had slashed his balls' weight from the groin.
Unburdened, now she understood the pain
of this *menarche*. These whitened fingers seeking
the redemption of her drum from earth;
the sacred drum of sacrifice, Cybele!
Shaking at the empty bull-skin; trembling,
chanting to her gathering familiars:
'Go there! You, my likenesses, my exiles,
ever searching for this other place.
Who following have made my journey's semblance,
burnt with the erosion of this rapid
salt-edged wind; your bodies equally
unmanned through excess of this loving-hate.
You, who cannot stand here, rid yourselves
amongst this forest; let the swiftness of
your movement please her. Go there, to Cybele!
Where the shelling cymbal-voices clash;
the shuddering-hollow drums resound. To where
the flautist deeply mouths the curving reed;
and Maenads fling their raw and moistened heads,
mane-wreathed in ivy. Where the restless, shaking
goddess-pack habitually career.
To find this other place! Let us be gone!'
So the tribe of ecstasy in screech-chords,
every eel-tongue bloated, flicking out
in seizures of imagination; every
drum-skin bellow answered by the cymbal,
coiled towards the darkening Ida-green.
Before them, Attis clamoured senseless through
the thickening growth: a heifer still unbroken,
rasping, lung-burnt, chafing at the burden
of the yoke; the rush of Gallae drum beat
frenzied and stampeding at her trace.
At last within the goddess-woods, the wasted
pack fell in exhaustion—food beyond them,
starved of sleep—their eyes were overwhelmed;
their rabid furor lidding into night.
Attis woke to sun-snort. Rustling. Brittle-
timber torched by eyes. Until horizons
reared and broke: a white horse sped across
the corrugated sea to earth, and trampled
every shadow underneath its hooves.
Sleep deserted Attis for the brided
arms of Pasithea. And so, abandoned
to the furor-memory of loss,
in anguish she retraced that shoreward path;
where, looking to the sea's peripheral
immensity—veiled behind the onset

of these woman-tears—she cried in grief
as any mourner, leaning to her home:
'And have I left you, City bearing me,
and City of my birth: a slave escaping
domination for these dominating
woods of Ida; to be lost forever
in the frozen cunt-lairs of the savage;
to approach that hidden wilderness?
Where are you—eyes that want you mine—now I
may speak outside that brief parenthesis
of ecstasy? And have I lost you: forum,
wrestling school, gymnasium; the taste
of cinders, burning here, from hearth and track.
And have I lost you, poor and poor, again
this heart's wild turn of grief. What form has not
been mine: this Attis, woman, man; this Attis,
youth or boy. My body oiled and massive
ever hard between you, cradle-locked
in arguments of flesh. My doorway crowded;
threshold warmed with visitors. And there!
The sun itself has led me, Attis, from
the bedroom under canopies of flowers ...
By what name shall I now be known? As *she*,
the goddess-slave, the handmaid of Cybele?
Maenad, half-himself, the "I" of penis
ever lost? And shall I now abide
forever in these forest slopes of Ida,
smothered in the whitenesses of snow
and ice; beneath these flinted peaks, forever
forested alone with wandering boar,
or wooded with the deer. Beloved City,
who will ever hear me now? And now
this deep regret. And now and now, this shame.'
Cybele listened to these words that flowed
between her red-stained lips. The chariot lions
having fallen silent, stirring—nostrils
spreading—searching for the stringent prey-blood
of her speech. And so the goddess, freeing
the lion (left, flock-tearing lion) cried:
'Relentless one, infuriate him! Stalk him
into madness! He who so desires
his freedom shall remain within my woods
eternally possessed. Now go! Your back
perpetually wounded by the lashing tail.
Endure this pain that every place might thunder
to your raging bellow. Let your mane
bleed rivers through the muscles of the neck!'
Self-goading into fury now, the beast slashed
blade to blade, until the vegetation

bled and whitened, foam-flecked, at its passage.
On the dampened shore-sand, lined by white,
girl-Attis stood against the marbled waves.
She heard the tide-wash ruptured once again
by padding feet—the lion broke towards her
out across the sand—and ran in terror
to the forest; to the wild enslaving
darkness spilling ever from the wound.

Man in Petersham

He's dropped his heart!
His heart has fallen to the footpath.
But no one seems surprised and least of all
the office girl whose stockings violin
across this empty road. He's dropped his heart!
It surely must be this and not his cigarettes.
The way he stares so long and makes no effort
to redeem it. And his suit is an immaculate grey,
and his shoes a duco white. And his feet are
frozen in the tiny refrigerators of his shoes.
With all the colours running out, he stares
upon his fallen heart. His mild-blue heart
shattered in its twenty filtered pieces.

Changing room

The breath's slow
drum-brush marks the end of Gillian's time.
Her hair's haphazard marathon, swaying
with the slowest jazz of afternoon. Detectives
wandering at her breast; the nipple's darker trilby.
A black thief hair, returning to its crime.

*

Now, amongst the sheets, there is
a trace of blacker hair, curled and blunt
as shorthand. I watch her move, the blankets
fanned across the mattress like a deal of cards.
Her foot beside an ashtray shell, its butted
cigarettes settled into parquetry. She dresses
as a child might in a changing room, all
half-under things. And what she'll do tonight
comes out of silence like a talking in her sleep.
She's leaving; and the similes are gone.
A borrowed room, and everything quite suddenly
and only like itself: this coat, this coat.
    This floor, this floor.

Alex Skovron

The composer on his birthday

I am thirty-five: next year Wolfgang
    will be dead. Young Franz lies buried in Vienna now
        three seasons under. Even the infant Arriaga's no doubt

notched his genius. High time for Hochzeit
    is the needle of an ailing mother, she spies
        a grandchild round every corner but I remain deaf

dreaming my firebirds & kalevalas, or a father of twenty who
    still had time. Already mirror-scratched, I'll soon be scored
        as the grim sheets grinning back, edentulous with

missed music: my curlicues stare bleak at the decay
    around them, tracked by a thin fate. What should have been
        the great romance of Chroma & Diaton is an Opus 1

Allegro fragment scattered lovesick
    on slippery timber. I sit to excavate knowing all musics
        are entrapped in this ivory but the keys

lie tacit, unbroken—neat bones of a cryptic enigma
    the solutions to which are infinite are
        impossible are at worst

satisfactory. Sebastian is smiling like a steep uncle, Bonn's
    mountain pulsates with laughter. My mother
        is weeping.

I must journey once more to Vienna.

Sentences

FOR RICHARD APPLETON

I seem to recall
a quaint time I thought hitherto
said like concerto
    hithérto
and albeit to echo Arbeit
    álbeit

My friend who drank
red wine and wrote encyclopaedias
confessed he'd crossed
segments of youth
mouthing misled like wise-old
    mísled

The ostrich has drunk all the sand

Some thugs
I know up north pronounced a black
dream to kill a million
years of promiscuity
proclaimed this drunken chiliad
its tone a skull
its eye
the broken claws of a dead metaphor
crossed
on a field free of language

Between dreams
is where I thought all things
likely as death

Or as words
which I enunciated softly
rummed by the solo music of the alphabet
on a planet crammed with pages
and the burnt
ghosts of lexicographers who knew
surely
the impossibility of mispronouncing
   pain

Albeit hitherto misled
the ostrich is drinking still

$\mathcal{W}$HAT MATTERS

The old roof creaking in the rain
A moth fussing about under the light
A mug of gold steam on a windy night
The impermanence of tunnels, a line of type
And the face inspecting itself
Like a stranger, bitterness
When its slants across the blade of the years
Love of course
Uninvited tears, a letter
From a faraway friend long thought lapsed
The stars in a child's eyes
The trust in its hand, music, sharp apples
The rent, a miniature wooden box given
As a memento, in which nothing is kept
Paper, wine, the mobius mystery of sex
Flaws forgiven yourself, a good bed slept
In, several books waiting patiently
Twenty years, a pen quietly leaking
Old pain, the old fears creaking

Alan Wearne

FROM THE NIGHTMARKETS

In this extract from the verse novel, Sue, a journalist, reviews major
people in her life: Ian, Louise, a clergyman uncle, and John, her lover.

SUE DOBSON
Today, a forecast for intermittent thunder and showers:
I see, I know, an architect's daughter in her grey and green
Methodist Ladies' College blouse, looking at the rains
moving onto the deciduous trees and pre-war bungalows
of Florizel Street, Burwood. When did I quit
calling it home? That winter into spring of going out
with Ian and his Edward G. Robinson impersonations?
The bistros seem packed with activists guilty
over their parents' quarter acre blocks
or their own. Who cares if frosted galleons
ride on the dining-room doors?
How colonial? But children are colonists:
recreating much, or acknowledging the other recreations.
          Somewhere a car horn plays 'Colonel Bogey',
telling the world what Hitler had,
and daughters of men who marched beefing that out,
say words and stories
which the fathers wouldn't think to tell
each other! Consider how these fighters
may have blushed at their best-man's instant telegram:
its *springing on the inner spring!* My parents
wedded for love I always think.
Some time in the post-war eastern suburbs
they're besotted; then there's the daughter
and Florizel Street and somewhere a car horn
and, by then, me telling Ian or Joe words
and stories, besotting *them*. At the market
I bought this photograph: three members of
the Women's Land Army rest, smile, before the camera
in an English field; their hair scarved;
they have checked blouses, overalls.
          'Was anything,' I asked Louise,
'less sour, more comradely?' It's framed
and hangs next to one of my mother
marching through Melbourne with the WAAF.
Do you understand women who'd never heard
of fascism joining to fight it?
Why not? It's the same street that
we've marched down for much the same.
          'Haven't you had enough,' Louise cried out,
'from those nasty shrill petticoat pigs of
Women Who Want To Be Women?' Whose

presumptuous farrago implies that you and I, your
mother and my mother didn't want to be women.
Or, if these women *want* to be women, what
are they now? Only dumbos could construct
such conundrums. Yet I've my own. I mean,
is being a lover-biographer a mere re-run of
the perpetual back-room gal with shades of
new, improved whore? May be. However,
I'll not submit my life, or any life,
to some tick-where-applicable purity checklist.
I'm quite aware that women or men may
exist for the convenience of another's fears,
even their own, but will risk that.
Sure the Glenferrie Station crrrea-tures still haunt.
Often I think this town is more than over-choked
with Los Creepos: twisted virgin boys
that called me 'titless', etcetera.
I try to imagine their mothers, their wives and daughters.
Or, as Ian put it: 'I try conjuring y'average lezzo-seppo,
Ms Diesel Dyke. But can't get past a vision of
her old man. Th'poooor bugg-ahs!'
        Well, cousin, seems this letter is coursing back
to where I began it, family life,
and where that can only be, for starters, reduced to
a pragmatic administrative unit; perhaps.
Take it from there.
        It's time to shut off the cassette, roll
further numbers. You may not receive my rave (as it's become).
Seems I'm using your address more
as a form of beacon, some reference point,
with questions turning to be my answers.
Having seen a pattern of heroes, am I
to always stand beside, watch and chronicle
men who haven't quit their dreams?
(Once more my demure, flinty cousin? Well,
just once more.) I think of a cleric striding round
a verandah bellowing 'The Riff Song',
with great Gothic clouds layered over
the Riverina skyline—as if he could
remain in that mean town, shout at its burghers,
'Strike me! strike me!' come the apocalypse
or Melbourne. 'P'pa must stand and fight—he *must*,'
you always mused, dabbing your temples with
four seven eleven while the rest
retreated to their rooms with pre-storm mee-grains.
        And Ian, who, after his revelations, pilloried the Porker,
stood over the freeway, watching the city's
homebound trail. 'I've got him,' in his quiet glee,
'I've got him!' The cars turned to 'Newsview',

hearing of governments in flux, floundering through
the public groundswell. Ian loved it.
       'Sure I'm "pleying th mairn". I've got him, and
I'll get him again! I'll get him again! It's not enough
to keep them choking in their own trough.
I mean, I'm not in this the way
a businessman is into making money;
self-justifying leaps of morality I can't believe.
I only want, and I want him out.'
       We kept standing over the freeway/
The Porker became a consul. His party
right-side-upped and, with an er-Cap'n at
an er-helm was steady as she er-goes.
       'That's when I quit,' said John. 'I want to thank
your friend, offer a hand—but even *he*,
he—anyone would think that
single-contract tendering apexed corruption!
Ha ha. Allow me to tell you!' He hasn't yet,
but stood looking out his bay windows.
There was work to be done, and he was
impatient for an aide to tap the shoulder,
indicate that, yes, canting and ranting
had ceased, the call had risen, embattlement
was turning to attack; he would be needed.
No aide appeared, only the biographer:
a house guest profering interest rather than
infatuation (well, we trust).
All that's needed is Sue and her right mind
to keep on strutting with her don't-shit-me look
right up to and past any who've judged
that is her lover? *That*? Or deem yours truly
among the Golddiggers of nineteen eighty.
What fun to know something *is* different.
To buggery if the bistro-gossips decree
this grazier as playboy, Teddy Kennedy style.
Yes, and Lenin joined Rotary!

       So, after a day's writing, any evening I'll visit,
have visitors, smoke exo, play tracks, chat; not try
to spend my thoughts on John McTaggart, Junior:
off somewhere working, to bring down a government,
rescue the country; if he phones he phones.
I can rest up for weeks (or try),
glad of any serenity after these months
of manic rooting. Some friends stay annoyed.
They'd love continual, breathless, senseless
adoration and, much to their glib chagrin,
don't get it. Well, yo ho ho, vacuity
wasn't my strong point; return, say in October,

after, when, if, we've sorted this one.
    Clouds have banked enough, there's rain starting.

Ken Bolton

Beginning the new day

POEM WRITTEN LATE AT NIGHT WITH DRANSFIELD'S INSPECTOR OF TIDES & ASHBERY'S SOME TREES

just write great first lines.
From every corner comes a distinctive offering.
in the third line explain that the line above was stolen.

this gives you the rules for a poem
the second line is stolen,
&, in the third line, this is explained.

dawn reveals a fact to me: an endless rolling of smoke across my
    window (not trees, not cloud);
The road so strangely lit by lamps
is not revealed, but apposite—a borrowed line

it now reveals the scene that has been created, out of the night:
high over the city. Angels
are they angels? as this borrowed line suggested?—

the smoke curls now from left to right … not 'like a spent hypothesis'
'the white is too painful'
a line that seemed untrue, when it suggested itself, but possible,

then true. & then 'pain' & 'white' pass, magically,
this is perhaps a day of general honesty
independently   high over the city   'angels' now seems true.

The smoke curls with just that confidence
'& Dick gives Genevieve a swift punch' suggests
in its serene displacement, like the angels visiting____in that
    painting of Piero's, *The Nativity*,—so displaced.

Similarly the clouds of smoke seem just themselves, in the lightening air,
    each
joining a neighbour, as though speech
were theirs, ignoring us (as I think of myself), with the independent
    reality of borrowed lines

like the line that says
'I wish I did not have to write the instruction manual …'
& you don't—the day achieves itself despite the lines you've chosen

though through them you've seen.

Laurie Duggan

AUSTRALIA

I like the way we've
been able to fuck things here
as good as anywhere else
in only half the time.

DRIVE TIME

The New Nationalism winks
from its track suit
and slips a few extra dollars
into the hip pocket
of the Quiet Achiever.

HOLOCAUST

Australia has escaped the holocaust.
The surviving cultural artifacts are
Zen Buddhism, Australian Rules Football
and talk-back radio. The poetry
that develops from this takes on titles
like 'Late Night Eclogue: Rinzai and Barassi'.
Pupils are beaten with the Master's cane
for asking stupid questions like: 'What
is a shirt-front?' 'How can I escape
from my alcoholic husband?'

THE MYSTERIES

Everything happens at once.
We miss most of it.
The kettle boils over
and puts out the fire.

THE TOWN ON THE TEN DOLLAR NOTE

Too much history
and the place becomes a mausoleum:
the chemist closes for lunch;
the museum stays open all the time.

*B*LUE HILLS 21

Out at the twelve-mile mark
peppercorn seed equals memory.
A lizard flits under rubble
between the sleepers, on the line where
trains 'rocket to impossible destinations';
overhead, pale green semiconductors,
a sky full of cirrus.
          It's spring:
the peppercorns hang, an innocent aura
of ten year olds sharing cigarettes
in a hollow of compacted earth
under the waiting room.
And the lunatic who pushed a barrow
from the station to the newsagent,
infantile in middle age, what burst gland
disposed of him?

*B*LUE HILLS 23

In this town a dance is
the dance.
          The chill
of shoulder straps, Friday night
outside the Main Hotel,
a sacrifice for style.
          Sunday, the glint
of a flute in the trees up the Mitchell's bank;
snatches of Mozart: skewed notes running off the scales.

The path goes on endlessly, crackling with twigs.
Auxiliary generators whine over the agistments.

Across the river,
white branches lean in the wind
that blows down from the Divide.

FROM *T*HE EPIGRAMS OF MARTIAL

I XVIII
You watered down red
   from the Hunter Valley
with a cask of factory white
   and called it rosé.
Your guests were fair game
   but did the Hunter have to die?

III XVII
An enormous quiche
was placed on the table
by a gloved waiter.
Steve anxiously blew upon it.
The quiche cooled
and it was all his.

III XLVII
Range Rovers carry
the 'mountain-fresh' odour
of aftershave
'up the country'.

V LI
Shorthand writers
    crowd around the man
        with a cricket bat
who can barely read two words
    off an idiot card
        for a TV commercial.

VIII XX
Dransfield, who wrote
    200 poems each day,
was wiser than his editor
    who printed them.

X IX
With my quick feet,
    my nimble syllables,
the bit fast in my teeth,
    and an unspared crop,
I, Martial, am a nag
    lengths behind Phar Lap.

FROM THE ASH RANGE

8:2   DEAD WARRIORS
Dead warriors, return to camp
placed on a skin, the legs drawn up
        and tied to the chest
the skin thrown over the head
bound lightly round the neck.
        A small area
facing the sea or lake cleared,
the mourners chant the victim's

life and deeds,
cover themselves with red and white clay,
white rings around the eyes; the women
        lament at a distance.
The life of the dead man re-enacted
mourners dig with sharpened sticks
        a deep pit
lined with bark, leaves and twigs,
the possessions thrown in
        finally the body
in a sitting position .
facing the water;
        a cylindrical pit
with a side chamber
blocked in with pieces of wood.
        The dead
do not remain in the grave
but leave and return at will.

Alan Gould

Reykjavik

No doubt impatient with the bravura
of his bandit forebears, it took Arnason
three years of fortified headlands to win
this spot from a dozen jittery ascetics.
His sagacity shows still in the square
concrete homes lumped for no-nonsense with the Arctic's
muscle, and in the town's repute as venue
for chess celebrities and potentates
manoeuvring detente. The airport and hotels
have changed nothing. Thirty miles south of here
the Atlantic Rift crosses the coast and arcs
its one animus inland, its canals
take the island without fuss, bulge, divide it
cautiously, a millimetre a year.

South coast mechanic

We watch with two eyes, I reckon, outer and inner.
So I eat lunch slowly, one eye on the apprentices
where sheet-sunlight through the roll-a-door,
catches them in their huddle. They're guzzling soft drinks,
raucously outdoing each other in their scorn
for the latest model. *Yah, couldn' scrape*

the skin from off rice puddn', says the one
too young for his licence who they call Fucknuckle.

But speed is too like bolting your food—time
retaliates with indigestion or a curve's
slippy camber. Machinery's the same;
a job rushed is like marital discord;
the good mechanic is a lifelong bridegroom,
watchful, tender, deliberate. That's why
it's the slow watchful fellow from that lot who,
once he's done his time, I'll put on full wages here.

He's got good ears. It's ears let you see an engine
in X-ray, tappet squeak, a carby's ill-music.
But my other eye is on my fingernails, reflective-like.
There's grit under there goes back to Airforce days,
Trobriand nights of torsos gleaming to get
a Beaufighter's engines changed by dawn—
we did that—which would have been a week's work
for a peacetime crew. But that was efficiency,

not speed, the brain and hand in sync, in trance.
With machinery, I guess, it's the thought of sync,
those greased parts dancing behind their cowls,
which makes me fall in love over and over,
and me, the listening angel with a spanner,
repairing, refining. That thought cost me a wife.
She cleared out with the boy, benzine stench
and carburettor bits all over the white laminex

got to her, she said. Had a point.
Once I could improvise from a box of junk,
but now it's all kit-form; *Three days, lady,*
depending on the supplier. You should've bought
a paperback, eh! I've had honeymooners
find each other in my car yard, their campervans
waiting on a clutchplate; romance conked
beside a ditch for sump-oil, and that lover's moon

high above the cyclone fence; an image
for our times, you reckon? Domestic bliss;
my idea is a bed and fridge at the less
decorated end of a vast workshop, but
through habit I've kept the marriage weatherboards
with their empty rooms. As for the Cosmos,
sure, I've seen it, wheeling there above
the wire when I lock up of a winter's night.

The Grand Machine in sync, greased on air,
it's nice engineering, though wearing out, I'm told,
and spare parts, yeah, well, problems, foreign supplier.

Now which of my eyes was looking at that?

Jamie Grant

How to fold army blankets

Everyone's breath burst out of their mouths
just like the smoke breathed
from the lips of rifles facing the range,

that shattered man-made
hummock whose undigested belly-full
of shells would one day

stand to baffle archaeology. Each
morning we'd parade
outside the canteen, polished thoughts still wreathed

with figments strange
as dreams. Nights of fitful sleep on sacks of hay.
The mountain peak south

from the camp was blocked neatly as the tall
crown of my old slouch
hat. The days marched on a curve which always

returned to its start;
they finished with the prim geometry
invented to make

soldiers out of children—with heartless
domesticity
which scrubbed, aligned or folded whatever

we weren't expected
to salute. Imprisoned in those ways
we were taught the art

of folding the army's blankets—we'd take
the stitched seam over,
so, and *so*, till it became a flawless

cube of wool, reflected—
in shape at least—in the cold metal pans
they served our meals from.

Remembering that hard-earned skill, a bored
civil servant years
from his army days folded up the map

of Vietnam
the morning we left the camp. His office
must have been spotless,

with calf-bound volumes lined up into squads,
every paper-clip
gleaming. None of us knew a thing about

that room. The frost-smoke
mountains watched us as we started out
on another clear

cold morning. I longed to fold that country
like a rug which we
could stow forever out of mind. No one spoke.

His Nibs

Round-boled, the eucalyptus tree
puts one in mind of a stout worthy

burgher—the Lord Mayor in his robes,
perhaps, slyly addressed as 'His Nibs',

half-dressed before a pageant, and half
in disarray. Its peeling bark ruff

looks like a skin complaint, a collar
of loosening flakes, at once the colour

of rust, and stone, and of flesh—except
the papery scabs are incorrupt.

Beneath its insect-nibbled cloak, stitched
to resemble the intricate patched

surface on a geologist's maps
of the Outback, a white torso slips

in view, owning a sleek complexion
like a woman's before the invention

of the cancerous pastime, sun-bath.
Its limbs, the means through which a tree draws breath,

embark at the level of a man's
skull to pursue divergent plans,

as water running downhill seeks out ways
without resistance—and yet their maze

flows upward, feeding on nourishment
of light. Its end is embellishment:

a shiny peruke of downward-hung
leaf-silk, an oil-textured shantung

in pale green, comprising foliage
almost grassblade-slender. At each stage

of growth, the trunk has added a ring
as if there were someone honouring

its worth in new-struck chains of office;
but jewel-red sap-stains compromise

such honour, leaking from joints and seams
in the cream-bland integument. Dreams

reinvent these lurid sap-trails
as welling shotgun-pellet holes

in the unlucky corpse who revealed
the graft of His Nibs, lying in a field.

Susan Hampton

Ode to the Car Radio

My right eye leaking blood coming home
from Casualty, patched, pirate view, & changing gears
past Rooms to Let $12 p.w. beside Surry Hills Smash Repairs
& a beer gut emerging from a pub door at ten, well,
you can picture the general scene
& click! clear as glass, the flute opening
to Prokofiev's *Romeo and Juliet*, cool & sweet
as a parkful of wet trees. Or the time
when a Sutherland aria came blasting through
the stink of rubber at a stop light in Lidcombe,
the volume accidentally on full & I grinned,
mouthing at surprised traffic-jammed faces.
Stopped for a milkshake at the corner of Norton
& Marion Streets, watching clouds coast by
the asbestos-looking steeple of that church—
Pachelbel's *Canon* (I want it played at my funeral)
and the church sailed in towards the city, freed,
the fierce white clouds stayed still.

Diesel fumes from a 470 to Lilyfield spread upward
to Mahler being grandiose, & disappear past a balcony
where an old man (knees spread like a cellist)
reads a newspaper, bowing the strings with scrawny
sun-bitten arms. Oxy-gear lights a Brandenburg Concerto,
car brakes are violins, a jay-walker is moved on
by a French horn. Before too long,
a jack-hammer in Woolloomooloo sounds reasonable
with pizzicato in one ear. The green brush graffitist
writes FRASER IS THE HILTON BOMBER to a Haydn trumpet
& during the downpour after a southerly buster, Debussy
dances on factory rooftops & front lawns &
the whole of Sydney heaves & drifts as the radio
lets out its congruous, incongruous love.

Kate Jennings

My GRANDMOTHER'S GHOST

I asked my father about your girlhood, how you met
my grandfather, but he had forgotten, or never knew,

and so it goes; I have to cosset my few thin facts.
I loved to rummage in your dressing-table drawers,

a busy spy sending puffs of pink face powder
into the air and finding cards with panels of muslin

stitched with violets, and snaps of the ruins of Baalbeck,
souvenirs of my grandfather's travels courtesy the Kaiser.

You were raised in a house with clay floors, and it was
your job to damp the dirt down with wet tea leaves.

(This you told me when I complained about housework.)
You were nearly blinded by sandy blight and flinched

at the telling. I imagined an unrelenting dust storm,
a furious wall of grit, and you flailing, your arms

outstretched, eyes blasted in biblical retribution.
I was numb with anger at the world's injustices

when you died, so I failed to mourn or even miss you.
Later, I needed to talk with you, but I couldn't find

your headstone in the whiskery cemetery grass. Instead
you visited me on Forty-Eighth Street in New York,

a standard-issue ghost, soft around the edges and alive
with a sweet glow. 'You've come a long way,' I said.

You answered, 'And so have you. But not far enough.'
Then you faded, and I slept, untroubled.

Jennifer Maiden

THE ANGLO-SAXONS' XMAS

Mistletoe cankers the glades
where we hide. In the sky
their fires are feasting.
At the green fortress all banquet
on ale-doused pig. We steal
entry like a legend from them
axing out the raucous psalter
sung on tongues of beasts
& pray

PREAMBLE

I remember you dancing: almost
a debutante in what was
almost a country town.
There was no programme but
pearl sandals, a sequined purse
& your face was lavished with oils
& corals until you were
more obviously corruptible
    'presentable'
to the mayoress, & to dance
with footballers erudite
in percentage play.

    But
I preferred you on cracker night,
evading the ritual suttee,
bungers in your pocket,
shoving a shoulder against me
rough with loneliness.
    All people
have their natural smells:
some musk or ether
dettol or arpege,
but yours is something
more like gunpowder—
not burnt-out char but damper
something discarded & deeper
fierce as the over-primed squibs
which flared in the undergrowth.

ANOREXIA

Kelly sharpened is powerful, asexual and yawns,
curls up on tartan cushions with pick-me-up arms,
viewed by no one but cat, video, grandmother.
She is cranky with Nan's tabby. He is sleek
and haughtily whores, meanwhile demanding all
the messy food and closeness they can muster.
She ate last night and will not eat this week.
Her body lives off itself like anger.
It was once too dumb, too soft, too tall.
She bites her mouth because it's still a stranger.

CHAKOLA

Were there more people here?
Seventy years ago when the child
my father had his sight and ran
along the banks of the Numeralla
such a clear quick little river
such a crisply-lighted river
horizoned by mountaineous clouds
and the cloudy mountains, dark
in air as sharp as thirst. Were
there congregating families in the wind-
used Boy's Hall with the stained glass cross
or was this the school my grandfather taught,
was this his first promotion from
driving his buggy each day in turn
to towns on either side of Braidwood? Was
this the battered big chimneyed house
he brought quick Nell and seven children to?
Was the eighth child born here to
the youngest of the 'wild' Feeney girls?
My father was the fourth, the second boy.
My three year daughter rides the grey seesaw
which is bearded with cobwebs and whittled
down by many weathers, primary force.
She says 'You used to teach here.' I say 'No:
your great grandfather did, and your father
played here.' But *you* say 'You mean
grandfather.' And yes, that's where the sense
of self slips up of course—in history.
Maybe we're all an 'I' as we confront
the past, the broken ford, the Numeralla,
gleaming with sunlit absence.
When we return perhaps the ford will be
rebuilt and we will take her to the town.
I don't think it was here yet that his cousin
threw the stone which slowly turned him blind.
Although so far I have only been here twice
I remember Chakola clearly and its light
tightens my eyes in dreams, has heaviness.

As we drive back the suicidal sheep
scuttle before the car, so slow, and so
sane-seeming in the late May afternoon.
What sense have I of the boy who was here?
The wind which brittles leaves and swirls
at the river's pace whets wit's edge on
warm fields and country rooms. The sense
of him is in that not the ruins. I have

no echo of him playing here unless
the landscape gave back nothing but his voice.

Vicki Raymond

THE MERMAIDS' LAGOON

'To die will be an awfully big adventure'—*Peter Pan*

Look at it this way, Peter:
you are about to start
a whole new career as a corpse.

Of course, you'll have to learn
to keep your mouth shut.
For you, that's the hardest part.

Then, there's the glassy stare
when a live person swims past:
just copy the fish.

After a few days afloat,
you'll hardly know yourself.
You'll have grown up at last.

THE PEOPLE, NO

You never hear 'the People' now:
that thundering, slightly frightening sea
has been oiled flat.
But 'people' you hear everywhere,
a baby chirrup sensuously drawn out.

The People used to be a little
too fond of crowds for their own good.
Like movie extras, they
were sent from place to place, kept standing
long hours in the sun and, finally,
given their fortnight's pay.

People, on the other hand,
were sensitive, and cared;
and they agreed they needed
to keep their weight down, running
around the park each morning.
No wonder that they superseded

that poor old dinosaur, the People,
who smoked, and never understood
that to survive you have to be quite small,
and sometimes seem not to be there at all.

Let's hear it, then, for people,
their sensitivity and taste,
their sets of values
like sets of willow pattern,
so delicate, so easily replaced.

John Forbes

EUROPE: A GUIDE FOR KEN SEARLE

Greece is like a glittering city
though only in a political speech

but Italians believe in *bella figura*
& mis-use the beach. In Germany there's

Kraftwerk & acres of expressionist kitsch.
Oil-rich Norwegians don't need to ski

they just like it & Iceland is famous
for its past. Doing their physical jerks,

a quiet pride permeates the Swedes.
Denmark is neither vivid nor abrupt

& Belgians have a ringside seat
to observe the behaviour of the Dutch.

The French invented finesse but it's
their self-regard that intrigues us.

We pity the English, though they get on
our wick, pretending to understand us

& Scotland is old-fashioned like a dowry
but unusual, like nice police. Mention

Ireland & you've already said enough.
The Spaniards are not relaxed about sex

& tourists are attracted to this. Some
Portuguese exist entirely on a diet of fish

but rich cakes, finance & guest workers
sustain the Swiss. Consult my *By Trailbike*

& Hot Air Balloon Through Middle Europe
for details of the Austrians & Czechs

but don't forget Bavaria's Oktoberfest
or that Rococo architecture was designed

to be passed out under, pissed, & it's
aesthetically edifying to do this.

For the rest: give Russia a miss,
the Poles will appreciate hard currency

but only as a gift & the fleshpots of
Split will leave you a physical wreck.

This guide stops short at the Balkans,
as it omits the Finns. I won't apologise

—many guides to Australia include
New Zealand or leave out Tasmania.

No doubt some thorough American manual
can give you the lowdown on Europe's margins

but mine, designed for only one traveller,
is better written & much shorter.

Besides, if you remove the art, Europe's
like the US, more or less a dead loss

& while convenient for walking
& picturesque, like the top of a *Caran*

D'Ache pencil case or a chocolate box,
what do you make of a landscape

that reminds you of itself? Is this why
the people are sure they're typical

not standard? I can't advise you on this
but I know how I enjoyed myself: though

knocked out by what convinced me
'Great Art' without inverted commas is

(but not because of this) I hung around
with other Australians & hit the piss.

$\mathcal{D}$EATH, AN ODE

Death, you're more successful than America,
even if we don't choose to join you, we do.
I've just become aware of this conscription
where no one's marble doesn't come up;
no use carving your name on a tree, exchanging vows
or not treading on the cracks for luck
where there's no statistical anomalies at all
& you know not the day nor the hour, or even if you do
timor mortis conturbat me. No doubt we'd
think this in a plunging jet & the black box recorder
would note each individual, unavailing scream
but what gets me is how compulsory it is—
'he never was a joiner' they wrote on his tomb.

At least bingeing becomes heroic & I can see
why the Victorians
so loved drawn out death-bed scenes:
huddled before our beautiful century, they knew
what first night nerves were all about.

*S*PEED, A PASTORAL

it's fun to take speed
& stay up all night
not writing those reams of poetry
just thinking about is bad for you
                    —instead your feelings
follow your career down the drain
& find they like it there
among an anthology of fine ideas, bound together
by a chemical in your blood
that lets you stare the TV in its vacant face
& cheer, consuming yourself like a mortgage
& when Keats comes to dine, or Flaubert,
you can answer their purities
with your own less negative ones—for example
you know Dransfield's line, that once you become a junkie
you'll never want to be anything else?
        well, I think he died too soon,
as if he thought drugs were an old-fashioned teacher
& he was the teacher's pet, who just put up his hand
        & said quietly, 'Sir, sir'
        & heroin let him leave the room.

*L*OVE POEM

Spent tracer flecks Baghdad's
bright video game sky

as I curl up with the war
in lieu of you, whose letter

lets me know my poems show
how unhappy I can be. Perhaps.

But what they don't show, until
now, is how at ease I can be

with military technology: e.g.
matching their *feu d'esprit* I classify

the sounds of the Iraqi AA—the
thump of the 85 mil, the throaty

chatter of the quad ZSU 23.
Our precision guided weapons

make the horizon flash & glow
but nothing I can do makes you

want me. Instead I watch the west
do what the west does best

& know, obscurely, as I go to bed
all this is being staged for me.

On Tiepolo's Banquet of Cleopatra

Any frayed waiting room copy of *Who*
could catch this scene: flash Euro-
trash surveys a sulky, round faced
überBabe who's got the lot—what else
could this painting mean, except that
superstars can will their luck, or
just how little raw envy's hidden by
contempt, so words like 'Wow! Great
Tits!' or 'Comic Opera Wop' sum up
the observer, not Antony & Cleopatra
attached to pets & entourages—our
contemporaries minus coke & sunglasses.
What's that pearl without price she's
dropping in her glass? A mirror of
their self-regard, replaced by each
other's glances. Still, it glows, blue
& blank at the centre like their hearts,
flanked by idlers on balconies leering
& placing bets. But if they suggest *Eros*,
what role does *Agape* play in this—
downstairs & screaming, being shown the
Instruments? You wish, voyeur, you wish.

Philip Salom

Sight

Sun, wind, on my forehead.
For hours I gaze at the ocean.

Soul's recollection
breaks through me: I am both hunter

and prey?
              From fierce eye and talon

the osprey stares
through the golden-louvred sea.

THE WIND HAS PANELS

Not the seminar kind. The wind has panels
like an endless series of opening doors
but far more subtle than doors: I think
of panels in Thailand, where the walls of houses

fold out and air moves like a calming sexual act,
like ecstasy, like walking inside the wind
when panel after panel admits you. Forget
the days when they don't, when knocking there

buffets and resists you. On the common days
like these, fights break out on the corner, someone
is shot. A Jumbo crashes after take-off
looking, in devastation, like it hit the sky head on

and mountainous. Was refused admittance.
Such is the grief in families of the victims.
Their faces crease and flatten, worn back
by wind, pushed flat by the panels in the wind.

The wind has dreams. It dreams its panels
altogether cease, like Buddha's final meditation,
like Christ's emphatic vision of the will of God.
Yet the wind awakens. The wind has panels.

RECOGNITION

FOR PRAMOEDYA ANANTA TOER

His words are so dangerous they're praised,
pored over. His life, therefore, given this
grammarians' surveillance: these men all
turn him like the dial of a telephone,
reporting—they hear the voices Marx and Lenin
but actual proof among the lines and plots so
difficult to find.
        Only the recognised
suffer from such brilliance, their genius
given by the most perceptive, the equal
genius of the judges. And given on the morning
of awards: the Handcuffs for Fiction, the
Shackles for Political Essays, the government's
Fellowship of Compulsory Silence.
        Mnemonists
had once supported him: each prison wall,
floor, ceiling, each face listening, each
breath or voice, everything he looked upon,
stories in each of them, and only later

pages to put them on.
      Now only the state
shall publish him, the logo with its
parallel bars and labouring islands, and
his name not merely larger than the title
but larger than the text.
      Now only spirits
—the banned prints pale from the photocopier's
ghost, and ten years off the reader's life
for having them. In Paradise there are
many artists, oh yes, it's full of them.
But not any art.
      Now merely a man again,
free to consider where his mind has been,
his irony of house arrest and house of nations:
each house as shadowy as wayang
where only one man does the voices.

*P*OEMS OF DISSOCIATION

7

Is there a brothel in the opposite apartment?
Sensitivities at $4 a minute? There
in the airspace racketting above the poem
a blunt-nosed, skidless greenish helicopter
is advertising condoms. But what
are these women doing? I wonder for months.
Across the street, day and night, but night
most oddly, the windowed walls
shine appliance white, and women sit in white.
Are they icing wedding cakes? Do they sew?
Why is it somehow like an operation?
If they face East is there a double facing West
black with women in lingerie black?
Imagination makes a question for the shock
or want of balance, a dialogue of answers
made in images. Is it the ache of surfaces
where neighbours are far too often strangers,
one way mirrors? It takes a wink, a nod.
Assuring nothing. Nothing's certain.

So the building empties, its fire-alarm howling
like a sick kid. The pavement fills with workers
from an illustrated children's book: each face
determinedly different, each patch made simple
like a mended knee ... the artist learnt too well
Leonardo's dictum: never make your people
look like brothers (sisters). Closer up, they *do*.
Nowhere in this crowd of extras, nowhere
talking and smoking under the demented siren

are women dressed in refrigerator white.
Now, the wall dark again, the streetglow
ochre-ing and a line dividing day from reason
they sit inside the white-walled room
white-dressed, with white, and working.

Andrew Sant

OUT OF THE WOOD

If X-rays are nearsighted
our craftsmen have looked into wood
like visionaries; whose hands

have been sympathetic
as healers', fingertips touched
what is not yet visible,

as if the vibrations
of the thunderously toppled trees
are stored there for release;

and so compelling is this energy
they have to refine and polish their wares
like love or scrap them completely.

Consider the huon-pine bowls and vases—
one man has entered a two-thousand-year-old
tunnel of cellulose with sharp tools

and imagined them, he jokes,
to be as perfectly preserved
as sacred artefacts in an Egyptian tomb;

a treasure-house jammed
with nameable goods and
clearly not visible

in the panel of light
the superfast chainsaw revealed
when the huge tree unbalanced from its hinge.

Now I, loving their drive
for discovery and embracing it
expectantly, see our jostling trees

with a curiously deepened pleasure
in the way the conductor's baton-maker might have
before I saw him playfully

raise his polished batons,
in the absence of an orchestra, as if he heard
startling music alight from the wood.

COVER-UP

It occurred to me that since our house was built in the 1860s
it must be made of convict bricks; now, scouring a wall, it occurs to me
      again
that behind plaster and paint there are convict bricks,
some with a sweaty thumbprint signature, convict colophons,
baked into orange clay and as permanent as those other inscriptions,
the welts of the lash that encouraged these walls piecemeal out of the
      ground;
and it occurs to me that each brick forms part of an unwritten history
      blasted
by a hell-fire that could bake a million bricks: a few thousand here
with solid life-everlasting behind plaster and paint.
I could expose and study them, they are those convicts' only
      gravestones
as befits the anonymity of those wearers of dun-coloured uniforms
but I'll keep them sealed off, not only for practical purposes
but also from better society. I think of the brogue of the Irish
and the witty cockney tale-spinners exiled in Tasmania
behind the hugely substantial indifference of distance;
and I am walled in, a keen listener amongst the dumb bricks, with
      windows
wide-open to admit the fresh breeze, the sail-raising westerlies.

Nicolette Stasko

MY NURSE AND I

AFTER FRIEDA KAHLO
FOR CHRIS
I am twined in the great trees
by the river
my hair a flock
of cockatoos
settling in branches
everywhere I am open
to the night
feeling the sky   the slope
and distance of mountains
with their wings
my eyes the dark creatures
tunnelling through earth
scraping at roots
in my veins leaves
the creaking of gang gangs the sighing
of rain

THE MURMURING OF MANY TONGUES

On our first night at Depot
we make love   knitting the delicate
bones of the dead
with our own
around us the ghosts
of the eucalypts
whisper in the rain   a canopy
of ancient trees filled
with the shadows
of owls
even here it is winter   the terrace
covered with leaves

inexplicably   we find
ourselves weeping
holding each other
we mourn for all the past
lovers who have lain
in this bed
for friends
making love here when
they were young
we mourn for ourselves
a firmament of stars planets
and clouds arches
over the house   and a pale moon
shines on the surface of the sea
beneath it
large fish feed
in darkness

in the morning
we are unable
to rise with the first light
later   all we know
is   the finding of a fragile
and most perfect shell
in a newly formed
tide pool   its minute spikes
hardening as we hold it
translucent
up to the sun
a child running
along the clean curve
of the beach   white froth

flicking her ankles
the glimpse of a lyrebird
disappearing
into the ferns
by the side of the road

Stephen Edgar

GONE A MILLION

Danae's kicked away the sheets,
Her hand strokes where she's moist with juice.
Between her legs is counted out
The gold ejaculate of Zeus;

Money well spent. You get the picture?
(Titian. Worth millions.) Cut to now.
The drive-in wedding bar is full,
The celebrant's asking what priced vow

They'll buy, while family and friends
Urge them on, crying, 'Take the lot'
(Though prudently laying side bets down
On when they'll split and who'll get what).

Instead of a ring receipts are stuck
Upon each shyly proffered sex.
A few invited couldn't come
But in their place are propped the cheques

They decently sent, or telegrams
Of latest offers. Gifts! Yes, theirs
The rare coins, special mintages,
Money, debentures, money, shares.

But enough. Dissolve. Alone at last
With the promise of the bridal suite,
Their limpid eyes large with desire,
They reach for the cash heaped at their feet–

She, like reclining Danae,
Her hand on a dime-tumescent sock,
Caresses herself; he, not outdone,
Wraps a greenback round his cock—

Till finally (and stroke for stroke)
Having made their love (shrewd newlyweds)
Last hours (and grow at twelve per cent)
They come together in separate beds.

THE SECRET LIFE OF BOOKS

They have their stratagems too, though they can't move.
They know their parts.
Like invalids long reconciled
To stillness, they do their work through others.
They have turned the world
To their own account by the twisting of hearts.

What do they have to say and how do they say it?
In the library
At night, or the sun room with its one
Curled thriller by the window, something
Is going on,
You may suspect, that you don't know of. Yet they

Need you. The time comes when you pick one up,
You who scoff
At determinism, the selfish gene.
Why this one? Look, already the blurb
Is drawing in
Some further text. The second paragraph

Calls for an atlas or a gazetteer;
That poem, spare
As a dead leaf's skeleton, coaxes
Your lexicon. Through you they speak
As through the sexes
A script is passed that lovers never hear.

They have you. In the end they have written you,
By the intrusion
Of their account of the world, so when
You come to think, to tell, to do,
You're caught between
Quotation marks, your heart's beat an allusion.

ALL WILL BE REVEALED

In the nudist camp identity is lost
Behind disguise.
See, over all the fashions of the self,
Whatever size,

They're slipping on identical pink suits
Of nakedness.
On either sex there stretches, nips or droops
Its single dress.

Where have they gone, the friends who brought me here?
Where are the strangers
Hiding? The eyes like bullets aimed against
Uncertain dangers

Ricochet from nudity's blank walls.
In such a place
One might devise a nightclub for dresstease
Where they could face,

To whistles, randy cries of 'Get it on!',
Themselves as lewd
Performers who would strut their bump and grind,
Beginning nude,

Discarding part by part their bare accord,
Till they finessed
The erotic climax of true self-display,
Completely dressed.

Peter Goldsworthy

Piano

Each night I return to this discipline:
a straight-back on a hard bench
in an unheated room, sometimes uncooled,
embarked on Czerny without end
or pun, an unsmiling bondage.

The piano is the heaviest thing
I own: heavier than a set of weights
or a complicated exercise machine, heavier
than a small car and travelling further.

Allowed inside it will not be ignored.
It expands to fill the biggest room.
A planet, it draws me
past armchairs, past cooling meals,
past better versions by other people
reproduced.

Yet it contains no music.
Nor are there images to be had inside:
no moonlight or sunken churches,
no picturesque exhibitions.
If I push back the lid I find
only notes: black and white,
loud and soft, sharp and flat.

The wrong alone are of interest:
as long as there is error
there is hope, there is a day's hard work,
there is perfection to be again disproved.
As for hands: a kind of mob
which must be broken.
This delinquent right index, that lazy left little.
Even you, thumbs—yes, you, in the middle—
have whittled toothpicks on demand,
have moved holes from here to here

as I sit upright, nightly:
stern-faced, rod-backed,
posed as if before a mirror
or on a starting-block, facing the music,
aiming to break the minute waltz.

A STATISTICIAN TO HIS LOVE

Men kill women in bedrooms, usually
by hand, or gun. Women kill men,
less often, in kitchens, with knives.
Don't be alarmed, there is understanding
to be sucked from all such hard
and bony facts, or at least a sense
of symmetry. Drowned men—an
instance—float face down, women up.
But women, ignited, burn more fiercely.
The death camp pyres were therefore,
sensibly, women and children first,
an oily kind of kindling. The men
were stacked in rows on top. Yes,
there is always logic in this world.
And neatness. And the comfort
of fact. Did I mention that suicides
outnumber homicides? Recent figures
are reliable. So stay awhile yet
with me: the person to avoid, alone,
is mostly you yourself.

CIMETIÈRE PÈRE LACHAISE

1

Even in Paris graveyards there are queues: tourists
clutching phrase-books and muttering the Basic Expression:
If Only There Weren't So Many Tourists.
Officials sell roses and a map of fashionable tombs:
the whereabouts of celebrities, more famous for being dead.

I wander among rows of upright granite phone-booths,
checking Names and Dates and Numbers. At Oscar's
the crowd is thickest: a line of men waiting to phone home.
At Gertrude's? Only women, who watch me suspiciously.
Music and the sound of heated English draws me to another plot
thick with anglophones: teenage backpackers swigging wine
and listening to a cassette of the Doors. No phone-booth here,
the grave is flat; a broken rock, a hewn name: *Jim Morrison*.
He was my age, I tell them. None of you were born.
Jim Lives a child says, and passes me a bottle.
I sit and sip and listen to the noise of Resurrection:
*The Body Didn't Look Like Jim. The Death Certificate
Was Forged. Someone Saw Him, Risen, In Galilee ...*
The horizontal door, a granite slab, stays shut, the cassette ends.
Lennon was killed by the CIA, someone mutters;
the worshippers disperse, wanting to believe, and finding it easy.

2

I remember when it was easy. I remember
my first shave with Ockham: everything
is a conspiracy. For a time I sit alone
among the Gauloise stubs and scattered empties
and disconnected stone phone-boxes.
The past is a text, I read this morning
in a book review in last night's *Paris Soir*.
If so its words are difficult to read, a text
cleansed of conjuctions. Unconnected things
come back, scattered across distant pages:
school, too many years ago, and drunken weekend nights,
and Jim—and Jimi, and Janis—and someone else now gone,
a girl I knew who set odd precious nights on fire.
Perhaps a cemetery far from home is no fit place
to flip back through the past, but everywhere
of late seems far from home, including home.
So many things have gone unimportant,
so many lusts and angers have come to seem
fake orgasms, like wearing a black armband
the day that Hendrix died, feeling a public sadness
I'd never privately earned. These days I prefer Chopin,
his grave is over there. As for seasonal beliefs,
I have no faith in resurrection, or in anything else right now
except the need for tidiness. I rise and bin my bottle,
and walk away clutching my map of the dead
and my single long-stem rose, bypassing Gertrude and Oscar,
searching somewhere between Chopin's grave
and Proust's, for the Tomb of the Homesick Tourist,
open-doored, perhaps, as if ready to receive.

Robert Harris

The enthusiast

The brutal man
who angry with every heart
turned all his friends to enemies
and sought perfection everywhere
perfection could not either live or last,

who mocked and sneered and spoke and struck
all weaker things perpetually,
who strafed his wife and bombed his child
until his neighbours intervened

would stalk to his shed, his Ogre's lair
peopled with compliant tools

to conduct the harping saw through wood,
with fifing chisel define the joint,
then urge the odd, dull rustle of the plane
to level and clean like several
violins.

Riding over Belmore Park

Riding across the town in a dirty carriage
to read at the library Modern Jewish Poets
I thought of last war's troops in rain at Central,
then the junkies of a decade ago. Men younger

than I am have died for allowing moonlight
to rest on a button. A few have followed
by serum hep., some went ga-ga tripping
& stayed that way, but none of this happened often.

Enough to sense empty chairs on rare occasion,
enough to long for McAuley's baroque sarcasm
to flay alike counsel to rebel, and the nuclear lobby.

What do the Jewish Moderns say
to someone as well dressed as I am?
The vile rooms are not far. I survived them.

Tambaroora remembers

for Henry Lawson

The wind blew him south, on a day like this,
here to the Come-and-find-it Flats
'with Ballarat Adolphus and a mate of Ballarat's'.

I read him again and thought of them
arriving, just as the day closed …

It shook me when the shades who passed
laid down a dusty quid.
The timber-getter's hands which worked on
while he slept. I've met men who had
round shoulders from starting work at thirteen,
humping sacks in a granary,
or who've had nervous breakdowns building Fords.
It's part of the job in Completely-Knocked-Down,
an initiation that comes back
in lessening cycles.
These reasons can find their triumphant redress,
a skill at golf,
a clutch of good-looking daughters,
or resolve will sparkles into a word like *musician*
for some orange-peeling nine year old.
To cry onto laminex out of fatigue
at fifteen is wrong, but it may help forty
to shift a fridge more nimbly.
There are imageries as there are silences
too ready to honour these subjects,
I live and I am glad to live
where the cartons hold either milk or ammunition,
where the rites of indignation
or origin as a bygone amniosis
suffice no internal *émigré*. Also
there's half a lifetime or more
in the secular, classless state
of a certain response, a tinge of expectation
like the mad little smile that poets see
from time to time. Did Lawson
see it? Inevitably.

He spoke for the truly dumb.
Those ministers had chased away
or towns surrendered on a whim.
He well knew how push comes down to shove
and hung upon the keenest pegs of feeling
ungainly human love.

Tonight a vanished town has rejoiced
though I was alone here, reading.
Carved lamb, brought logs, put out her best
to remember the episode.
A day the weather was in the west
and the wind's feet in the north.

Rod Moran

LEADERS

Some will arrive there on the steel flat sea.
Black barges of calculated iron
will unload by moon-light the common troops:
their leader will be a proud just Lion.

Still others will spin down the lunar air
of politics, sounding shrill words of peace.
In smart cafés by wine-light they will sell
kind schemes: their loved leader will be a Thief.

And the keen Liar will invade by ruse
the full hearts of the grim well-intentioned,
as they clamour for the Lion's good might,
ignoring all the Thief never mentioned.

Liar and Thief and the proud just Lion
will construct their usual walls and wire:
the Liar will govern, the Lion stalk,
the Thief will cruelly mock the buyer.

THREE STUDENTS AT THE UNIVERSITY INVOKE BILLY GRAHAM

In the precincts of imperfect knowledge,
three students invoke Billy Graham.
A cassette preaches upwards at pure light.
They understand this stipple of sun
as God's thumbprint on the day's warm season;
wonder at the finches that pirouette,
mad and shrill on these high thin stems,
as the birds-that-God-built.
There is for them no wonder self-sufficient,
no beauty minus the drafting marks
of smart Design, Divine and Nifty Whim.
Billy's voice climbs upwards,
lost in the static of the highest boughs.

Chris Mansell

Amelia Earhart flies out from Lae, New Guinea

there are no gods
you can please yourself
what rivers you rush up and down on
what roads you ignore
what patch or rift of landscape
you choose to fly over

but remember this
you cannot choose whether
to stay or fly

the inevitable path
has you to fetch
and your wings will stick
in some tacked-down horizon
somewhere

     Fly out Amelia!
from my old town
Fly out! from its fecund green green green
from the red green red green brown
of the Flame Flower lianas.
Fly from the Poinsettia leaves
Fly from the bluer blue sea
where the earth falls off
where the water pushes
and pulls at your unconscious feet
blue at the horizon
     Amelia. This premonition
Take care you do not
wedge your craft
in this interstitial depth

    *   *   *

We have waited for years
It has always been so.
To wait with the embroidery in the lap
To grow big bosomed and comfortable
To grow mild and stupid
and happy.

Waiting for your return
as if you were a man
or a dream
has a certain helpless futile charm

we are locked with our eyes
to that horizon—
Did you fly over Salamaua
or perhaps Finschafen?
What part of the map
what sector of the sky
should we watch

As we stand on the black sand beach
imagine your flight
straight ahead
over the isthmus Salamaua
string of sand
can't imagine the gun emplacements
there yet

The waves cannon down
on the open side and lap the lee edge
of the bay
and coral fish
dip their snouts
into the rusted struts
of the ship *Tanya Maru*

We watched it twenty years
slowly slipping off the edge
of the reef

One morning it was gone
we hadn't noticed it go
it was suddenly an absence

It's been more than forty years
the women wait
Amelia

Kevin Hart

PASCAL

Mathematics to Religion in twenty years—

a record for any age, always aware
of both sides, he balanced like the smile
on his own face, forever ready to
collapse in pain or laughter.
'I want to show you a *new* abyss,' he cried.

No one looked up. One by one he raised
their eyes, but as they stared their smiles

were afraid of him and what they saw—
an attic floor covered with Euclid, proven
and by an unread boy at night.

A life of brilliance awaited him:
stars withdrew to order at his glance,
the world slowly unfolded itself—
its fine print showed him patterns, laws.
He smiled—and then—divided life in two,

quivered like the edge of a flag,
confessed mortality, started his search
for God, Embracer of Contradictions.
It was no good. He had long retired
behind His eager henchman, Death.

What could be done? Logic moved back.
He wagered with God, and lost—quickened
a life of thought that did not please,
died begging a priest to give him peace:
he thrust his forty years behind him

as a man builds a wall and then jumps over it.

GYPSOPHILA

Another day with nothing to say for itself—,
gypsophila on the table, a child's breath
when breath is all it has to name the world

and therefore has no world. It must be made:
her shadow sleeping on the wall, the rain
that pins fat clouds to earth all afternoon,

a river playing down the piano's scales.
This is the strangest of all possible worlds
with foam upon the beach, the sea's dead skin,

and lightning quietly resting in each eye.
Like gypsy camps or love, it must be made,
undone, then made again, like the chill rain

that falls without hope of climbing back,
content to leave its mark, for what it is,
upon the window or in the child's mind.

Gypsophila on the table, rain outside,
the child will tune the world to her desire
and make another world to keep in mind:

these breaths of air in which we softly wrap
the rain's glass stems to let them fall again
in sunlight, or flower for ever in the mind.

A world of things with nothing at all to say,
a margin that absorbs our silences:
the child must take the lightning from her eye

and place it in the sky, her shadow must
be told to fall asleep. This strangest world
in which we say *Gypsophila, Baby's breath*—

Reading at evening

The day is heavy, dragged down by the sun
that looks into each window one last time
and finds old air now aching with the heat,

the windows becoming mirrors, and a clock
still hedging its bets, pointing this way and that.
Soon nothing but darkness outside, as though the day

disclosed its one assumption at the end
when there's no time to argue about truth,
no common ground for talk, as with a man

who finds the standard metre slightly short.
The house stands still and cracks its swollen joints.
There is a volume open on the desk

and inside proofs that books do not exist;
you sit it on your knees, its argument
a cat's eyes piercing the liquid evening,

possessing a knowledge difficult to grasp
as though it rested just behind the page,
upon the silence before you touched the book.

The cat is sleeping on the cool verandah
where a full moon looks down, boiled white as bone,
now perfectly round, chastised all yesterday

in Paris by the standard metre that rests
bathed in blue light, immaculate in glass,
a powerful relic of a martyred saint.

The book continues, brilliant to the end,
and then, at midnight, the clock adds its applause.
Outside, the cat is chasing its own tail.

Shane McCauley

CHIN SHENT'AN'S HAPPY MOMENTS

He had the audacity and fortune
To list thirty-three of them. A veritable
Inner furnace to huddle around
During the rainy season; the only
Problem was to decide how much of any
Experience was material, how much spiritual.
Chin listed a friend's arrival after
A decade's absence, the planting of banana trees,
Explosion of fireworks, descent of snow,
The sharp knife slicing the greenest
Water melon, release of a captive wasp,
And twenty-seven more experiences
To recall in cold moments when
Low grey clouds bearded with rain
Appear some mimicry of the heart.
From his articles he extracted and
Refined an essence called happiness,
The long dance of spirit with the senses.
When death approached he wishes to see
A broken kite-string, and eat some honey.

Dorothy Porter

MY MOTHER

My mother is a politician

and a good one

she loves power
she loves paper-work

that edge
that knot in her lip
   can send a scribe
      or general
         to the pot
            with a griping gut!

my father plays
   in his inoffensive way
with his health
   or his harem

Mummy plays
　　with gods
Mummy frightens
　　iron.

GOD-WATCHING

I watch the morning ritual
of Thoth, the sacred ibis.

He grooms his feathers
with his fussing hook beak
then shits
with a quick squirt
on a library of papyrus.

Strange behaviour
for the god of scribes!

DAWN

The full moon
in a blank sky

I itch
with lightness

then a blood ball rises
over the cowed rocks

Aten looks at Himself
in the moon

and smashes it.

TONY'S CHARM

Tony is charming
and comfortable

his poems are depressed
like sleeping pills

I got to page three
of his *Selected*

but Tony's generous
with his time

he talks about Mickey
with laid-back affection

'A nice kid'
he says

'her poetry was awful
but she was a nice kid'

we light up
in chummy silence

'a really nice kid'
he sucks down
    a deep drag

'I haven't seen her for months'

his hands lie still
and bland

'not for months.'

TONY'S COMPANY

Tony's voice
is a lullaby Mogadon

but he likes a joke

we snigger through
my time
in the poetry scene

but even
with the passionfruit smell
of a Brisbane night

Tony's company
is hard cold work

like defrosting fridge.

FRANGIPANI

I thought poets
were broke

Tony's house
is high and airy

the breeze carries
frangipani from the garden

from his long verandah
he can watch the Brisbane River

does he sit sipping his tea
in some fragrant twilight

and write
his miserable poetry?

Adrian Caesar

Accents

In Lancashire my vowels were fettled.
From Mancunian carpenters and Irish farmers
my tongue is broad, grooved and furrowed—
I call a spade a bloody shovel
spit tanners when I'm thirsty
and from me mam learnt
cross-eyed people sken like whelks
and those who have no guts
are easily could or cowed are nesh,
and if you die you go to Dicky's medder.
        At university down south
answering cut-glass questions
on Matthew Arnold's misery
my prof said, 'of course, dear boy, these days
an accent like yours is all the rage.'
I wished the proper girls agreed
and heard the high-pitched tinkle of
their scorn at my slow invitations
to the dance as if they swallowed
perfect sound with mother's milk
so from their lips could only issue
the music of the filthy rich.
        I left it in the early days
of rot and unemployment
Mrs Thatcher laying waste
with perfect elocution
to health and education
whilst the inner cities sweated
there was blood on the streets
and shouting in accents
I could recognise.
I knew which side I should be on
but flinging bricks at coppers
was not my scene—
between culture and anarchy
what escape?
        So to Australia where I met a girl
who liked my thick-voiced mumblings
of love and lovin'
as our tongues touched
and others too were generous
though for some I was still the enemy—
playing the wrong games
my voice a rep for Empire

'you're a sour faced Pom' I heard one scream,
and another on first acquaintance
'about the accent
you'll have to do something with that
you need to become a real Aussie fella
there's nothing finer on earth' she spat.
I couldn't imagine she meant
I should be black
and so I've tried to work on G'day, fair dinkum
flat out like a lizard drinkin
no worries mate and she's right
but now I've nearly mastered these
I'm three times out of fashion
I should be Greek, Slav or Italian.
So I like my vowels best
dancing on this democratic page
where they aim to partner yours
whose accent idiom origin don't matter
as long as you'll allow
that my tongue was branded in Lancashire
though now it wags and plays its games
between invented nations.

Uneven tenor

Sometimes you think how lucky they are
to have the kind of gift that others love
but after the applause, encore,
the singer must pack his props
wipe off the smiles and tears
go home to face the ordinary music,
while those who have clapped and cheered
take home their perfect images and sounds
to grace lives with the illusion
of something, someone, extraordinary.
They do not spare a thought
for his family dealing with tantrums,
the ego massive as his belly,
matched only by fears
of losing voice or worse
of losing fame.
He stuffs himself for comfort
dreams of being slim, but vanity
enables him to ladle charm
that persuades his wife each day
to iron the handkerchief
she folds into his pocket
to prop Otello, Rodolpho, Radames,

and after the high notes
he thinks of her when in the dressing room
he blows his nose and blots the tears
of a cuddly crocodile.

Philip Harvey

THE FICTION EXPLAINS THE FACT

This year the bicycle ducked past the gelignite of incendiaries, the
    napalm
From choppers left Bambra Road and Bealiba Road like outer Hanoi.
You had to deliver main evidence through enemy lines without
    detection,
Snipers and tacticals at every mailbox, but you always made it to the
    front gate.
Home from school there was chemist round, countless bottles of the
    enigmatical Linctus
For housebounds with manners, and Mrs Rubinstein with her secret
    five-dollar tip.
Dinner would be grace, the adults first, speak your turn and pronounce
    it well—
Views from the father's end on absurdities of archdeacons, the villainies
    of Liberals,
Questions from the mother's end on what your friend had said, and
    how are the greens.
Evening might be basketball, an hour of the past participle in French,
A session on the backstep polishing cadet brass, an experimental
    cigarette in the woodshed.
And if sleep was still that slide into the otherworld you could not
    explain
Then still, it was safe, and you would not die, and the moonlit garden
    was still.
Waking was more ugly blackheads, the same tensing shower, the same
    navy blue uniform,
And the back streets on your bicycle were just the first dull class of the
    day.
Caspar the Friendly Ghost, Kanga, Wingnut, the Skull, Smiley and
    Poofter—
If the teachers didn't fire, at least some knowledge you barely noticed
    took root.

Peter Rose

Imagining the Inappropriate

Not exactly difficult after a day
spent outfacing dyslexia, consoling
Brahmins in their shag-piled bunkers,
central heating syruping laments.

Kind of the novelist
to descant in Cornish journals
on Vision in the Flinders Ranges;
sweet of the expatriate
to proffer a triolet;
admirable of the Czech soprano
to bare her Butterfly in Narrabri;
oracular of Oscar to civilize
such a turd-shaped continent;
always hilarious when Tarkovsky
and Truffaut send us their cameos.

But why New South Wales in the first place,
for God's sake?
Why am I writing this in Croydon,
in a city named after
an impotent prime minister?
Why does that median strip over there
commemorate a dead mayor?
Why is it that only our rivers run real?
How do we manage to keep a straight face
under this Ruritanian lace?

Imagine waking in astoundment's land,
the ungazetted paradise,
kingless, ruleless, griefless, anthemless,
whose only currency lurks
at the bottom of a lake
and is therefore unattainable,
where the libraries are our legislatures,
cavatinas our major export,
euphorics firing dogma.

Name me a republic
rousing and ringing
as a coital cry,
whose vivid flora
no colonizing nose
has penetrated.

TRUE CONFESSIONS

Unversed in Latin,
incapable of Greek,
Kant for me a clausal blur
never ceasing to haunt,
like mystic Russia
and Lord Elgin's marbles,
I am profoundly ignorant
of Hinduism, and deeply fazed
when the subject of Australian wines
is raised, as it often is
during sophisticated dinners.
Like Candide's hapless spinners
or Hulot in Guermantes
I lack the front.
Asked to spell metempsychosis
I blush; hounded for the right
meteorological term for
a squeamish genus of cloud
(even, absurdly,
what makes the sky blue)
I would doubtless fail
any Mastermind audition.
As for childhood,
it never ceases to amaze that
when Mozart wrote lovesick arias
I was more absorbed
in penile heavens.
I am not Björn Borg,
nor alas was meant to be.

THE WALL

The great wall is universal.
The great wall is what you dream about,
Vast and sacred and amorphous.
The great wall is there for all of us to see,
To run our hands over,
To train vines and paint murals.
Graffiti mocks a buttress
And the great wall rides a tremor
Like a blond his seismic wave.
Built by mullocks to withstand attack
She is man's one great insurmountable fact,
Totem-sheer, moon-inane.
All through history they gathered here

To barbecue tough hairy juiceless boars.
They wiped their hands on leaves
Instead of napkins, but they too had
Their flasks and flans and prodigious sleeps.
Pasty-faced women snuck off behind a Blackboy
To gossip about this one's ostentatious pav.
The good went for intramural strolls, raving on.
This one set his sights on a raised rock
And found five black snakes sunning themselves.
How he ran and ran through the writhing gorge
Where idiots and mystagogues alike dangled
From trees. There was blossom too,
Pink and cherubic—ditto lovers,
Nature's unreconstituted lambs.
Too-imaginative youths convinced themselves
That a queer sunstreak engendered life.
Others, auto-didacts and -erotics,
Lost themselves in Teach Yourself books
Or Greatest Ever Novels.
Wondering how close they'd come
To leading interesting lives,
Those subliminal drifts through Lambinet.
An elderly couple took a rug,
Some even recklessly made love,
Sprawled beneath the desecrated arch
Where soot was already forming,
The very spot where centuries later
A child would be sacrificed,
Sacrificed and buried beneath
The great wall rank and universal,
The smeared, roseate, immitigable wall.

Dog days

for Gwen Harwood

After the blazoned festival,
the luminous photography,
the row of intelligent banners,
Chinese lanterns glowing
in their plane trees;
after the committees,
the televised rehearsal,
the tense unbibulous launch,
one window open only
on a city impossibly far:
it is with more than relief
that I walk an aged beagle,
my unliterary but truly

civilized friend, who
tolerates our sentimental
one-sided conversation,
veering on aromatic detours,
tugging at the dewy grass
like a class traitor.
Enervation too accompanies me,
pulling on its choker collar,
dogging me like a mal de flanc.
Hungry, needful in my own way,
I memorize faces of joggers
and strollers, young men
with first gingery moustaches,
tweaked by impertinent sisters;
marvel at the multiplicity of
children, the kaleidoscope
of human hair, lank, curly,
titian, punk-onyx. Only
an Indian boy, pigeon chest
pursing with fright, resists
the flirting of an aged beagle.
Then a phrase moving through
my heart, through my blood,
like one last slow rapture.
The exquisite Indians.
How it struck us simultaneously
as we sat in that bar years ago,
drinking beer after our crazy
cycle round the island.
The exquisite Indians.
Incantation of envy almost.
Around us belched and swaggered
Cowes's boozy youth, commercial
T-shirts bulging and stained.
No silk here. One glance,
and you left our window perch,
joined the couple posing their
grinning black-eyed children
against a war memorial,
offered to frame them,
clasped and bewildered,
against a vast immartial sea,
came bounding, buoyantly, back,
as if we could shed racial inanity
for a moment in that disco bar.
Now I am far from ocean,
far from strait, long separated
from that known blue whelm.
Gathering night will not ferry me

to some convivial harbour
for wine and fish and company.
It is retreat that I seek
in my urban, secular way,
following a concrete path
sorrelled for municipal tastes.
Around me, like a lethargic chorus
slow to assemble, a bar
too late for 'Va, pensiero',
unfurls the missioned blossom,
nature's sold-out epiphany.
Now only the budless witch-elm
drags its heels, gothic, misshapen
amid spring's muscular shield.
Like an extra I move through
groves of wattle fiery as
sharp pain, a beautiful migraine.
Disentangling olfactory dogs
I skirt the grey-haired women
in their tonish slacks,
give way to electric daughters
executing their power walk,
that absurdest strut in history.
But I'm not even watching,
or listening. The opera is over,
the point made and the Hebrews
gone home. Before I know it
I've reached the eucalypt
where I always turn—I'm not
sure why: habit, superstition,
predictable as a panting jogger
consulting his wrist, above all
sentimental about nature,
even this tenuous reserve
five minutes from a freeway.
But I'm not even drifting,
lost in a welled atavistic sleep
to renege on life. I remember
reaching this outermost gum,
bluish bourne of the known,
in a similar trance, bleak,
catatonic, chain-smoking
underneath it for an answer,
so intent on solitude
I rued the human dot slowly
dilating on the horizon.
Today it is an old beagle
waddling towards me,
discreet, wary, just smiling,

like a timid man visiting
a mentor of whom he's unsure—
victim of some wilful malady.
So I frisk her ears, dance about,
declaim the poems she fails to hear.
Now I'm like a West Highland
terrier let off its chain,
indulging in a moment's
boundless, futuristic dynamism—
except I long in my own way
for the faint impress of the collar,
the slow bruise of the familiar,
the sharp tug on the gnostic leash.

THE BEST OF FLEETWOOD MAC

The gulf between a mute, elementary
kitchen and the more garrulous
maisonette is so mandatory,
so legalistic, as to entice only choirs
of staring cats and matted kittens,
broodily attuned to dementia of plumbing,
like wizards of the waiting-room.
Across this torpid lantern-jawed strip
down which randy beams tilt
when you least expect,
the Best of Fleetwood Mac
winds down on its crusted track,
convulses like an urban journey,
as if some grave, dilating guitarist,
the Seneca of Woodstock, digits
and features crippled in surprise,
reckons with the Parousia of Marketing.
Now only the uxorious pigeon's
captious insight rides the novel air,
affronting limb-locked plane tress;
and a transcendental Spitfire
bombarding our sluttish suburb
with sachets of pink detergent.
But this is another century,
another kind of phoney war,
the politicians' noses powdered
on one side like fruity overtures.
When at last I am free to begin,
when I plug these dubious imaginings,
I find I have no appetite for laundry
or maundering—not as free as I thought.
What shall I do with this thing, this life?

Where shall I bury it, dragging
a recusant spine over terminal ice?
In the bright mauve curtainless cell
opposite mine, confronting it even
like a glib date capable of one lisped taunt,
a precocious Jewish boy, on holidays
from California, lambasts his adoring aunts,
listing all their mortal deficiencies:
trite coffee, falsetto chat,
fond talk at midnight through a wall.
Now and then, exploding their shy defences
like the brilliant attorney he aspires
to be, he consults my herby sill,
sane jury of thyme and fennel and marjoram,
to watch them batten on his rhetoric.

Judith Beveridge

MAKING PERFUME

So, that summer I picked everything:
the hibiscus that shut at six o'clock,
the white-pollened flower
I called the Baker's Daughter,
the yellow rose that lasted weeks beyond its season
and the great pale flower with a cold look—
Queen in the Tower.

Then I took some bottles from their cupboards
and their lids twirled off and their perfume
came three voices high in my head.
I lined them like wineglasses on the sill
and filled each with petals and water
and gave them keyboard names like
Chandelier and Tier on Golden Tier.

I remember how I lived that summer
in a room with a thousand windows in blue and green.
I'd stay out late to pick and soak the petals
and pour them into bottles and bury them in the earth
with a made-up name for a simple flower plus water.
Later, I'd wash and line the bottles on the sill
and read their labels until each one rang

a terrace of bells in my head.
I mourned the bottles I named for my heroines of hopeless love
and stood them in kitchentapwater
and stored them out of the light.

I dreamt of Balls, dinner roses,
a women gently naming herself to herself.

Now, I wonder whatever happened to Lavinia,
the Fourteen Nights, Ballet Blanc,
the fragrance in the blue twirled bottle
I named Pirouette.
Months later I probably poured them down the sink.

But no-one suspected that summer
why my eyes were suddenly circled with a dark pencil,
why my cheeks had the faint glow of day,
why I swished my skirts as I moved.

I kept the bottles with me, moved them about the room
vowed not to open them for seven years,
and named them after the girl kept at home
who never stopped saying as she stirred her pots:
'O, I wish, I wish, I wish … '

THE CATERPILLARS

On the headland to the lighthouse,
a brown detour of caterpillars
crimped end-to-end across the road.

Poke away the pilot and the line
would break up, rioting,
fingering for the scent.
Put him back, they'd straighten.
You could imagine them humming
their queue numbers.

I've only seen such blind following
in the patient, dull dole queues,
or old photos of the Doukhobors
the world's first march of naked people.

I watched over the line for hours
warding off birds whose wings, getting close,
were like the beating of spoons
in deep bowls. I put a finger to the ground
and soft prickles pushed over,
a warm chain of hair.

This strange sect, wrapped in the sun
like their one benefit blanket
marched in brotherhood and exile.

Later, a group of boys
(their junta-minds set on torture),
picked off the leader.
Each creature contorted,

shut into its tight burr.
I could only stand like a quiet picket
and watch the rough panic.

I remember them, those caterpillars,
pacifists following their vegetable passion—
lying down in the road and dying
when they could no longer touch each other.

S. K. Kelen

A TRAVELLER'S GUIDE TO THE EAST INDIES

1

To arrive anywhere tonight
you travel a road lit only by fireflies
to towns whose names really
mean 'tomb of a hundred martyrs'.
Invisible birds sing tinkling vowels
—words from a time
before history invaded.

Frogs roar louder and louder
kickstarting a generator.
Trees, pagoda, the moon
a shaking world in lagoon waters.

Beware the regiments of the kangaroo!
Progress follows without emission controls.
Across, say, the Banda Sea or clouded mountain ranges
a world lost for ten thousand years
soon adjusts to ghetto-blasters and minibuses.

Western airliners overhead: missiles
that deliver foreign exchange.
Banyan trees grow sideways through the air.
Shouts and shrieks of barter and cash
amplify in a packed bazaar.

Crowds ebb and swell, laughing.
Trays of trinkets, batiks, sweets, fruit
and vegetables all laid out on small grass mats.
Beggars harangue pointing at their children.

A legendary pickpocket, Dusk, splashes red over the sky.

2

In Sumatran cities transvestites caterwaul
after visitors' fair skin.
Bus races over cliffs are a diversion

most prefer to miss, likewise a tiger
loose in a longhouse
though if one wears the brass ring a shaman prescribes
a tiger's friendship is assured.
Indeed you'll be invited home to its lair
& there smoke pipes of jungle grass,
receive potent amulets as gifts.

Kalimantan monkeys and wildcats screech like brakes
before a crash. Honeybears and orang-outangs,
singing laments, carry giant lilies to hideaways
as all the forests are felled
so throw-away-teak-chopsticks
adorn Japanese bowls.

Whilst animist priests fill an earth station's dish
with rice, square rigged ships ply old spice routes.
On deck, gladly corrupted sailors swig arak
and drunk as baboons on durians their minds
swim off to the Roaring Forties.

Gig Ryan

ALREADY

You're back from Melbourne
and already sadness floors you.
Belief flows out, his face deadlocked
and your friends playing Largactyl-piano
to the orange empty lookout street.
It doesn't seem like an occasion, or war in Poland,
it's just Enmore
and a man falls down the steps.
The waterfront is on strike
and our useless fuel blows the house out.
The more you talk the more vacuous it gets,
as I walk away from the conversation
like a soul
slipping out of death.

I have deliberately made my brain smaller,
but the cliff is free.
From the plane, clouds on an invisible shield
spread to their horizon, then curve.
I wake up like a soldier,
and fire. I have deliberately made my mind blank
for you to talk to, and now between sweetness and revolt
my mouth is hurting on your skin
and means dying.

Poem

The day is beautiful
He doesn't love me
Pieces of me fly in formation
across the sky's blue lung
Clouds of white hope
the beautiful afternoon
drifts like childhood
The green and yellow trees
fountain over you
Vines of memory
your rubbed face
Cars come home from work
The day is beautiful
its white christening shawl
its winding cloth

Rent

1

Always, he manages to weed around to sex
I mean it doesn't matter if we start on work
or books or sport
or the contemplative jog he gets from presenting
what to me is fuel
He pushes another port across
This time it's the barmaid
Yesterday it was the astringency of souls
I chip in, trying to imagine liking anyone

2

To loosen up and, for a change, be social
I throw it back
It's sort of an advance in that you talk
or argue more like
He orbits, and after the joint you're poleaxed to the chair
Though he's letting down his blue face, it's no fun
compared to what you wanted, a gem a heap

Anthony Lawrence

GOANNA

I was standing outside the killing shed,
ankle deep in skulls that knock and roll when you kick them.
I was thinking about the way a sheep dies,
the knife in behind the wind-pipe, the head
snapped back over the knee,
when a black goanna ran up my back
and fixed its claws into my neck.
Its tongue was flicking in my ear.
I screamed and reached behind me,
trying to lift its claws from my skin.
The sharp pain, the fear, the way a sheep dies.

SOOTY OYSTERCATCHERS, VENUS TUSK FISH

A pair of sooty oystercatchers are probing
an oyster-blistered mantle of exposed reef
with their red beakspikes. I've found it's
often best to wait a few days before turning
such things into poetry, but the accurate
wading and stabbing of the birds demands
immediate attention.
            After they'd gone,
in a shallow pool flushed by a rising tide
I discovered, like a piscatorial arrowhead
blunted by refraction, the bleaching frame
of a Venus tusk fish. Its parrot beak
had been worn smooth by the waves, or more
probably, by the oystercatcher's nervous hammering.
            So I record this now to get things
absolutely right; to contain observation's
fine-winged mariposa, monogrammed into a rock
pool's black plumage of diminishing shadows—
the birds' departure, the arrangement
of white bones in a magnified frame.

I scatter a handful of tusk-fish scales on the wind.
First they are like small cloudy windows,
then a flock of distant birds turning side-on
into the sun. Each scale has a blue and orange
mandala at its centre: the dark-hued,
slime-protected watermarks of death.

Sarah Day

Apple

You offer me an apple.
In your language, the word resonates
a difference—mellow, moribund,
earthen. *Apple*, in mine it's crisp.
One thinks of Newton,
mass plummeting
that's sprung from tree, leaf,
branching into ether, fingering space.
I think of a green, hard surface,
resistance sheer like water's thin skin.
It is late Spring. Autumn at home.
Windfalls will be strewn
worm-pecked; pale bellies
already loaming in grass. In towns
the waste, fermenting on pavements.
Three seasons here since apple time.
You select from the store
and give. Proud, resourceful.

This loose, sack-shrunk mammary
brown-skinned, empty
is not what I fancied.
Crumpled, dried old flower.
You would eat it?
Apparently. You peel its rough contracted skin,
I think of an old face;
the flesh beneath is white,
concentrated, sweet; paring back
to what was always vigorous and there.
Locked in an old body.
First expression, carried through a lifetime.
Sweet flesh and the star
pattern of the kernel,
nursing five ideas of apple trees.

Chaos

Ovid was wrong. Chaos is no
unordered mass except for those
in its welter. It is hard to see the pattern
when you are the lines that construct

or the lemniscate you are riding.
The abyss, for example, could not be louder

than in this room. Strapped to this chair,
I'm at the epicentre of chaos,
now, before the currents bolt.
But if you are on the outside
counting away my clanging seconds,
champagne corked, it's all clear;
killer of wives, children, mothers—
Presto! Order has commenced, is restored.
Chaos Ovid, is frigid, calculated
as this inert combination of hot wires.
As my hand with a knife raised.
As my mind on most days.
It's only mad, confusing at the centre.

You are the yellow soup
in the chrysalis, awaiting a miracle;
blind faith and caterpillar memory
and no foresight. No distance to view
the alchemy from which the moth swims,
substance from will. Etched wing forms
folded inchoate in ether, are unseen;
you have no eyes. Process has no eyes.
The confusion is the caterpillar's
as it must have been the earth's.

Deep in primordial swamp
in the blackening peat-bog,
ideas lie enfolded, reversed fossils
of forests, cities, people.
Turn on your TV news,
suspend history a moment on the screen;
the present's an impasse of doubt, a koan,
but today's riddles unwound yesterday.
Model of absurdness, the centre,
the subatomic paradox, thoughts turn
at a distance into this chair, this floor,
me. A dead hyacinth, a dry gourd—
viewed too close, autumn's over the hill,
a mockery of summer. Those who saw
the first autumn must have seen
the end of everything.
On yesterday's news there's a semblance
of shape, coherence,
design is impossible to argue
on the greens of killing fields.
People are the evidence that of time,
distance, order is born
though in stepping back to view
the choreography, a foot may whirl
into the gyre of a madder dance.

IMPERIUM ROMANUM

Here's the culmination of genius and law
languid on the shore of the glittering Mediterranean,
a fresco of athletes, trumpeters and modern gladiators,
towels rippling like togas in late Siena light.
These legendary bodies spawned the globe;
men of vision and invention, the great civilisers.
There is majesty now, grand indifference to dissolution
that Trajan not divine his world in tatters
and his company still swim like Neptunes
through a sea of plastic bags and excrement;
that leaden waves still slap the littered sand.
Like the tableaux fading to oblivion in dusty streets
and on church walls, it is hard not to see this posturing
as allegory and visualise the short-lived swordfish
rise and sink on the horizon, one last time.

Paul Hetherington

RESONANCES

Caught in the process
of observing the day—
each leaf, it seems,
separate and conspicuous—

the articulate earth,
the resonance of what we do not see
but which informs us,
writing our existences,

I am at a loss with words,
full of a sense of place,
like a child exploring a garden,
finding the fallen berries,

the hard green apples,
the yellow lime still sour,
like disappointment,
the unfolding scarlet flower.

FARMING

A farm and creek, tussocks, sleety rain
that curtains the barn with silver-grey, the smell
of seepage in old timber, blackberry spills

that scramble across pocked water during squalls,
the slow falling of light, and insect shrill.

And then your gestures, gathered during tea
on the long verandah, hands that sketch and scrawl
air eddying from stone, frame old hills
crowding our distance. Your family comes here
in looping phrases, benign now, generous

in anecdote as they were not in life,
their failings sympathetic. Then your laugh
startles me from your narrative, we stand
on the undulating ground of sentences
brisk with ideas, with dig and heft and fall.

Kathleen Stewart

LITTLE THINGS

When you go inside someone else's house
and things
small and practical
have changed
it is sad.
Strange sadness that wishes for eternity
as if that would take the cake.

Can a somebody be jealous of moving things
as if they rubbed hips
as if each move and addition
were some traitorous kiss?

Little thing, plant, tin or spoon,
I envy your belonging.
Move, tiny objects,
dance, cup, bowl and spoon.
We are dying around you.

ANOTHER DEAD POET

Broken first heart, then spirit, then mind.
'And I am not a genius,' he said, quite sad.
Broke his head open, fried his brain,
then said, 'It's gone quite bad.' By then, it had.

They let him leave his bed, clutching a paper bag.
'Drop pill after pill if you will be well,' they said.
Sprinkling a path through the maze of his head.
'They've pointed the bone,' he said. They had.

Lionel G. Fogarty

FRISKY POEM AND RISKY

Regarding respects I'm fully
purchased within my own
exchanges
Please give my regards to our
God down and above
I would also like more spirits
so the list can be send
Before receiving your hearing
I had to write to a conference
Sincerely I'm yours against
all evil co-ordinators
I decided from myself stems
a meaning and a creation
The prices I payed in every
eye ear and tongue will
wish they gave the correct addresses
My project have been pulsed
by blacks, and repriced
rejected too personally politically
This document I place, will be
the birth shown
A division by me is true
of knowledge in poetry
I've got history information
My date rave into sane real
I am amended then lended
Are you prepared for the
Nee Nee who died
I anticipated my pissed mind
I wish to withdraw all
my poems from the
building and put in the
open spaces.
As for gardens of me growing
out to another country
I may do honestly
My heart ain't pure love
My brain ain't poison daze
Ngunda Bimiai spoke the message.
All I did was draw this.
All I did was pass on
But one thing they gave me
is my own selfing self.

Farewell reverberated vault of detentions

Today up home my people are
indeedly beautifully smiling
for the devil's sweeten words are
gone.
Today my people are quenching
the waters of rivers without grog
Today my people are eating delicious
rare food of long ago.
Tonight a fire is made round
for a dance of leisuring enjoyment
where no violence fights stirs.
Certainly my people are god given
a birthright of wise men and women
Our country is still our Motherland
Our desires ain't dying in pitifully
lusting over contempt and condition
Tonight my peoples sleep
without a tang of fear
No paralysed minds
No numbed bodies
No pierced hearts hurt
The screams of madness ends
The madly stretched endurance
are resisted with Murri faith
The enchantingly lonely
pains by white constipations
are pushed gaped nailed by
our emerging loves for
primitive's potentials.
Tonight overturned hells
brang surface innocent olds
Tonight my people don't wait
for successions of society
But yell, sing the souls to
our endless dreaming
Today my people have a Murri
Thirtieth century culture
but with care safe and snarls
Today my people feel precious as
human beings burials and birth
Mankind demands imperative love
for all, And my people never
wants to escalating barbarous century.
For now Today up home they free;
Tonight they learn to fight consciences.

Philip Hodgins

CATHARSIS

Beyond incorrigible death, childhood's small killings
are still there blinking up at me as I hoisted the bale
of hay. All a tabby mother's love and cunning were
undone by the necessity of feeding out. I counted seven.
Their softness began to stir as I took them away
from the haystack's labyrinth. They caught on my jumper
like roses. Behind the machinery shed I plunged
their new warmth into a bucket and watched tiny bubbles
escape from the paralysed struggle. Two minutes expired.
They came out cold and bony. I put them in a sack
and threw it in the dam and watched it sink.
Today it floated to the surface.

APOLOGIES

I'm sorry.
Because it's only possible
to think in clichés
when the end is really nigh
there won't be any standing back
to write like no one else.
Because it's really happening. The symptoms
wouldn't lie. The headaches,
sweating, swellings, loss of sight:
I'll hate this death
because it gives the meaning back
to words I never thought I'd have to use.
I can't explain. The words
are plain, the images obvious—
'This was the last work. Notice the crows.'

That's the way the symptoms really are—
not the body sending first calls now
and last calls now
but two married people
sitting in a hospital corridor
gazing down the length of sorrow.
Their only child will not bury them.
I must tell them how sorry I am.

Sant'Ivo della Sapienza

No square pegs or round holes here—
everything goes.
The corners of the hexagon
are jutting like reversed wings
of fighter planes from the next century
but they go back in design
to Hadrian's *Teatro Marittimo*
while the ground plan goes shrinkingly
up to the top of the dome.
Somewhere in between there's space
so thick and unified it's rabbit-proof.
Such an organism makes me think of flowers
and bees, or at my worst a cog.
Either way, as autonomy it changes to the carapace
where, without a change of style,
a Babel ziggurat is drilling Eastern air
and pyrotechnics are really conch.
On top of that, like its human counterpart,
the cross on dove on globe on cage miracle
is a balancing trick prolonged by believing.
But, disappointingly, even here
death has got past the caretaker
to discredit Borromini's biographies.
This delicate unity is an acceptance
whose membrane needs another coat of white.
In the final composition
all eyes are turned up
and the ribs are showing through.
Is this the dilatation of wisdom
or is it the fabulous triple echo?

The rabbit trap

So tense and yet it doesn't mind waiting,
sometimes for years: a quiet disused track
becoming in an instant the theatre
of sharp loud pain, of ready rusty teeth
embedded in the foot of some bushwalker
who never hurt another living thing.

So crude and yet it tricks the nimblest creatures,
jumping shut before instinct or reflexes
can swerve the victim from its struggling death,
and making no distinction between the one
intended animal and all the others;
the different species caught in this debate.

So fast and yet it takes the longest time
of any butcher's steel to do its job—
the sufferer might hang on for days

not knowing if the counting heart will stop
or if the smell of human predator
will come to bring the process up to date.

So sensitive and yet it is unfeeling,
always reacting badly to the slightest
pressure on the blood-stained centre plate,
the stage where little tragedies are played out
while back in some warm spot the mother's young
stare out as the world closes in on them.

Richard Allen

A GERMAN CHRISTMAS

Germany is a grey place with many factories.
Villages look like towns even when they're small.
In the beerhall where Hitler began his putsch
I remembered Bismarck & Weltpolitik & Lebensraum
& graveyards with famous names like Auschwitz & Belsen.

There was a rabbit in the snow of the Hofgarten
& when on Christmas eve I was jogging
& got lost on the far side of the forest
& gestured to a young cyclist
He accompanied me all the way home.

Some say the language is ugly
I say it depends who is speaking.

THE THOROUGHLY MODERN POEM

is a jug to be filled
a mouth to be fed
a closet to hide
the bones

a canvas unpainted
an instrument unplayed
a weapon ready
to kill

the thoroughly modern poem
ready aim fire

*T*WINS

two beautiful athletes
life and death
are racing
one another
soon enough
one will cross the line

Luke Davies

*A*ZARIA SONNET

> ' … and the Beasts of the Wild shall
> render asunder the Limbs of the Babes
> of the Earth … '
> Anastomosis III, iv

To join a religion like a Book Club …
unstable, but not beyond the sane.
To submerge in the poetry of codas—
'Go get thee run over by a train … '
How much hidden meaning do we act on?
National parks imbued with a wrathful God;
the knee-length-socks-Bermuda-shorts religion
treads outback where the Butcher-King has trod.

She stands ice-cold for the Twelve Tribes of Gosford,
her faith shall be the Bastion of Bland.
'Oh let thy people judge; be they struck down,'
(a non-prophetic husband takes the stand:
and the ghost of the enigmatic and amazing
Technicolor bibcoat stalks the barbecue-pit land.)

*T*RAINS

Everything I expected Vienna to be:
meat pies by choice rather than necessity.
The trains still came, as if all was expected
to go on as normal. Platform One was
the Hitler Express (with the distortion of memory
we smile a little and pretend they could have survived).
Platform Two the Red Star Special. The rubble
of the old world, Herr Hofenstahl, ah the money
greases notches in the bank balance now.
And at dawn each day from Moscow: everybody
knows it as the Emigrant Train. A journey to the fringe

of the world they've left behind; for us it's a new start
too. A change of money, change of engines, this
one brings a dining car. Three hours to Budapest.
Punished for not knowing which side they were on—
and always the railways were destroyed. The wide
Hungarian plains: once Alaric the Visigoth, banner
a black crow fluttering through the smoke and blood,
scared the wits, the daylights, the shit out of everyone.
But the railways outgrew the financiers who conceived them.
Budapest Station: 'Hot Dog', 'Bufé', 'Espresso'.
His eyes shifted, nervous. The camera makes it worse.
On Platform Eighteen, the busiest, I sold the daily papers
    from a booth.
And so we make for the terminus. Constantinople, always the
city of my dreams, and in slow motion dreams
the huge frothing engine crashes through the walls of the
Hagia Sophia. Mayhem all over like the Mosque at el-Aqsa
when Tancred and the Knights Templar burst in playing
choo-choos for the Lord, eternal salvation the prize.
I dreamed so much of trains, it must have meant they meant
    something immense.
The way the world would go, I guess. And on the busiest
    platform
I sold them all the news, or types of it. Eight years old,
I cried when they shot up the Commodore Hotel,
shoddy heroic palace of Beirut. Is there really a placed called
    Stamboul?
Trains, always trains. In the lobby of the Commodore an
    alcoholic journalist
ignores the parrot Coco mimicking the whistles of incoming.
    The telex
goes *click-click* just as the trains *chug-chug*: that's how we
    learn of Death.

John Kinsella

COUNTERPOINT

Counterpointing the death of twenty-eight
parrots so named because their call comes
twenty-eight twenty-eight twenty-eight
which is seven on three times a scatter gun's
twelve-gauge call, dumped by the boxful
four days into the new year and awaiting
the bull-dozer's shadowy blade. Maybe

they hung thickly about a farmer's fruit trees,
maybe they sported under the sprinkler
on his only patch of green lawn. Maybe.

ℒINKS

Every separation is a link ...
    Simone Weil

I
There are days when the world
buckles under the sun, trees blacken
to thin wisps, spinifex fires,
and white cockatoos, strangled
in telegraph wire, hang
dry and upside down.

II
I think only of thirst.
The drifting sand does not
lend itself to description,
the sketchy border trees
offer little protection
from the sun as we negotiate
the edge and fine line
between sand and vegetation.

III
I have always lived by the sea,
or travelling underground, have always
been concerned with water—the flooding
of mines, rain in dark forests,
the level of the tide.

IV
To see a waterbird, maybe a crane,
fly deep into desert, comes as no
surprise—we note its arrival and follow
its disappearance, discuss it over a beer,
and think nothing more of it.

V
And nights, contracting into cool winds,
when the sand becomes an astrolabe to the stars,
where in the reflection of the crystal spheres
we wander without direction, searching out
water flowers ...

The myth of the grave

I
A pair of painted quails
scurries across the quills of stubble
a flurry of rapid
eye movement

they shadow my walk
ostentatiously
lifting and dropping
into invisible alleyways

reaching the grave
I turn to catch them
curving back, stopped
by the windrows

the grave is a magnet
that switches polarity
when you reach it.

II
The epitaph is measured
by the size of the plaque,
or is it the plaque that's
measured by the epitaph?

It seems to matter.
Death becomes a question
of economy—the lavish are big
on ceremony, slight on prayer.

III
At a distance
sheep leave salt-licks
beside a dam and zig-zag
down towards the shade.

Grey gums bend with the tide
of the breeze, the midday sun
would carry their doubles
to the grave and fill the urns.

The ground dries and crumbles,
a lizard darts out of a crack
and races across the paddock.
Do ashes rest easily here?

IV

A fresh grave that holds three
generations is something you question
on a first encounter. How in life
would they have felt about sharing

a single room in a shoebox flat?
Maybe, at an instant, only one soul
is resident, the others entering the bodies
of quails, exploring the wastes of stubble.

Lisa Jacobson

FLIGHT PATH

that's my father
high up there
in his light
and improbable
sky machine
looking for clouds
small enough
to fly in

when I was
much younger
and knew
everything and nothing
of the world
he navigated me
around our nu-brick block
beneath the blazing
Sunday sun
then brought us
safely home

later when the girl
had changed her shape
so that it leant and curved
into herself more boldly
he moved in crisp formation with me
down the aisle
my hands
champagned with roses
my dress
white as cumulus
towards a man
whose love is constant

as a flight path
—and there unfathered me

these are still
the dazzling days
of lift off point and counterpoint
as father-daughter-husband
shift the angles
of their separate flights
from wing to wing
and dip and fall
but never
disappear

Tracy Ryan

ℐN THE FIRST PLACE

In the first place was something other than this.
I know that, though I couldn't tell you
where the first place was.

It was somewhere between the fur and
looking slightly ridiculous
with our sleek skin on

or perhaps even earlier.
I wish, I wish I could remember
the way back there.

The trees, the earth, look familiar.
They call me back to before
we got separated.

I want to lie down beneath them
become what I was in the first place
in the first place where we knew how to

mate and die without talking
of love because
love was obvious

love the first time and the first place.

Judith Bishop

Passage of winter precluded; or, death imagined

Then it seemed a white angel
crossed your breath; your voice unhusked,
grain by grain it grew visible.
Paused lucid by the garden bath,
the angel drew sharp breath;
pinched between grasses,
its voice grew thin and low.
The roots of common weeds,
upturned, dried from morning
into winter.

I neither dared look down, nor back:
for then it drew the earth about it;
water, and teeming soil;
shadowed in flight the waters of Land's End,
their foetal love of a globe
flat as leaves decayed
& skeletal

Since that day, my mother, your hands
have knotted, be-ribboned as aches
fluttering—
white cloth fragments—
Mother   I fear most the angel's eyes,
whose look is single—
single as: *How will I ever yield
these tatters of our bed's defence?*

On arriving

Arrival is a way of growing convex: the hemisphere's
two prongs sprouting rails back to the place one's left,
the moon-soft belly of the curve displacing fear; a mild
voluptuousness settles in its folds.

Imagination reflexes to the earliest arrivals: circling
their parturient garden, growing into it, fingering its nubs
and stones: recalling only void, then the seamlessness of time
struck open by expectant blue.

The end of the platform that inhales one to the sky
is superficial, profound. Temple-arches in the city, rocks beside a shore,
silver buildings to the edges of the aqueous suburbs.
(But this is 1920s-style Milan, and not a model.)

Arriving gives the *arriviste*, the one who's come so far.
And then, it offers the unparented child, the near-sighted
lover, the connoisseur of selves, the untested and the trying
the milk of its impressions—adored, accepted or feared opacity.

I'll step out: the morning's crisp:
the city a mute and unembraceable globe. Match to this
the lover's undeterred pursuit of keys; her radiance; and this:
a blind feeling for the new.

Acknowledgments

We wish to thank copyright holders for permission to reproduce the following material:

Robert D. Fitzgerald: 'Eleven Compositions Pt III: Roadside' and 'The Wind at Your Door' from *Forty Years' Poems* (Angus & Robertson 1965). **A. D. Hope**: 'The Lingam and the Yoni', 'Moschus Moschiferus', 'Hay Fever', 'Spätlese', 'The Mayan Books' and 'Inscription for a War' from *Selected Poems* (Angus & Robertson 1992). **Elizabeth Riddell**: 'Tom', 'The End of the Affair' and 'Wakeful in the Township' from *In the Midnight Courtyard* (Angus & Robertson 1989) and 'Suburban Song' from *Forebears* (Angus & Robertson 1961). **Roland Robinson**: 'Drifting Dug-out', 'Curracarang' and 'Captain Cook' the Estate of Roland Robinson. **John Blight**: 'Cormorants', 'Garfish', 'Black' and 'The Limousine' from *Selected Poems 1939–90* (University of Queensland Press 1992). **Kenneth Mackenzie**: 'Sick Men Waking', 'An Old Inmate' and 'The Awakening' from *The Poems of Kenneth Mackenzie* (Angus & Robertson 1972). **David Campbell**: 'At the Sheep-dog Trials' from *Speak with the Sun* (1949); 'The House Rises' from *The Miracle of Mullion Hill* (1956); 'Mothers and Daughters' from *Poems* (1962); 'Strzelecki', 'The Wolf of Gubbio' (part of *Red Bridge*) and 'Deaths and Pretty Cousins' from *Deaths and Pretty Cousins* (1975). **John Manifold**: 'The Tomb of Lt John Learmonth, AIF' and 'Fife Tune' from *Collected Verse* (University of Queensland Press 1978). **Judith Wright**: 'The Trains' from *The Moving Image* (1946); 'Camphor Laurel' from *Woman to Man* (1949); 'Request to a Year' from *The Two Fires* (1955); 'Brush Turkey' from *Birds* (1962); 'To Another Housewife' from *The Other Half* (1966); 'Finale' from *Alive: Poems 1971–72* (Angus & Robertson 1973); 'Counting in Sevens' from *Fourth Quarter and Other Poems* (1976). **James McAuley**: 'Vespers', 'The Inception of the Poem', 'Because', 'In the Huon Valley', 'Holiday', 'Moulting Lagoon' and 'Explicit' from *Collected Poems 1936–70* (Angus & Robertson 1971). **Amy Witting**: 'To the Unborn', 'Beast of Burden' and 'Lillipilli' from *Beauty is the Straw* (Angus & Robertson 1991). **Oodgeroo of the tribe Noonuccal**: 'Nona', 'Ballad of the Totems' and 'We are Going' from *The Dawn is at Hand* (Marion Boyers 1966). **Rosemary Dobson**: 'One Section' from *In a Convex Mirror* (Angus & Robertson 1944); 'Country Press' from *Ship of Ice* (Angus & Robertson 1948) and 'Drowned Person' from *Over the Frontier* (Angus & Robertson 1978). **Gwen Harwood**: 'A Simple Story', 'The Lion's Bride' and 'A Scattering of Ashes' from *The Lion's Bride* (Angus & Robertson 1981); 'Daybreak' from *Poems* (Angus & Robertson 1963); 'At the Arts Club' from *Poems: Volume 2* (Angus & Robertson 1968); 'Oyster Cove' from *Selected*

Poems (Angus & Robertson 1975); and 'Schrödinger's Cat Preaches to the Mice' from *Bone Scan* (Angus & Robertson 1988). **Lex Banning**: 'Nursery Rhyme', 'Ixion' and 'Captain Arthur Phillip and the Birds' from *Apocalypse in Springtime* (Edwards & Shaw 1956). **Dimitris Tsaloumas**: 'September', 'Autumn Supper' and 'The Grudge' from *Falcon Drinking* (University of Queensland Press 1988). **Alexander Craig**: 'Sea at Portsea' from *When No One is Looking* (1977). **Dorothy Hewett**: extract from 'Testament' from *Windmill Country* (Overland 1968); 'The Witnesses' from *Rapunzel in Suburbia* (Prism 1975); and 'Summer' from *Peninsula* (Fremantle Arts Centre Press 1994). **B. R. Whiting**: 'Our Sad Monarchies', 'Splitting Firewood' and 'Blind Chess' from *The Poems of B. R. Whiting* (Sheep Meadow Press 1991). **David Rowbotham**: 'The Rattle in the Marquee' from *New and Selected Poems 1945–93* (Penguin 1994). **Vincent Buckley**: 'Natura Naturans', 'Sheela-na-Gig', 'One put down his notebook' and 'Introvert and Horseman' from *Last Poems* (McPhee Gribble 1991). **Laurence Collinson**: 'Bedmanship' and 'Night and Day' from *Hovering Narcissus* (Grandma Press 1977). **J. R. Rowland**: 'Children at Wee Jasper' from *The Feast of Ancestors* (Angus & Robertson 1965) and 'Cicadas' from *Sixty* (Angus & Robertson 1989). **Francis Webb**: 'Vase Painter' and 'Nessun Dorma' from *Cap and Bells: The Poetry of Francis Webb* (Angus & Robertson 1991); 'End of the Picnic' from *Birthday* (Angus & Robertson 1953); 'Five Days Old' from *Socrates and Other Poems* (Angus & Robertson 1961); 'Canobolas', 'Airliner' (extract from *Clouds*) and 'Legionary Ants' from *The Ghost of the Cock* (Angus & Robertson 1964). **Bruce Beaver**: 'Cow Dance' from *Under the Bridge* (University of Queensland Press 1961); 'The Red Balloon' from *Open at Random* (University of Queensland Press 1967); 'Death's Directives III' from *Death's Directives* (University of Queensland Press 1978); 'Silo Treading' from *As It Was* (University of Queensland Press 1979). **Peter Porter**: 'The Sadness of the Creatures' from *The Last of England* (Oxford University Press, UK 1970); 'An Australian Garden' from *Living in a Calm Country* (Oxford University Press, UK 1975) and 'Wish We were There' from *The Chair of Babel* (Oxford University Press, UK 1992). **R. A. Simpson**: 'Evening' from *Words for a Journey: Poems 1970–85* (Melbourne University Press 1988) and 'All Friends Together' and 'My Funeral' from *Poems from Murrumbeena* (University of Queensland Press 1976). **Bruce Dawe**: 'City Lovers', 'The Rock Thrower', 'Teaching the Syllabus', 'Returned Men' and 'Henry Artenshaw's Canaan' from *Sometimes Gladness* (Longman Cheshire 1979) and 'From the Outset' from *This Side of Silence* (Longman Cheshire 1990). **Evan Jones**: 'Address to the Pure Scholars', 'Study in Blue', 'Language, Talk to Me', 'Instructions to a Servant' and 'Insomnia' from *Left at the Post* (University of Queensland Press 1984). **Philip Martin**: 'Dune Ship' from *A Flag for the Wind*

(Longman Cheshire 1982) and 'A Certain Love' and 'Dream Poem' from *New and Selected Poems* (Longman Cheshire 1988). **Keith Harrison**: 'The Island Weather of the Newly Betrothed' from *Points in a Journey* (Macmillan, London) and 'Here' from *A Burning of Applewood* (Black Willow Press, Northfield, Minnesota). **Jennifer Strauss**: 'Aubade' and 'What Women Want' from *Labour Ward* (Pariah Press, Kew 1988); 'Tierra del Fuego' from the author. **Vivian Smith**: 'Summer Sketches, Sydney', 'There is No Sleight of Hand', 'Tasmania' and 'At the Parrot House, Taronga Park' from *Selected Poems* (Angus & Robertson 1985). **Fay Zwicky**: 'Waking' from *Isaac Babel's Fiddle* (1975); 'Reading a Letter in Amsterdam' from *Ask Me* (University of Queensland Press 1990) and 'Talking Mermaid' from *Poems 1970–92* (University of Queensland Press 1992). **William Grono**: 'The Way We Live Now' and 'The Critic' from *On the Edge* (Freshwater Bay Press 1980). **Barry Humphries**: 'A Threnody for Patrick White' from *Neglected Poems and Other Creatures* (Angus & Robertson 1991). **David Malouf**: 'The Crab Feast' from *Poems 1959–89* (University of Queensland Press 1992). **Chris Wallace-Crabbe**: 'Introspection' from *The Emotions are Not Skilled Workers* (Angus & Robertson 1980); 'The Fall of the West' and 'The Home Conveyancing Kit' from *The Amorous Cannibal* (Oxford University Press, UK 1985); 'God' from *I'm Deadly Serious* (Oxford University Press, UK 1988); 'For Crying Out Loud' and 'And the World was Calm' from *For Crying Out Loud* (Oxford University Press, UK 1990); and 'Trace Elements' from *The Rungs of Time* (Oxford University Press, UK 1993). **Randolph Stow**: 'Seashells and Sandalwood', 'As He Lay Dying', 'Jimmy Woodsers' and 'The Singing Bones' from *A Counterfeit Silence* (Angus & Robertson 1969). **Katherine Gallagher**: 'Poem for the Executioners' and 'It is Written' from *Fish Rings on Water* (Forest Books, Chingford, UK 1989). **Rodney Hall**: 'Madam's Music', 'Hydra' and 'The Public Turns to Its Hero' from *Selected Poems* (University of Queensland Press 1975). **Antigone Kefala**: 'Prodigal Son' and 'Ultimo Bridge' from *Thirsty Weather* (Outback Press 1978). **Thomas Shapcott**: 'Light on the Water', 'Advice to a Politician', 'Elegy for Gertrude Langer' and 'The City of Home' from *Selected Poems 1956–88* (University of Queensland Press 1989). **Judith Rodriguez**: 'Family', 'Eskimo Occasion' and 'The Mahogany Ship' from *New and Selected Poems* (University of Queensland Press 1988). **Les Murray**: 'The Broad Bean Sermon' and 'The Mitchells' from *The Vernacular Republic* (Angus & Robertson 1976); 'Laconics: The Forty Acres', 'The Future' and 'Rainwater Tank' from *Ethnic Radio* (Angus & Robertson 1977); 'Poetry and Religion' from *The Daylight Moon* (Angus & Robertson 1987); 'The Tin Wash Dish' and 'Ariel' from *Dog Fox Field* (Angus & Robertson 1990); and 'Pigs' and 'Eagle Pair' from *Translations from the Natural World* (Isabella Press 1992). **j. s. harry**: 'One, in the motel' and 'Coming and going: peripatetic poet' from *The Deer Under the Skin* (University of Queensland Press 1971); 'If ... & the Movable Ground' from *A Dandelion for Van Gogh* (Island Press 1985); and 'An Impression of Minimalist Art in the Late Twentieth Century' from *The Life on Water and the Life Beneath* (University of Queensland Press 1995). **Clive James**: 'The Crying Need for Snow' and 'The Book of My Enemy has been Remaindered' from *Peregrine Prykke's Pilgrimage Through the London Literary World* (1976) and 'Reflection in an Extended Kitchen' (*New Yorker* 1996). **Mudrooroo**: 'I've Met Them All' and 'Oldering' from *The Garden of Gethsemane* (Hyland House 1991). **Peter Steele**: 'Futuribles', 'Wednesday' and 'The Academy of Contempt' from the author. **Syd Harrex**: 'Atlantis' from *Atlantis and Other Islands* (Kangaroo Press) and 'Libran Birthday' from *Inside Out* (Wakefield Press 1991). **Elizabeth Lawson**: 'Valentia Street Wharf' from the author. **Geoffrey Lehmann**: 'Bird-watching with Mr Long', 'The Spring Forest', 'Not Yet Found' and 'The Golden Wall' from *Spring Forest* (Angus & Robertson 1992). **Jan Owen**: 'Twilight', 'On Stradbroke', 'Window' and 'The Transmutation' from *Night Rainbows* (Heinemann 1994). **Geoff Page**: 'My Mother's God', 'Immovable Feasts' and 'Ulcer' from *Human Interest* (Heinemann 1994). **Andrew Taylor**: 'The Bell Birds', parts 1, 2, 3 from *The Cool Change* (University of Queensland Press 1971) and 'The Old Colonist' from *Ice Fishing* (University of Queensland Press 1973). **Alan Alexander**: 'Northline' and 'Street Parade' from *Northline* (Fremantle Arts Centre Press 1987). **Julian Croft**: 'Timetable' from *Breakfasts in Shanghai* (Angus & Robertson 1984); 'Amica' and 'Darkie Point' from *Confessions of a Corinthian* (Angus & Robertson 1991). **Roger McDonald**: 'Probably Jack', 'Mangalore' and 'Recent Archaeology' (University of Queensland Press). **Jennifer Rankin**: 'Dragon Veins', 'I am chasing the end of that rainbow', 'Love Affair 36' and 'Storms' from *Collected Poems* (University of Queensland Press 1990). **Nigel Roberts**: 'Dialogue with John Forbes' from *In Casablanca for the Waters* (Wild & Woolley 1977) and 'The Gull's Flight' from *Steps for Astaire* (Hale & Iremonger 1983). **Silvana Gardner**: 'Friendship with Benito' from *When Sunday Comes* (University of Queensland Press 1982). **John Tranter**: Sonnets Nos 5, 13, 35 from *Crying in Early Infancy* (Hale & Iremonger 1977); 'Country Verandah' and 'The Guides' from *Under Berlin* (University of Queensland Press 1988); and 'Old Europe' from *At the Florida* (University of Queensland Press 1993). **Robert Adamson**: 'A Final Spring' and 'Holding' from *The Law at Heart's Desire* (Angus & Robertson 1982) and 'Blue Feathered Sonnet' from *The Clean Dark* (Angus & Robertson 1992). **Caroline Caddy**: 'King George Sound' from *Letters from the North* (Fremantle Arts Centre Press 1985) and 'The Snow Queen' from *Conquistadors* (Penguin 1991). **Tim Thorne**: 'Reds' from *Red Dirt* (Paperbark Press 1990). **Alison Clark**: 'Breathless' and 'Reclaiming the Feminine' from the author. **Robert**

Gray: 'The Meat Works' from *Creekwater Journal* (Angus & Robertson 1974); 'A Day at Bellingen', 'Karl Marx' and 'Aubade' from *The Skylight* (Angus & Robertson 1983); and 'The Girls' from *Certain Things* (Heinemann 1993). **Mark O'Connor:** 'The Cuttle Bone' from *Poetry in Pictures: The Great Barrier Reef* (Hale & Iremonger 1988). **Peter Skrzynecki:** 'Wallamumbi' from *Head Waters* (Lyrebird Press 1972). **Lily Brett:** 'The First Job' and 'The Guarantee' from *The Auschwitz Poems* (Scribe 1986). **Gary Catalano:** 'A Poem is Not' and 'Slow Tennis' from *Selected Poems 1973–92* (University of Queensland Press 1992). **Dennis Haskell:** 'No One Ever Found You' and 'One Clear Call' from *Abracadabra* (Fremantle Arts Centre Press 1993). **Martin Johnston:** 'No. 5 Directions for Dreamfishing' (from *Uncertain Sonnets*); 'Goya's Colossus', 'No. 2 Biography', 'No. 6 The Café of Situations' and 'No. 11 Of Time and Typing' (from *In Transit: A Sonnet Square*) all from *Selected Poems and Prose* (University of Queensland Press 1993). **Rhyll McMaster:** 'Flying the Coop', 'Set to Music' and 'The Lost Jackaroos' from *On My Empty Feet* (Heinemann 1993). **Graham Rowlands:** 'Elusive' and 'Marking Secondary School Papers' from *Selected Poems* (Wakefield Press 1992). **Michael Dransfield:** 'Purcell', 'Goliard', 'Fix', 'Minstrel', 'No, but I saw the movie' and 'Psyched Out' from *Collected Poems* (University of Queensland Press 1987). **John A. Scott:** 'Catullus 63' from *St Clair* (Picador 1990) and 'Man in Petersham' and 'Changing Room' from *Selected Poems* (University of Queensland Press). **Alex Skovron:** 'The Composer on His Birthday' and 'Sentences' from *The Rearrangement* (Melbourne University Press 1988) and 'What Matters' from *Sleeve Notes* (Hale & Iremonger 1992). **Alan Wearne:** 'Sue Dobson' (extract from *The Nightmarkets*) (Penguin 1986). **Ken Bolton:** 'Beginning the New Day' from *Selected Poems 1975–90* (Penguin 1992). **Laurie Duggan:** 'Australia' (extract from *Dogs*), 'Drive Time', 'Holocaust', 'The Mysteries', 'The Town on the Ten Dollar Note', 'Blue Hills No. 21' and 'Blue Notes No. 23' from *Blue Notes* (Picador 1990); 'The Epigrams of Martial', I xviii, III xvii, III xlvii, V li, VIII xx and X ix from *The Epigrams of Martial* (Scripsi 1989); and 8.2 'Dead Warriors' (extract from *The Ash Range*) (Picador 1987). **Alan Gould:** 'Reykjavik' from *Formerlight: Selected Poems* (Angus & Robertson 1992) and 'South Coast Mechanic' from *Momentum* (Heinemann 1992). **Jamie Grant:** 'How to Fold Army Blankets' from *The Refinery* (Angus & Robertson 1985) and 'His Nibs' from *Mysteries* (Heinemann 1993). **Susan Hampton:** 'Ode to the Car Radio' from *Costumes* (Wild & Woolley 1981). **Kate Jennings:** 'My Grandmother's Ghost' from *Cats, Dogs & Pitchforks* (Heinemann 1993). **Jennifer Maiden:** 'The Anglo-Saxons' Xmas', 'Preamble', 'Anorexia' and 'Chakola' from *Selected and New Poems of Jennifer Maiden* (Penguin 1990). **Vicki Raymond:** 'The Mermaids' Lagoon' and 'The People, No' from *Selected Poems* (Carcanet 1993).

John Forbes: 'Europe: A Guide for Ken Seale', 'Death, an Ode' and 'Speed, a Pastorale' from *The Stunned Mullet* (Hale & Iremonger 1988); 'Love Poem' and 'On Tiepolo's Banquet of Cleopatra' from the author. Philip Salom: 'Sight' from *The Projectionist* (Fremantle Arts Centre Press 1983); 'The Wind has Panels' and 'Recognition' from *Feeding the Ghost* (Penguin 1993); and 'Poems of Dissociation No. 7' from *The Rome Air Naked* (Penguin 1996). Andrew Sant: 'Out of the Wood' and 'Cover-up' from *Brushing the Dark* (Heinemann 1989). Nicolette Stasko: 'My Nurse and I' from *Abundance* (Angus & Robertson 1992) and 'The Murmuring of Many Tongues' from *Black Night with Windows* (Angus & Robertson 1994). Stephen Edgar: 'Gone a Million' from the author; 'The Secret Life of Books' and 'All will be Revealed' from *Corrupted Treasures* (Heinemann 1995). Peter Goldsworthy: 'Piano', 'A Statistician to His Love' and 'Cimetière Père Lachaise' from *This Goes with That: Selected Poems 1970–90* (Angus & Robertson 1992). Robert Harris: 'The Enthusiast' from *Localities* (1973); 'Riding over Belmore Park' and 'Tambaroora Remembers' from *The Cloud Passes Over* (1986). Rod Moran: 'Leaders' and 'Three Students at the University Invoke Billy Graham' from *Against the Era* (Fremantle Arts Centre Press 1988). Chris Mansell: 'Amelia Earhart Flies out from Lae, New Guinea' from *Redshift/Blueshift* (Five Islands Press 1988). Kevin Hart: 'Pascal' from *The Departure* (University of Queensland Press 1978); 'Gypsophila' and 'Reading at Evening' from *Peniel* (Golvan Arts Press 1990). Shane McCauley: 'Chin Shent'an's Happy Moments' from *Deep-sea Diver* (Fremantle Arts Centre Press 1987). Dorothy Porter: 'My Mother', 'God-watching' and 'Dawn' from *Akhenaten* (University of Queensland Press 1994); 'Tony's Charm', 'Tony's Company' and 'Frangipani' from *Monkey's Mask* (Hyland House 1994). Adrian Caesar: 'Accents' and 'Uneven Tenor' from *Hunger Games* (Polonius 1996). Philip Harvey: 'The Fiction Explains the Fact' from the author. Peter Rose: 'Imagining the Inappropriate', 'True Confessions' and 'The Wall' from *The House of Vitriol* (Picador 1990); 'Dog Days' and 'The Best of Fleetwood Mac' from *The Catullan Rag* (Picador 1993). Judith Beveridge: 'Making Perfume' and 'The Caterpillars' from *The Domesticity of Giraffes* (Black Lightning Press 1987). S. K. Kelen: 'A Traveller's Guide to the East Indies' from *Atomic Ballet* (Hale & Iremonger 1991). Gig Ryan: 'Already', 'Poem' and 'Rent' from *Excavation* (Pan Macmillan 1990). Anthony Lawrence: 'Goanna' from *Dreaming in Stone* (Angus & Robertson 1989) and 'Sooty Oystercatchers, Venus Tusk Fish' from *The Darkwood Aquarium* (Penguin 1993). Sarah Day: 'Apple' from *A Hunger to be Less Serious* (Angus & Robertson 1987); 'Chaos' and 'Imperium Romanum' from *A Madder Dance* (Penguin 1993). Paul Hetherington: 'Resonances' from *Mapping Wildwood Road* (National Library of Australia Pamphlet Press 1990) and 'Farming' from *Shadow Swimmer* (Molonglo Press). **Kathleen Stewart:** 'Little Things' and 'Another Dead Poet' from *Snow* (Heinemann 1994). **Lionel Fogarty:** 'Frisky Poem and Risky' and 'Farewell Reverberated Vault of Detentions' from *New and Selected Poems: Munaldjali, Mutuerjaraera* (Hyland House 1996). **Philip Hodgins:** 'Catharsis', 'Apologies' and 'Sant' Ivo della Sapienza' from *Blood and Bone* (Angus & Robertson 1986) and 'The Rabbit Trap' from *Up on All Fours* (Angus & Robertson 1993). **Richard Allen:** 'A German Christmas' and 'The Thoroughly Modern Poem' from *The Way Out At Last* (Hale & Iremonger); 'Twins' from *Hope for a Man Named Jimmy* (Five Islands Press). **Luke Davies:** 'Azaria Sonnet' and 'Trains' from *Absolute Event Horizons* (Angus & Robertson 1994). **John Kinsella:** 'Counterpoint' from the author; 'Links' from *Night Parrots* (Fremantle Arts Centre Press 1989); and 'The Myth of the Grave' from *Eschatologies* (Fremantle Arts Centre Press 1991). **Lisa Jacobson:** 'Flight Path' from *Hair & Skin & Teeth* (Five Islands Press). **Tracy Ryan:** 'In the First Place' from *Killing Delilah* (Fremantle Arts Centre Press 1994). **Judith Bishop:** 'Passage of Winter Precluded' and 'On Arriving' from the author.

Details for the acknowledgments are as supplied by copyright holders. Every effort has been made to trace the original source of all material contained in this book. Where the attempt has been unsuccessful the editor and publisher would be pleased to hear from the author/publisher concerned, to rectify any omission.

INDEX OF FIRST LINES

Index of poets and titles